THE COMPLETE
JAPANESE VERB GUIDE

THE
COMPLETE
JAPANESE VERB
GUIDE

compiled by

THE HIROO JAPANESE CENTER

Charles E. Tuttle Company
Rutland, Vermont & Tokyo, Japan

The Hiroo Japanese Center is a private Japanese language school located in central Tokyo.

Published by the Charles E. Tuttle Company, Inc.
of Rutland, Vermont & Tokyo, Japan
with editorial offices at
2-6 Suido 1-chome, Bunkyo-ku, Tokyo 112

Library of Congress Catalog Card No. 89-50023
International Standard Book No. 0-8048-1564-x
First edition, 1989
Ninth printing, 1994

Printed in Japan

CONTENTS

ACKNOWLEDGMENTS

We wish to thank the following people for their help with the publication of this book: first, our students, who in one way or another have both guided and prodded us to seek new and better approaches to teaching Japanese; and second, Richard Ryan, Peter Moore, Ross Story, and Erick Homsher, who were all kind enough to help out with the tedious job of proofreading. Special gratitude is due to the Charles E. Tuttle Company for offering editorial guidance and personal encouragement.

> Hiroo Japanese Center:
>   Kazuo Ishii, Michiko Kono,
>   Yuko Miyazawa, Naomi Nagano,
>   Hitoshi Watanabe, Naomi Watanabe

Tokyo, Japan

INTRODUCTION

Fluency in a language cannot be attained without a solid understanding of that language's verbs and their usages. Especially with Japanese, it is crucial for the student to master verbs in order to be able to communicate effectively.

In Japanese, the importance of the subject-verb relationship is not stressed as it is in Indo-European languages such as English. In English, verb forms change depending on whether the subject is singular or plural, first person or second person, and so on. Thus, for the verb "to go," one says "I *go*" and "He *goes.*" More complicated are some of the many languages whose verb forms change depending on whether the subject is feminine or masculine.

In Japanese, however, verbs are not affected by their subjects in this manner; it does not make any difference whether the subject is singular or plural, or first person or second person. This, plus the fact that there are relatively few exceptions to the rules, makes Japanese verbs relatively less complicated to learn than those of many other languages. Once the students master certain rules for making such forms as the *masu*, imperative, *te,* and conditional forms, they will be able to apply these rules to almost any verb.

Of course, the students should be aware that while any form can in theory be made from any verb, forms of some verbs are seldom used in ordinary situations. Along with the main entries and their example sentences, this introduction will help the student learn both the conjugation and the usage of Japanese verbs.

VERB GROUPINGS

One way to approach Japanese verbs is to classify them into three major groupings according to the way they are conjugated when spelled with Roman letters. (This classification method does not apply when they are written in the Japanese syllabary.) These groups are:

Group 1: The *u*-dropping conjugation
Group 2: The *ru*-dropping conjugation
Group 3: Irregular conjugation

Knowing which group a verb belongs to enables one to determine the stem of a verb.

Group 1: (the *u*-dropping conjugation)

Most of the verbs in Group 1 are easy to recognize. With the exception of *suru* and *kuru,* if the ending of the plain (dictionary) form of a verb is anything but *-eru* or *-iru,* the verb belongs to this group. As shown below, to determine the stem, simply drop the final *-u* ending. The *masu* forms are then made by attaching *-imasu/-imasen* to the stem.

VERB	MEANING	STEM	MASU FORM	MASEN FORM
aru	to have	ar-	arimasu	arimasen
dasu[1]	to take out	dash-	dashimasu	dashimasen
isogu	to hurry	isog-	isogimasu	isogimasen
iu	to say	i-	iimasu	iimasen
kaku	to write	kak-	kakimasu	kakimasen
kau	to buy	ka-	kaimasu	kaimasen
matsu[1]	to wait	mach-	machimasu	machimasen
nuru	to paint	nur-	nurimasu	nurimasen
omou	to think	omo-	omoimasu	omoimasen
shinu	to die	shin-	shinimasu	shinimasen
tobu	to fly	tob-	tobimasu	tobimasen
toru	to take	tor-	torimasu	torimasen
yomu	to read	yom-	yomimasu	yomimasen

[1] Verbs ending in *-su* and *-tsu* have a *sh* stem and *ch* stem respectively.

If the ending of a verb is either *-eru* or *-iru,* one must consult a reference source to determine if it belongs to Group 1 or Group 2. A small percentage of verbs ending in *-eru* and *-iru* do belong to Group 1, and likewise form their stem by dropping the final *-u* ending. Confusion may arise when words spelled the same have different meanings. For example, the word *kiru,* accenting the *ki* syllable, means "to cut" and belongs to Group 1; its stem is *kir-.* On the other hand, the *kiru* that accents the *ru* syllable means "to wear" and belongs to Group 2; its stem is *ki-.* In the same manner, the word *kaeru,* accenting the *ka* syllable, means "to return" and belongs to Group 1; its stem is *kaer-.* The *kaeru* that accents the *e* syllable, however, means "to change" and belongs to Group 2; its stem is *kae-.* Sometimes, there are no pronunciation differences, as exemplified by *iru.* Thus, while the word *iru* meaning "to need" belongs to Group 1, *iru* meaning "to exist" belongs to Group 2. Both are pronounced the same.

Examples of Group 1 verbs whose endings are *-eru* or *-iru* are listed below. The stem is formed by dropping the final *u* ending; the *masu* forms, by attaching *-imasu/-imasen* to the stem.

VERB	MEANING	STEM	MASU FORM	MASEN FORM
hairu	to enter	hair-	hairimasu	hairimasen
kaeru	to return	kaer-	kaerimasu	kaerimasen
shiru	to know	shir-	shirimasu	shirimasen

Group 2: (the *ru*-dropping conjugation)

Most verbs ending in *-eru* or *-iru* belong to this group. The stem is formed by dropping the *-ru* ending, and the *masu* forms are made by adding *-masu/-masen* to the stem.

VERB	MEANING	STEM	MASU FORM	MASEN FORM
ageru	to raise, give	age-	agemasu	agemasen
dekiru	to be able	deki-	dekimasu	dekimasen
iru	to be	i-	imasu	imasen
kangaeru	to think	kangae-	kangaemasu	kangaemasen
miru	to see	mi-	mimasu	mimasen
taberu	to eat	tabe-	tabemasu	tabemasen

11

Group 3: (irregular conjugation)

This group has only two verbs, *kuru* "to come" and *suru* "to do." Their verb forms are shown in their respective entries in the main text of this book.

Verb stem + adjuncts

Many adjuncts are attached to the verb stem to alter the verb's original meaning. Some of the more common examples are listed below.

    a. *Kare no Nihon-go wa wakari-yasui.*
      His Japanese is easy to understand.

    b. *Kanojo no Nihon-go wa wakari-nikui.*
      Her Japanese is difficult to understand.

    c. *Watashi wa benkyoo shi-tai desu. Shigoto wa shi-takunai desu.*
      I want to study. I don't want to work.

    d. *Kare wa Nihon e iki-tagatte imasu.*
      He wants to go to Japan.

    e. *Terebi o mi-nagara, shokuji shimashita.*
      I ate while watching television.

    f. *Ame ga furi-soo desu.*
      It looks like it will rain.

    g. *Kanojo wa eiga o mi ni ikimashita.*
      She went to see a movie.

    h. *Kono kanji no yomi-kata ga wakarimasen.*
      I don't know how to read this kanji.

    i. *Isogi-nasai.*
      Hurry up.

EXPLANATIONS OF VERB FORMS

Following are explanations and examples of each of the verb forms listed in the main entries.

The Plain Form

The plain form, including the plain forms of the present, past, conditional, presumptive, volitional, potential, passive, causative, and causative passive forms, is used in everyday conversation among friends, family, and other close relationships. The present tense of the plain form of verbs sometimes is called the "dictionary form."

Note that there is a slight change regarding the conjugation of the negative forms of verbs such as *kau, iu,* and *omou*—Group 1 verbs that have the final *-u* preceded by a vowel. Instead of attaching *-anai/-anakatta* to the stem of these Group 1 verbs, *-wanai/-wanakatta* is attached to make the negative forms. Thus, *kau* becomes *kawanai, iu* becomes *iwanai,* and *omou* becomes *omowanai.*

The plain form generally is used as follows.

1. In informal conversations:
   a. *Ashita tomodachi ni au?*
      Will you meet your friend tomorrow?
   b. *Un, au.*
      Yes, I will.
   c. *Uun, awanai.*
      No, I won't.
   d. *Kinoo tomodachi ni atta?*
      Did you meet your friend yesterday?
   e. *Uun, awanakatta.*
      No, I didn't.

2. Within a clause of a complex sentence:
   a. *Kare wa ashita kuru to iimashita.*
      He said he would come tomorrow.
   b. *Kare wa ashita iku ka doo ka wakarimasen.*
      I don't know whether he will go or not tomorrow.
   c. *Kare wa aruku'n desu ka.*
      Will he walk?
   d. *Kare ga oshieru no wa Getsuyoobi desu.*
      He teaches on Mondays.
   e. *Kare ni ashita hanasanai yoo ni itte kudasai.*
      Tell him not to talk tomorrow.

f. *Gakkoo e kuru toki tomodachi ni aimashita.*
I met a friend of mine on my way to school.

3. Before adjuncts:
a. *Raishuu tegami o kaku tsumori desu.*
I intend to write a letter next week.
b. *Kare wa mata kuru hazu desu.*
He is supposed to come again.
c. *Kare wa Amerika e kaetta soo desu.*
I heard he went back to the United States.
d. *Tomodachi ni denwa shita hoo ga ii desu yo.*
You should call your friend.
e. *Igirisu ni itta koto ga arimasu ka.*
Have you been to England?
f. *Paatii de nonda-ri tabeta-ri shimashita.*
I ate and drank at the party.
g. *Koko de tabako o suwanai de kudasai.*
Please don't smoke here.

The Masu Form

The *masu* form is often referred to as the "polite form." Suitable for a wide range of circumstances, the *masu* form is considered a polite, conventional way of speaking. Note that the present *masu* form covers both the English present and future tenses. The present *masu* form is made by attaching -*imasu*/-*imasen* to the stem of Group 1 verbs, or -*masu*/-*masen* to the stem of Group 2 verbs. The *masu* forms for the potential, passive, causative, and causative passive forms are made by dropping the final -*ru* syllable, and attaching -*masu*/-*masen*. For the *masu* forms for the humble and honorific forms, refer to the entries for *naru, nasaru, suru,* and *itasu.*

a. *Ashita dekakemasu ka.*
Will you go out tomorrow?
b. *Iie, dekakemasen.*
No, I won't.

c. *Kesa shinbun o yomimashita ka.*
Did you read the newspaper this morning?

d. *Iie, yomimasen deshita.*
No, I didn't.

e. *Piano o hikimasu ka.*
Do you play the piano?

f. *Ame ni furaremashita.*
I was caught in the rain.

g. *Moo ichido yaraseraremashita.*
They made me do it one more time.

The Imperative Form

The imperative (command) form is said by a superior to an inferior. This form is made by adding *-e* to the stem of Group 1 verbs, and by adding *-ro* to the stem of Group 2 verbs. For negative imperatives, add the adjunct *na* to the plain present form of the verb. Note that with some verbs, the imperative form conventionally is not used; students should avoid using this form if it has been set inside parentheses in the main entries.

a. *Suware.*
Sit down.

b. *Okane o tamero.*
Save your money.

c. *Shizuka ni shiro.*
Be quiet.

d. *Dare ni mo iu na.*
Don't say this to anyone.

A less harsh way to make a command is to use *nasai*. Add *-i* + *nasai* to the stem of Group 1 verbs, and *-nasai* to the stem of Group 2 verbs. *Shi-nasai* and *ki-nasai* are for *suru* and *kuru*.

a. *Suwari-nasai.*
Sit down.

b. *Kaku no wa yame-nasai.*
Stop writing.

The Te Form

The *te* form can be considered to be the Japanese equivalent of the English gerund. For most verbs, the *te* forms are made as follows:

Group 1 verbs:
1. Change the *-ku* ending to *-ite*.[1]
   aku (to open)   *aite*
2. Change the *-gu* ending to *-ide*.
   sawagu (to be noisy)   *sawaide*
3. Change the *-su* ending to *-shite*.
   hanasu (to speak)   *hanashite*
4. Change the *-bu, -mu,* and *-nu* endings to *-nde*.
   tobu (to fly)   *tonde*
   yomu (to read)   *yonde*
   shinu (to die)   *shinde*
5. Change the *-ru* and *-tsu* endings to *-tte*.
   kaeru (to return)   *kaette*
   katsu (to win)   *katte*
6. Change the *-u* ending when preceded by a vowel to *-tte*.
   kau (to buy)   *katte*
   iu (to say)   *itte*

[1]One exception is *iku* (to go); the *te* form is not *iite,* but *itte.*

Group 2 verbs: Change the *-ru* ending to *-te.*
     miru (to see)   *mite*

Group 3 verbs: See the individual entries for *suru* and *kuru.*

To make the *te* forms of the potential, passive, causative, and causative passive forms of verbs, change the *-ru* ending to *-te.*

1. State of Doing

The *te* form, when combined with *iru/imasu,* indicates a state of doing; in other words, a state where the action is continuous.

  a. *Ima nani o shite imasu ka.*

    What are you doing now?

b. *Nihon-go o benkyoo shite iru.*
   I'm studying Japanese.
c. *Yuube hachi-ji goro watashi wa tegami o kaite imashita.*
   I was writing a letter at about eight o'clock last night.

2. Present Perfect

The present perfect tense is also indicated by the *te* form. It is made by combining the *te* form with *iru/imasu.* Note that the *te iru* form is often used in Japanese for conditions that are not always indicated in English by the present perfect tense.

a. *Eiga wa moo hajimatte imasu ka.*
   Has the movie started yet?
b. *Iie, mada hajimatte imasen.*
   No, it has not started yet.
c. *Ame wa yande iru.*
   The rain has stopped.
d. *Michi wa migi ni magatte iru.*
   The road curves to the right.
e. *Kare wa futotte imasu.*
   He is fat.
f. *Kare wa chichi-oya ni nite imashita.*
   He looked like his father.
g. *Tanaka-san o shitte imasu ka.*
   Do you know Mr. Tanaka?
   Iie, shirimasen.
   No, I don't.
h. *Kanojo no namae o oboete imasu.*
   I remember her name.
i. *Nihon-go no jisho o motte imasu.*
   I have a Japanese dictionary.
j. *Kissaten de matte imasu.*
   I'll wait for you at the coffee shop.

3. Recording Events

The *te* form is used when recording events according to a time sequence.

In some cases, where one action stops and another starts is not always clear.

a. *Resutoran ni haitte, koohii o nonda.*

   I went into a restaurant and had some coffee.

b. *Roku-ji ni okite, uchi o dete, hachi-ji ni kaisha ni tsuita.*

   I got up at six, left the house, and reached the company at eight.

c. *Tomodachi ni atte, eiga o mite kara, uchi ni kaerimashita.*

   I met a friend, saw a movie, and then went home.

d. *Kaban o motte kimasu.*

   I'll bring my briefcase.

e. *Paatii ni tomodachi o tsurete ikimasu.*

   I'll take my friend to the party.

4. Something Caused Something

The *te* form is used to indicate that something happened, something that caused something else (often an emotion).

a. *Tegami o yonde, anshin shimashita.*

   Having read the letter, I was relieved.

b. *Nyuusu o kiite, bikkuri shita.*

   I was surprised to hear the news.

c. *Byooki ga naotte, ureshii.*

   I'm glad you got well.

5. Giving and Receiving

The *te* form is used with verbs such as *ageru* and *morau* to indicate giving and receiving. The level of politeness required for a particular situation dictates which verbs follow the *te* form; for instance, a person of lower status rarely would use *ageru* to a superior. In the examples below, notice how the verb following the *te* form changes according to the degree of politeness. (See also pages 24–26 for an explanation of honorific and humble speech.)

a. *Tomodachi wa shashin o misete kuremashita.*

   My friend showed me some photos.

b. *Sensei wa shashin o misete kudasaimashita.*

   My teacher (kindly) showed me some photos.

  c. *Tomodachi ni shashin o misete moraimashita.*
     I got my friend to show me some photos.

  d. *Sensei ni shashin o misete itadakimashita.*
     I got my teacher to show me some photos.

  e. *Tomodachi ni shashin o misete agemashita.*
     I showed some photos to my friend.

  f. *Sensei ni shashin o misete sashiagemashita.*
     I showed some photos to my teacher.

  g. *Tanaka-san wa haha ni shashin o misete kuremashita.*
     Mr. Tanaka showed my mother some photos.

  h. *Shachoo wa chichi ni shashin o misete kudasaimashita.*
     The president of the company showed my father some photos.

  i. *Haha wa Tanaka-san ni shashin o misete moraimashita.*
     My mother got Mr. Tanaka to show her some photos.

  j. *Chichi wa shachoo ni shashin o misete itadakimashita.*
     My father got the president of the company to show him some photos.

  k. *Imooto wa tomodachi ni shashin o misete agemashita.*
     My younger sister showed some photos to her friend.

  l. *Imooto wa sensei ni shashin o misete sashiagemashita.*
     My younger sister showed some photos to her teacher.

6. With Other Verbs and Adjuncts

  The *te* form is also used with other verbs and adjuncts.

  a. *Haitte mo ii desu ka?*
     May I come in?

  b. *Sawatte wa ikemasen.*
     Don't touch.

  c. *Doa o nokku shite mimashita.*
     I tried knocking on the door.

  d. *Ashita juu-ji ni kite hoshii desu.*
     I want you to come at ten o'clock tomorrow.

  e. *Heya o sooji shite okimashita.*
     I cleaned the room (to have it ready in advance).

  f. *Gohan o tabete shimaimashita.*
     I finished the meal.

The Conditional Form

One way to make the conditional form for all verbs is to drop the final -*u* and add -*eba*. Thus *furu* becomes *fureba*. The negative conditional form is made by dropping the final -*i* of the plain negative form and adding -*kereba*; therefore, *furanai* becomes *furanakereba*.

Another way to make the conditional form is to add the adjunct *ra* to the past plain forms or past *masu* forms, such as *futta ra, furanakatta ra, furimashita ra,* or *furimasen deshita ra.* In this book, to help students understand how to make this *ra* conditional form, it is written as two separate words (*futta ra*). Students should be aware, however, that it conventionally is written as one word (*futtara*).

While there are slight changes in nuance between the forms using *ra* and the forms using -*eba,* in many cases, they can be used interchangeably with little difference in meaning.

a. *Ame ga fureba, uchi ni imasu.*
   Ame ga futta ra, uchi ni imasu.
   Ame ga furimashita ra, uchi ni imasu. (polite)
   If it rains, I'll stay home.
b. *Jisho o mireba, wakarimasu.*
   Jisho o mita ra, wakarimasu.
   If you check the dictionary, you will understand.

Generally speaking, when a specific request follows the conditional clause, or if the sentence has the meaning "when something happens, I will do this," the form using *ra* is preferred over the form using -*eba*.

a. *Kare ni atta ra, yoroshiku to itte kudasai.* (correct)
   If you meet him, please say hello for me.
   Kare ni aeba, yoroshiku to itte kudasai. (incorrect)
b. *Nyuu Yooku ni tsuita ra, renraku suru tsumori desu.* (correct)
   When I reach New York, I intend to get in touch with you.
   Nyuu Yooku ni tsukeba, renraku suru tsumori desu. (incorrect)

The Presumptive Form

This form, indicating that something probably will happen, is made by adding the adjunct *daroo/deshoo* to the plain positive or negative forms of a verb.

- a. *Kare wa kuru daroo.*
  He'll probably come.
- b. *Kare wa konai deshoo.*
  He probably won't come.
- c. *Kare wa kuru deshoo ka.*
  I wonder if he will come.
- d. *Ame ga furu deshoo ga, ikimasu.*
  It will probably rain, but I'll go.
- e. *Kare wa mita daroo.*
  He probably saw it.
- f. *Kare wa konakatta deshoo.*
  He probably did not come.

The Volitional Form

This form indicating volition is made by adding *-oo/-imashoo* to the stem of Group 1 verbs, and by adding *-yoo/-mashoo* to the stem of Group 2 verbs. One should note that for some verbs, the volitional form conventionally is not used; students should avoid using this form if it has been set inside parentheses in the main entries.

- a. *Rainen Nihon e ikoo to omoimasu.*
  I think I'll go to Japan next year.
- b. *Saifu o kaeshimashoo.*
  Let's return the wallet.
- c. *Nichiyoobi ni eiga o miyoo to omou.*
  I think I'll see a movie on Sunday.
- d. *Yamemashoo.*
  Let's quit.
- e. *Benkyoo shimashoo.*
  Let's study.

The Potential Form

This form, expressing possibility or capability, is made by adding *-eru/-emasu* to the stem of Group 1 verbs, and by adding *-rareru/-raremasu* to the stem of Group 2 verbs. The negative form is made by adding *-enai/-emasen* to the stem of Group 1 verbs, and *-rarenai/-raremasen* to the stem of Group 2 verbs. For the potential forms of the honorific and humble forms, refer to the entries for *naru, nasaru, suru,* and *itasu.* Recently, the potential forms of Group 2 verbs have come to be constructed like Group 1 verbs; since this is considered unacceptable by many, in the main entries, this more colloquial form is listed underneath the standard form.

Also note that for some verbs, the potential form rarely is used; students should avoid using this form if it has been set inside parentheses in the main entries.

a. *Ashita juu-ji goro aemasu ka.*
   Can I meet you about ten o'clock tomorrow?
b. *Ashita aenakereba, asatte wa doo desu ka.*
   If I cannot meet you tomorrow, how about the day after?
c. *Nan-ji goro deraremasu ka.*
   About what time can you go out?

The Passive Form

The passive form conveys the idea that something was done to you and you were adversely affected. It is formed by adding *-areru/-aremasu* to the stem of Group 1 verbs (*-wareru/-waremasu* for verbs ending in two vowels such as *omou*), and *-rareru/-raremasu* to the stem of Group 2 verbs. The negative form is made by adding *-arenai/-aremasen* to the stem of Group 1 verbs (*-warenai/-waremasen* for verbs ending in two vowels), and *-rarenai/-raremasen* to the stem of Group 2 verbs. Note that the potential and passive forms of Group 2 verbs are identical and that both transitive and some intransitive verbs can be used in a passive sentence. Also note that for some verbs, the passive form is rarely used; students should avoid using this form if it has been set inside parentheses in the main entries.

a. *Doroboo ni okane o nusumaremashita.*
My money was stolen by the thief.
b. *Uchi ni kaeru tochuu de, ame ni furaremashita.*
On my way home, I was caught in the rain.
c. *Minna ni mitsumerarete, komatta.*
I didn't know what to do because everyone was staring at me.

The Causative Form

This form, conveying the idea of making someone do something, is formed by adding *-aseru/-asemasu* (*-asenai/-asemasen* for negative forms) to the stem of most Group 1 verbs. For Group 1 verbs that end in two vowels, such as *utau,* the causative is formed by adding *-waseru/-wasemasu* (*-wasenai/-wasemasen* for the negative forms) to the stem. For Group 2 verbs, the causative is formed by adding *-saseru/-sasemasu* to the stem (*-sasenai/-sasemasen* for negative forms). Note that with some verbs, the causative form rarely is used; students should avoid using this form if it has been set inside parentheses in the main entries.

a. *Kare wa musuko o kaimono ni ikaseta.*
He made his son go shopping.
b. *Kanojo wa kodomo ni piano o narawasemashita.*
She made her child learn to play the piano.
c. *Watashi ni harawasete kudasai.*
Please let me pay.
d. *Sono koto wa moo sukoshi kangaesasete kuremasu ka.*
Could you please let me think it over some more?

The Causative Passive Form

This form conveys the idea of "I was made to do something and was adversely affected by it." It is formed by adding *-aserareru/-aseraremasu* (*-aserarenai/-aseraremasen* for negative forms) to the stem of most Group 1 verbs, and *-saserareru/-saseraremasu* (*-saserarenai/-saseraremasen*) to the stem of Group 2 verbs. For Group 1 verbs that end in two vowels, such as *utau,* the causative passive form is made by adding *-waserareru/-waseraremasu* (*-waserarenai/*

-*waseraremasen* for negative forms) to the stem. As with the potential forms, in colloquial speech, causative passive forms of Group 2 may be formed similarly to the Group 1 verbs. In the main entries, this non-standard form is listed below the convential forms. Also, for some verbs, the causative passive form is rarely used—such cases are marked off by parentheses in the main entries.

a. *Shigoto de Hon Kon ni ikaseraremashita.*
I was made to go to Hong Kong on business.
b. *Watashi-tachi wa uta o utawaseraremashita.*
We were made to sing a song.
c. *Kare wa sensei ni takusan benkyoo saserareta.*
He was made to study a lot by his teacher.

POLITE LANGUAGE: HONORIFIC AND HUMBLE SPEECH

The use of polite language, that is, of honorific and humble forms, is an integral part of the Japanese language, and it is recommended that the student be at least familiar with it. In general, honorific speech is used when the subject is, or is related to, someone else, and humble speech is used when the subject concerns yourself or that which is associated with yourself. Basically, there are three situations which require the use of polite language.

1. A speaker uses polite language to an in-group member (such as someone in his school or company) when that person is senior in age or status. Thus, a worker uses both honorific and humble speech (depending on the subject) when speaking to his boss, as does a student to his teacher. Also, a worker would generally use honorific language when speaking to a fellow worker when the subject is their boss.

If, however, a worker is talking about either himself or his boss to a person who does not belong to his in-group, humble language is used. Thus, a worker would use humble language to describe his boss's actions if he were talking to someone in a different company.

2. In general, a speaker uses polite language to a non-in-group person, unless that person is clearly junior in age or status to him. Thus, a worker uses polite language to a president of another com-

pany, as well as to a worker at another company when speaking about that worker's president.

If the speaker is of the same social status as the person he is talking to, whether polite language is used or not depends on how well the two people know each other. If they are just casual acquaintances, honorific and humble speech usually are used.

3. When the speaker is not sure of the social status of the person he is talking to, usually he will opt for polite language. Thus, people meeting for the first time tend to use polite language with each other.

How to Make Honorific and Humble Verb Forms

Note that many verbs have special honorific and humble verb counterparts. One example is the verb *iku* (to go), whose humble form is the verb *mairu,* and whose honorific form is the verb *irassharu.* These special counterparts are listed in the main entries.

For those verbs not having such counterparts, the honorific and humble forms can be made as follows:

1. Honorific: *o* + verb stem + *ni naru*

The most common way to make an honorific form out of a verb is to add *o* to the verb stem, and then follow it with *ni naru.*

    a. *Sensei wa hon o o-yomi ni narimasu.*

      The teacher reads the book.

    b. *Tegami o o-kaki ni narimashita ka.*

      Have you written the letter?

Though used with less frequency, a politer honorific form can be made by replacing *ni naru* with *nasaru: o* + verb stem + *nasaru.*

    a. *Ano e o o-kai nasaimashita ka.*

      Did you buy that painting?

    b. *Futari no kekkon no koto o o-kiki nasaimashita ka.*

      Did you hear about their marriage?

2. Honorific: *passive form*

The passive form of verbs also is used to express politeness.

    a. *Tanaka-san, kinoo hon'ya ni ikaremashita ka?*

      Mr. Tanaka, did you go to the bookstore yesterday?

b. *Sensei wa denwa de sugu kotaeraremashita.*
The teacher answered immediately by telephone.

3. Honorific: *doozo* + *o* + verb stem + *kudasai*

A polite way of making a request is to add *doozo* and *kudasai* around the *o* + verb stem.

a. *Doozo o-kake kudasai.*
Please have a seat.

b. *Doozo o-meshiagari kudasai.*
Please start eating.

4. Humble: *o* + verb stem + *suru*

With most verbs, the humble form can be made by adding *o* to the verb stem, and then following it with *suru*.

a. *Ashita, shachoo-shitsu ni o-kaeshi shimasu.*
I will return it to the president's office tomorrow.

b. *Mina-sama ni kyuuryoo ni tsuite o-hanashi shitai to omoimasu.*
I would like to talk with everyone about salaries.

Suru generally can be replaced with *itasu*: *o* + verb stem + *itasu*.

a. *Suutsu-keesu o o-mochi itashimasu.*
Let me carry your suitcase.

b. *Suu-fun-kan no uchi ni o-yobi itashimasu.*
I will call for you in a few minutes.

TRANSITIVE AND INTRANSITIVE

In Japanese, verbs classified as transitive take a direct object, and thus use the particle *o*.

a. *Watashi wa tegami o kakimashita.*
I wrote a letter.

b. *Mado o shimete kudasai.*
Please close the windows.

A verb classified as intransitive does not take a direct object, and *usually* does not use an *o* as a particle.

a. *Kyuuryoo ga agarimashita.*
Our salaries went up.

b. *Kabe ni e ga kakatte iru.*

There is a picture hanging on the wall.

In Japanese, some intransitive verbs use the particle *o,* as shown below. These intransitive verbs tend to have meanings referring to motion, and used with *o,* give the idea of "going through a defined area."

a. *Watashi wa kooen made hashirimashita.*

I ran to the park.

b. *Watashi wa go-fun de koosu o hashirimashita.*

I ran the course in five minutes.

In cases where a verb has both a transitive and intransitive form, the form more commonly used is listed first; for instance, (intrans. and trans.). Note the change in meanings of such verbs.

a. *Shigoto ni isogu.*

Hurry to work.

b. *Shigoto o isogu.*

To work faster.

Note:

The romanization system used in this book is a modification of the Hepburn system. Double vowels are used instead of macrons, and *n* (rather than *m*) is used before *b, m,* or *p.* Also, all characters used here are part of the list of 1,945 characters prescribed for everyday use by the Ministry of Education. Those verbs with characters not in that list are written in *hiragana.*

KEY TO SYMBOLS AND ABBREVIATIONS

( )   The verb forms enclosed in parentheses are rarely used in modern Japanese, and thus it is advisable that the reader avoid using them.

        IMPERATIVE   (are)
        TE FORM   atte

,   The comma is used in the example sentences to help the student understand the meaning of the sentence. Its usage in some sentences may differ from conventional grammatical usage.

;   In the verb definitions, a semi-colon differentiates a) two different verbs pronounced similarly, or b) the transitive and intransitive cases of a verb.

    a) 話す to speak; 離す to keep away; 放す to set free, let go: (all trans.)

    b) 出す to put out, send, pay, submit: (trans.); begin doing: (intrans.)

:   The colon is used to indicate that all preceding verbs are either transitive or intransitive.

    開ける to open; 空ける to empty, keep the day open: (both trans.); 明ける the day breaks: (intrans.)

*   The asterisk is used in the verb definitions to indicate that the student should refer to the note at the bottom of the page.

trans.   transitive

intrans.   intransitive

lit.,   literally

caus.   causative

A GUIDE TO JAPANESE VERBS

上がる to go up, rise, get nervous, to finish, enter: (intrans.)

		Affirmative	*Negative*
PLAIN FORM:	PRESENT	agaru	agaranai
	PAST	agatta	agaranakatta
MASU FORM:	PRESENT	agarimasu	agarimasen
	PAST	agarimashita	agarimasen deshita
IMPERATIVE		agare	agaru na
TE FORM		agatte	agaranakute
CONDITIONAL:	PLAIN	agareba	agaranakereba
		agatta ra	agaranakatta ra
	FORMAL	agarimashita ra	agarimasen deshita ra
PRESUMPTIVE:	PLAIN	agaru daroo	agaranai daroo
	FORMAL	agaru deshoo	agaranai deshoo
VOLITIONAL:	PLAIN	agaroo	
	FORMAL	agarimashoo	

	Affirmative		*Affirmative*
POTENTIAL	agareru	HONORIFIC	oagari ni naru
			oagari nasaru
PASSIVE	agarareru	HUMBLE	(oagari suru)
			(oagari itasu)
CAUSATIVE	agaraseru		
CAUS. PASSIVE	agaraserareru		
	agarasareru		

Examples:

1. *Kyuuryoo ga agarimashita.*
   My salary went up.
2. *Bukka ga dondon agaru deshoo.*
   Prices will rise more and more.
3. *Supiichi o suru toki, itsumo agarimasu.*
   When I make a speech, I always get nervous.
4. *Ame ga agatta ra, dekakemashoo ka.*
   When it stops raining, let's go out.
5. *Enryo shinaide, doozo oagari kudasai.*
   Don't hesitate. Come in please.

上げる to raise, lift, give, (attached to a verb) finish: (trans.)

		Affirmative	*Negative*
PLAIN FORM:	PRESENT	ageru	agenai
	PAST	ageta	agenakatta
MASU FORM:	PRESENT	agemasu	agemasen
	PAST	agemashita	agemasen deshita
IMPERATIVE		agero	ageru na
TE FORM		agete	agenakute
CONDITIONAL:	PLAIN	agereba	agenakereba
		ageta ra	agenakatta ra
	FORMAL	agemashita ra	agemasen deshita ra
PRESUMPTIVE:	PLAIN	ageru daroo	agenai daroo
	FORMAL	ageru deshoo	agenai deshoo
VOLITIONAL:	PLAIN	ageyoo	
	FORMAL	agemashoo	

	Affirmative		*Affirmative*
POTENTIAL	agerareru	HONORIFIC	oage ni naru
	agereru		oage nasaru
PASSIVE	agerareru	HUMBLE	oage suru
			oage itasu
CAUSATIVE	agesaseru		
CAUS. PASSIVE	agesaserareru		

Examples:

1. *Kaisha wa kyuuryoo o agemashita.*
   The company raised our salaries.
2. *Kaban o tana ni agemasu.*
   I'll put my bag on the shelf.
3. *Tomodachi no tanjoobi ni purezento o agemashita.*
   I gave a present to my friend on his birthday.
4. *Nihon-go o oshiete agemashoo ka.*
   Shall I teach you Japanese?
5. *Ronbun o kaki-ageta ra, renraku shimasu.*
   When I finish writing my thesis, I'll contact you.

開ける to open; 空ける to empty, keep the day open: (both trans.); 明ける the day breaks: (intrans.)*

		Affirmative	Negative
PLAIN FORM:	PRESENT	akeru	akenai
	PAST	aketa	akenakatta
MASU FORM:	PRESENT	akemasu	akemasen
	PAST	akemashita	akemasen deshita
IMPERATIVE		akero	akeru na
TE FORM		akete	akenakute
CONDITIONAL:	PLAIN	akereba	akenakereba
		aketa ra	akenakatta ra
	FORMAL	akemashita ra	akemasen deshita ra
PRESUMPTIVE:	PLAIN	akeru daroo	akenai daroo
	FORMAL	akeru deshoo	akenai deshoo
VOLITIONAL:	PLAIN	akeyoo	
	FORMAL	akemashoo	

	Affirmative		Affirmative
POTENTIAL	akerareru akereru	HONORIFIC	oake ni naru oake nasaru
PASSIVE	akerareru	HUMBLE	oake suru oake itasu
CAUSATIVE	akesaseru		
CAUS. PASSIVE	akesaserareru		

Examples:

1. *Mado o akete mo ii desu ka.*
   May I open the window?
2. *Ryokoo ni iku node, shibaraku ie o akemasu.*
   Since we are going on a trip, we'll be away from home for a while.
3. *Kondo no Nichiyoobi o akete oite kudasai.*
   Please keep this Sunday open.
4. *Yo ga aketa.*
   The day broke./The sun rose.
5. *Akemashite omedetoo gozaimasu.*
   Happy New Year.

* The intransitive *akeru* 明ける, meaning "the day breaks," generally has no imperative, volitional, potential, passive, causative, causative passive, honorific, or humble forms.

あきらめる to give up: (trans.)

		Affirmative	*Negative*
PLAIN FORM:	PRESENT	akirameru	akiramenai
	PAST	akirameta	akiramenakatta
MASU FORM:	PRESENT	akiramemasu	akiramemasen
	PAST	akiramemashita	akiramemasen deshita
IMPERATIVE		akiramero	akirameru na
TE FORM		akiramete	akiramenakute
CONDITIONAL:	PLAIN	akiramereba	akiramenakereba
		akirameta ra	akiramenakatta ra
	FORMAL	akiramemashita ra	akiramemasen deshita ra
PRESUMPTIVE:	PLAIN	akirameru daroo	akiramenai daroo
	FORMAL	akirameru deshoo	akiramenai deshoo
VOLITIONAL:	PLAIN	akirameyoo	
	FORMAL	akiramemashoo	

	Affirmative		*Affirmative*
POTENTIAL	akiramerareru	HONORIFIC	oakirame ni naru
	akiramereru		oakirame nasaru
PASSIVE	akiramerareru	HUMBLE	(oakirame suru)
CAUSATIVE	akiramesaseru		(oakirame itasu)
CAUS. PASSIVE	akiramesaserareru		

Examples:

1. *Tanaka-san wa tenshoku o akirameta.*
   Mr. Tanaka decided not to change his job.
2. *Kanojo wa kare o akiramerarenai.*
   She cannot give him up.
3. *Kono kikaku wa mikomi ga nai. Akirameyoo.*
   This plan has no chance of success. Let's give it up.
4. *Akiramete wa ikemasen.*
   You must not give up.
5. *Nani o iwarete mo, watashi wa akiramenakatta.*
   No matter what people said, I didn't give up.

飽きる to be tired of, fed up with: (intrans.)

		Affirmative	*Negative*
PLAIN FORM:	PRESENT	akiru	akinai
	PAST	akita	akinakatta
MASU FORM:	PRESENT	akimasu	akimasen
	PAST	akimashita	akimasen deshita
IMPERATIVE		(akiro)	(akiru na)
TE FORM		akite	akinakute
CONDITIONAL:	PLAIN	akireba	akinakereba
		akita ra	akinakatta ra
	FORMAL	akimashita ra	akimasen deshita ra
PRESUMPTIVE:	PLAIN	akiru daroo	akinai daroo
	FORMAL	akiru deshoo	akinai deshoo
VOLITIONAL:	PLAIN	(akiyoo)	
	FORMAL	(akimashoo)	

	Affirmative		*Affirmative*
POTENTIAL	(akirareru)	HONORIFIC	oaki ni naru
			oaki nasaru
PASSIVE	akirareru	HUMBLE	(oaki suru)
			(oaki itasu)
CAUSATIVE	akisaseru		
CAUS. PASSIVE	akisaserareru		

Examples:

1. *Shigoto ni akimashita.*
   I'm tired of my job.
2. *Kanojo wa kare ni akita yoo da.*
   She seems to be fed up with him.
3. *Benkyoo ni akita ra, sanpo shimasu.*
   When I'm tired of studying, I take a walk.
4. *Nani o yatte mo sugu akiru.*
   Whatever you do, you soon get tired of it.
5. *Kare no iu koto ni kiki-akita.*
   I'm fed up with listening to what he says.

開く to open, begin; 空く to become vacant, be free: (both intrans.)

		Affirmative	*Negative*
PLAIN FORM:	PRESENT	aku	akanai
	PAST	aita	akanakatta
MASU FORM:	PRESENT	akimasu	akimasen
	PAST	akimashita	akimasen deshita
IMPERATIVE		(ake)	(aku na)
TE FORM		aite	akanakute
CONDITIONAL:	PLAIN	akeba	akanakereba
		aita ra	akanakatta ra
	FORMAL	akimashita ra	akimasen deshita ra
PRESUMPTIVE:	PLAIN	aku daroo	akanai daroo
	FORMAL	aku deshoo	akanai deshoo
VOLITIONAL:	PLAIN	(akoo)	
	FORMAL	(akimashoo)	

	Affirmative		*Affirmative*
POTENTIAL	(akeru)	HONORIFIC	oaki ni naru
			oaki nasaru
PASSIVE	(akareru)	HUMBLE	(oaki suru)
			(oaki itasu)
CAUSATIVE	(akaseru)		
CAUS. PASSIVE	(akaserareru)		

Examples:

1. *Jidoo-doa ga aita.*
   The automatic door opened.
2. *Kagi ga kowarete, to ga akanai.*
   Since the key is broken, the door won't open.
3. *Ginkoo wa juu-ji ni aku soo desu.*
   I heard the bank opens at ten o'clock.
4. *Sono seki wa aite imasu ka.*
   Is that seat vacant?
5. *Doyoobi wa isogashii kedo, Nichiyoobi nara aite imasu.*
   I'll be busy on Saturday, but I'll be free on Sunday.

争う to fight, compete, dispute, contend: (trans.)

		Affirmative	*Negative*
PLAIN FORM:	PRESENT	arasou	arasowanai
	PAST	arasotta	arasowanakatta
MASU FORM:	PRESENT	arasoimasu	arasoimasen
	PAST	arasoimashita	arasoimasen deshita
IMPERATIVE		arasoe	arasou na
TE FORM		arasotte	arasowanakute
CONDITIONAL:	PLAIN	arasoeba	arasowanakereba
		arasotta ra	arasowanakatta ra
	FORMAL	arasoimashita ra	arasoimasen deshita ra
PRESUMPTIVE:	PLAIN	arasou daroo	arasowanai daroo
	FORMAL	arasou deshoo	arasowanai deshoo
VOLITIONAL:	PLAIN	arasooo	
	FORMAL	arasoimashoo	

	Affirmative		*Affirmative*
POTENTIAL	arasoeru	HONORIFIC	oarasoi ni naru
			oarasoi nasaru
PASSIVE	arasowareru	HUMBLE	(oarasoi suru)
			(oarasoi itasu)
CAUSATIVE	arasowaseru		
CAUS. PASSIVE	arasowaserareru		
	arasowasareru		

Examples:

1. *Karera wa yuushoo o arasotta.*
   They fought for victory.
2. *Suzuki-san wa Satoo-san to shooshin o arasotta.*
   Mr. Suzuki competed with Mr. Sato for the promotion.
3. *Ano hito to arasotte mo shiyoo-ga-nai.*
   It's no use competing with that person.
4. *Arasou no wa suki ja nai.*
   I don't like to compete.
5. *Ima wa ikkoku o arasou toki desu.*
   There's no time to lose now.

洗う to wash, inquire into, wash one's hands of an affair: (trans.)

		Affirmative	Negative
PLAIN FORM:	PRESENT	arau	arawanai
	PAST	aratta	arawanakatta
MASU FORM:	PRESENT	araimasu	araimasen
	PAST	araimashita	araimasen deshita
IMPERATIVE		arae	arau na
TE FORM		aratte	arawanakute
CONDITIONAL:	PLAIN	araeba	arawanakereba
		aratta ra	arawanakatta ra
	FORMAL	araimashita ra	araimasen deshita ra
PRESUMPTIVE:	PLAIN	arau daroo	arawanai daroo
	FORMAL	arau deshoo	arawanai deshoo
VOLITIONAL:	PLAIN	araoo	
	FORMAL	araimashoo	

	Affirmative		Affirmative
POTENTIAL	araeru	HONORIFIC	oarai ni naru
			oarai nasaru
PASSIVE	arawareru	HUMBLE	oarai suru
			oarai itasu
CAUSATIVE	arawaseru		
CAUS. PASSIVE	arawaserareru		
	arawasareru		

Examples:

1. *Te o araimashita.*
   I washed my hands.
2. *Koko de fuku o arawanai de kudasai.*
   Don't wash your clothes here.
3. *Yoku araeba kirei ni narimasu.*
   If you wash it well, it'll become clean.
4. *Keisatsu wa sono otoko no kako o aratta.*
   The police inquired into that man's past.
5. *Hayaku konna seikatsu kara ashi o arai-tai.*
   I want to change from living like this soon.

現れる to appear; 表れる to become visible, show: (both intrans.)

		Affirmative	*Negative*
PLAIN FORM:	PRESENT	arawareru	arawarenai
	PAST	arawareta	arawarenakatta
MASU FORM:	PRESENT	arawaremasu	arawaremasen
	PAST	arawaremashita	arawaremasen deshita
IMPERATIVE		(arawarero)	(arawareru na)
TE FORM		arawarete	arawarenakute
CONDITIONAL:	PLAIN	arawarereba	arawarenakereba
		arawareta ra	arawarenakatta ra
	FORMAL	arawaremashita ra	arawaremasen deshita ra
PRESUMPTIVE:	PLAIN	arawareru daroo	arawarenai daroo
	FORMAL	arawareru deshoo	arawarenai deshoo
VOLITIONAL:	PLAIN	(arawareyoo)	
	FORMAL	(arawaremashoo)	

	Affirmative		*Affirmative*
POTENTIAL	(arawarerareru)	HONORIFIC	oaraware ni naru
			oaraware nasaru
PASSIVE	(arawarerareru)	HUMBLE	(oaraware suru)
			(oaraware itasu)
CAUSATIVE	(arawaresaseru)		
CAUS. PASSIVE	(arawaresaserareru)		

Examples:

1. *Mori kara kuma ga arawareta.*
   A bear came out of the woods.
2. *Ichi-jikan matte mo kare wa arawarenakatta.*
   I waited for an hour, but he didn't appear.
3. *Byoojoo ni henka ga araware-dashita.*
   Changes in the symptoms began to appear.
4. *Kanojo wa kimochi ga sugu taido ni arawareru.*
   She soon shows her feelings through her manners.
5. *Yuki ga tokete, jimen ga araware-dashimashita.*
   Since the snow was melting, the ground began to be exposed.

現す to appear; 表す to show, express; 著す to write: (all trans.)

		Affirmative	*Negative*
PLAIN FORM:	PRESENT	arawasu	arawasanai
	PAST	arawashita	arawasanakatta
MASU FORM:	PRESENT	arawashimasu	arawashimasen
	PAST	arawashimashita	arawashimasen deshita
IMPERATIVE		arawase	arawasu na
TE FORM		arawashite	arawasanakute
CONDITIONAL:	PLAIN	arawaseba	arawasanakereba
		arawashita ra	arawasanakatta ra
	FORMAL	arawashimashita ra	arawasimasen deshita ra
PRESUMPTIVE:	PLAIN	arawasu daroo	arawasanai daroo
	FORMAL	arawasu deshoo	arawasanai deshoo
VOLITIONAL:	PLAIN	arawasoo	
	FORMAL	arawashimashoo	

	Affirmative		*Affirmative*
POTENTIAL	arawaseru	HONORIFIC	oarawashi ni naru
			oarawashi nasaru
PASSIVE	arawasareru	HUMBLE	oarawashi suru
			oarawashi itasu
CAUSATIVE	arawasaseru		
CAUS. PASSIVE	arawasaserareru		

Examples:

1. *Hannin ga sugata o arawashita.*
   The criminal appeared.
2. *Kimochi o umaku kotoba ni arawasemasen deshita.*
   I could not express my feelings well.
3. *Ano kanban wa nani o arawashite iru no deshoo ka.*
   I wonder what that sign means.
4. *Kabu no ne-ugoki o hyoo ni arawashite mimashita.*
   I tried to chart the fluctuations of stock prices.
5. *Kare wa nakunaru ichi-nen mae ni jiden o arawashimashita.*
   He wrote his autobiography one year before he died.

有る *or* 在る to be, have: (intrans.)

		Affirmative	*Negative*
PLAIN FORM:	PRESENT	aru	nai
	PAST	atta	nakatta
MASU FORM:	PRESENT	arimasu	arimasen
	PAST	arimashita	arimasen deshita
IMPERATIVE		(are)	(aru na)
TE FORM		atte	nakute
CONDITIONAL:	PLAIN	areba	nakereba
		atta ra	nakatta ra
	FORMAL	arimashita ra	arimasen deshita ra
PRESUMPTIVE:	PLAIN	aru daroo	nai daroo
	FORMAL	aru deshoo	nai deshoo
VOLITIONAL:	PLAIN	(aroo)	
	FORMAL	(arimashoo)	

	Affirmative		*Affirmative*
POTENTIAL	(areru)	HONORIFIC	gozaru*
			gozaimasu
PASSIVE	(arareru)	HUMBLE	(oari suru)
			(oari itasu)
CAUSATIVE	(araseru)		
CAUS. PASSIVE	(araserareru)		

Examples:

1. *Yuubin-kyoku wa eki no soba ni arimasu.*
   The post office is near the station.
2. *Jikan ga areba, tegami o kakimasu.*
   If I have time, I'll write a letter.
3. *Tanaka-san kara denwa ga arimashita.*
   There was a phone call from Mr. Tanaka.
4. *San-ji kara kaigi ga aru node, shitsurei shimasu.*
   Please excuse me. I must go since I have a meeting at three o'clock.
5. *Hon ni namae ga kaite aru.*
   There is a name written on the book.

* See *gozaru*, p. 73.

aruku

Group 1

步く to walk: (intrans.)*

		Affirmative	*Negative*
PLAIN FORM:	PRESENT	aruku	arukanai
	PAST	aruita	arukanakatta
MASU FORM:	PRESENT	arukimasu	arukimasen
	PAST	arukimashita	arukimasen deshita
IMPERATIVE		aruke	aruku na
TE FORM		aruite	arukanakute
CONDITIONAL:	PLAIN	arukeba	arukanakereba
		aruita ra	arukanakatta ra
	FORMAL	arukimashita ra	arukimasen deshita ra
PRESUMPTIVE:	PLAIN	aruku daroo	arukanai daroo
	FORMAL	aruku deshoo	arukanai deshoo
VOLITIONAL:	PLAIN	arukoo	
	FORMAL	arukimashoo	

	Affirmative		*Affirmative*
POTENTIAL	arukeru	HONORIFIC	oaruki ni naru
			oaruki nasaru
PASSIVE	arukareru	HUMBLE	oaruki suru
			oaruki itasu
CAUSATIVE	arukaseru		
CAUS. PASSIVE	arukaserareru		
	arukasareru		

Examples:

1. *Kooen o arukimashita.*
   I walked in the park.
2. *San-jup-pun aruite, yatto eki ni tsukimashita.*
   After walking for thirty minutes, we finally arrived at the station.
3. *Chotto arukoo ka.*
   Shall we walk for a while?
4. *Eki kara ie made aruite, go-fun gurai desu.*
   It's about a five-minute walk from the station to my house.
5. *Ashi ga itakute, arukemasen.*
   Since my leg hurts, I cannot walk.

* As with other verbs indicating movement, *aruku* may take a direct object, thus giving an idea of "going through a defined area." (*See* example 1.)

遊ぶ to play, enjoy oneself: (intrans.)

		Affirmative	*Negative*
PLAIN FORM:	PRESENT	asobu	asobanai
	PAST	asonda	asobanakatta
MASU FORM:	PRESENT	asobimasu	asobimasen
	PAST	asobimashita	asobimasen deshita
IMPERATIVE		asobe	asobu na
TE FORM		asonde	asobanakute
CONDITIONAL:	PLAIN	asobeba	asobanakereba
		asonda ra	asobanakatta ra
	FORMAL	asobimashita ra	asobimasen deshita ra
PRESUMPTIVE:	PLAIN	asobu daroo	asobanai daroo
	FORMAL	asobu deshoo	asobanai deshoo
VOLITIONAL:	PLAIN	asoboo	
	FORMAL	asobimashoo	

	Affirmative		*Affirmative*
POTENTIAL	asoberu	HONORIFIC	oasobi ni naru
			oasobi nasaru
PASSIVE	asobareru	HUMBLE	oasobi suru
			oasobi itasu
CAUSATIVE	asobaseru		
CAUS. PASSIVE	asobaserareru		
	asobasareru		

Examples:

1. *Dizuniirando de asonda.*
   We enjoyed ourselves at Disneyland.
2. *Tomodachi to geemu o shite asobu tsumori desu.*
   I intend to play some games with my friends.
3. *Kodomo-tachi to asonde agemashita.*
   I played with some children.
4. *Yoku asobi, yoku manabe.*
   Play hard and study hard.
5. *Doozo chikai uchi ni asobi ni kite kudasai.*
   Please come visit us soon.

当たる to hit, shine upon: (intrans.)

		Affirmative	*Negative*
PLAIN FORM:	PRESENT	ataru	ataranai
	PAST	atatta	ataranakatta
MASU FORM:	PRESENT	atarimasu	atarimasen
	PAST	atarimashita	atarimasen deshita
IMPERATIVE		(atare)	(ataru na)
TE FORM		atatte	ataranakute
CONDITIONAL:	PLAIN	atareba	ataranakereba
		atatta ra	ataranakatta ra
	FORMAL	atarimashita ra	atarimasen deshita ra
PRESUMPTIVE:	PLAIN	ataru daroo	ataranai daroo
	FORMAL	ataru deshoo	ataranai deshoo
VOLITIONAL:	PLAIN	(ataroo)	
	FORMAL	(atarimashoo)	

	Affirmative		*Affirmative*
POTENTIAL	(atareru)	HONORIFIC	oatari ni naru
			oatari nasaru
PASSIVE	(atarareru)	HUMBLE	oatari suru
			oatari itasu
CAUSATIVE	ataraseru		
CAUS. PASSIVE	ataraserareru		
	atarasareru		

Examples:

1. *Takarakuji de hyaku-man en ga atatta.*
   I won one million yen in the lottery.
2. *Kan ga atarimashita.*
   I was able to guess right.
3. *Ya ga mato no chuushin ni atatta.*
   The arrow hit the bull's eye.
4. *Sono eiga wa totemo atatta.*
   The movie was a great hit.
5. *Watashi no heya wa hi ga ataranai.*
   My room gets no sunshine.

当てる to hit, guess, put; 宛てる to address to: (both trans.)

		Affirmative	*Negative*
PLAIN FORM:	PRESENT	ateru	atenai
	PAST	ateta	atenakatta
MASU FORM:	PRESENT	atemasu	atemasen
	PAST	atemashita	atemasen deshita
IMPERATIVE		atero	ateru na
TE FORM		atete	atenakute
CONDITIONAL:	PLAIN	atereba	atenakereba
		ateta ra	atenakatta ra
	FORMAL	atemashita ra	atemasen deshita ra
PRESUMPTIVE:	PLAIN	ateru daroo	atenai daroo
	FORMAL	ateru deshoo	atenai deshoo
VOLITIONAL:	PLAIN	ateyoo	
	FORMAL	atemashoo	

	Affirmative		*Affirmative*
POTENTIAL	aterareru	HONORIFIC	oate ni naru
	atereru		oate nasaru
PASSIVE	aterareru	HUMBLE	oate suru
			oate itasu
CAUSATIVE	atesaseru		
CAUS. PASSIVE	atesaserareru		

Examples:

1. *Takarakuji o ateta.*
   I won the lottery.
2. *Kuizu no kotae o atemashita.*
   In the quiz, I guessed the right answer.
3. *Kono hako no naka wa nani ka atete goran.*
   Guess what's in this box.
4. *Hitai ni te o atete miru to, atsukatta.*
   When I put my hand on my forehead, it felt hot.
5. *Kore wa anata ni ateta tegami desu.*
   This is a letter addressed to you.

集まる to get together, assemble: (intrans.)

		Affirmative	*Negative*
PLAIN FORM:	PRESENT	atsumaru	atsumaranai
	PAST	atsumatta	atsumaranakatta
MASU FORM:	PRESENT	atsumarimasu	atsumarimasen
	PAST	atsumarimashita	atsumarimasen deshita
IMPERATIVE		atsumare	atsumaru na
TE FORM		atsumatte	atsumaranakute
CONDITIONAL:	PLAIN	atsumareba	atsumaranakereba
		atsumatta ra	atsumaranakatta ra
	FORMAL	atsumarimashita ra	atsumarimasen deshita ra
PRESUMPTIVE:	PLAIN	atsumaru daroo	atsumaranai daroo
	FORMAL	atsumaru deshoo	atsumaranai deshoo
VOLITIONAL:	PLAIN	atsumaroo	
	FORMAL	atsumarimashoo	

	Affirmative		*Affirmative*
POTENTIAL	atsumareru	HONORIFIC	oatsumari ni naru
			oatsumari nasaru
PASSIVE	atsumarareru	HUMBLE	(oatsumari suru)
			(oatsumari itasu)
CAUSATIVE	atsumaraseru		
CAUS. PASSIVE	atsumaraserareru		
	atsumarasareru		

Examples:

1. *Kitte ga takusan atsumatta.*
   A lot of stamps were gathered.
2. *Ashita nan-ji ni atsumareba ii desu ka.*
   What time should we meet tomorrow?
3. *Juu-ji ni atsumatte kudasai.*
   Assemble at ten o'clock.
4. *Kifukin wa amari atsumaranai daroo.*
   Contributions probably won't amount to much.
5. *Konsaato ni san-zen-nin gurai atsumarimashita.*
   About three thousand people gathered for the concert.

集める to collect, gather: (trans.)

		Affirmative	*Negative*
PLAIN FORM:	PRESENT	atsumeru	atsumenai
	PAST	atsumeta	atsumenakatta
MASU FORM:	PRESENT	atsumemasu	atsumemasen
	PAST	atsumemashita	atsumemasen deshita
IMPERATIVE		atsumero	atsumeru na
TE FORM		atsumete	atsumenakute
CONDITIONAL:	PLAIN	atsumereba	atsumenakereba
		atsumeta ra	atsumenakatta ra
	FORMAL	atsumemashita ra	atsumemasen deshita ra
PRESUMPTIVE:	PLAIN	atsumeru daroo	atsumenai daroo
	FORMAL	atsumeru deshoo	atsumenai deshoo
VOLITIONAL:	PLAIN	atsumeyoo	
	FORMAL	atsumemashoo	

	Affirmative		*Affirmative*
POTENTIAL	atsumerareru atsumereru	HONORIFIC	oatsume ni naru oatsume nasaru
PASSIVE	atsumerareru	HUMBLE	oatsume suru oatsume itasu
CAUSATIVE	atsumesaseru		
CAUS. PASSIVE	atsumesaserareru		

Examples:

1. *Watashi wa kitte o atsumete imasu.*
   I collect stamps.
2. *Seito-tachi o kootei ni atsumete kudasai.*
   Gather the students together in the school ground.
3. *Kare wa kifukin o atsumeru no ni isogashii desu.*
   He is busy collecting contributions.
4. *Atsumeta gomi o moyashimashoo.*
   Let's burn the trash we collected.
5. *Kanojo no fuku wa michiyuku hito no chuumoku o atsumeta.*
   Her clothes attracted the attention of passersby.

会う to meet; 合う to match, fit: (both intrans.)*

		Affirmative	*Negative*
PLAIN FORM:	PRESENT	au	awanai
	PAST	atta	awanakatta
MASU FORM:	PRESENT	aimasu	aimasen
	PAST	aimashita	aimasen deshita
IMPERATIVE		ae	au na
TE FORM		atte	awanakute
CONDITIONAL:	PLAIN	aeba	awanakereba
		atta ra	awanakatta ra
	FORMAL	aimashita ra	aimasen deshita ra
PRESUMPTIVE:	PLAIN	au daroo	awanai daroo
	FORMAL	au deshoo	awanai deshoo
VOLITIONAL:	PLAIN	aoo	
	FORMAL	aimashoo	

	Affirmative		*Affirmative*
POTENTIAL	aeru	HONORIFIC	oai ni naru
			oai nasaru
PASSIVE	awareru	HUMBLE	oai suru
			oai itasu
CAUSATIVE	awaseru		
CAUS. PASSIVE	awaserareru		
	awasareru		

Examples:

1. *Kinoo dare to/ni atta'n desu ka.*
   Who did you meet yesterday?
   Dare to/ni mo awanakatta'n desu.
   I didn't meet anybody.
2. *Itsu sensei ni/to oai ni narimasu ka.*
   When will you meet your teacher?
   Raishuu oai suru tsumori desu.
   I plan to meet him next week.
3. *Watashi to kare wa itsumo iken ga awanai.*
   My opinions always differ from his.

* The *au* 合う meaning "to match, fit" generally has no imperative, volitional, potential, and passive forms.

謝る to apologize; 誤る to make a mistake: (both trans.)*

		Affirmative	*Negative*
PLAIN FORM:	PRESENT	ayamaru	ayamaranai
	PAST	ayamatta	ayamaranakatta
MASU FORM:	PRESENT	ayamarimasu	ayamarimasen
	PAST	ayamarimashita	ayamarimasen deshita
IMPERATIVE		ayamare	ayamaru na
TE FORM		ayamatte	ayamaranakute
CONDITIONAL:	PLAIN	ayamareba	ayamaranakereba
		ayamatta ra	ayamaranakatta ra
	FORMAL	ayamarimashita ra	ayamarimasen deshita ra
PRESUMPTIVE:	PLAIN	ayamaru daroo	ayamaranai daroo
	FORMAL	ayamaru deshoo	ayamaranai deshoo
VOLITIONAL:	PLAIN	ayamaroo	
	FORMAL	ayamarimashoo	

	Affirmative		*Affirmative*
POTENTIAL	ayamareru	HONORIFIC	oayamari ni naru
			oayamari nasaru
PASSIVE	ayamarareru	HUMBLE	oayamari suru
			oayamari itasu
CAUSATIVE	ayamaraseru		
CAUS. PASSIVE	ayamaraserareru		
	ayamarasareru		

Examples:

1. *Kare ni ayamarimashita.*
   I apologized to him.
2. *Dooshite watashi ga ayamaranakereba naranai'n desu ka.*
   Why do I have to apologize?
3. *Okureta koto o kare ni ayamatta hoo ga ii.*
   You should apologize to him for being late.
4. *Handan o ayamatta kamo-shirenai.*
   I might have made a wrong judgment.
5. *Sono jiko wa untenshu ga ayamatte, handoru o kitta tame to mirarete imasu.*
   It seems the accident happened because the driver turned the wrong way.

* The verb *ayamaru* 誤る meaning "to make a mistake" generally has no volitional, potential, passive, humble, causative, or causative passive forms.

預かる to keep, take charge of: (trans.)

		Affirmative	*Negative*
PLAIN FORM:	PRESENT	azukaru	azukaranai
	PAST	azukatta	azukaranakatta
MASU FORM:	PRESENT	azukarimasu	azukarimasen
	PAST	azukarimashita	azukarimasen deshita
IMPERATIVE		azukare	azukaru na
TE FORM		azukatte	azukaranakute
CONDITIONAL:	PLAIN	azukareba	azukaranakereba
		azukatta ra	azukaranakatta ra
	FORMAL	azukarimashita ra	azukarimasen deshita ra
PRESUMPTIVE:	PLAIN	azukaru daroo	azukaranai daroo
	FORMAL	azukaru deshoo	azukaranai deshoo
VOLITIONAL:	PLAIN	azukaroo	
	FORMAL	azukarimashoo	

	Affirmative		*Affirmative*
POTENTIAL	azukareru	HONORIFIC	oazukari ni naru
			oazukari nasaru
PASSIVE	azukarareru	HUMBLE	oazukari suru
			oazukari itasu
CAUSATIVE	azukaraseru		
CAUS. PASSIVE	azukaraserareru		
	azukarasareru		

Examples:

1. *Anata no nimotsu o azukatte imasu.*
   I am keeping the luggage for you.
2. *Kore, azukatte moraemasu ka.*
   Can you keep this for me?
3. *Kaban wa doko de azukatte kuremasu ka.*
   Where can I leave my bag?
   Kochira de oazukari itashimasu.
   We'll keep your bag here.
4. *Tomodachi ga kodomo o azukatte kureta.*
   My friend took care of my child for me.

預ける to leave a person or thing under someone's care, deposit: (trans.)

		Affirmative	*Negative*
PLAIN FORM:	PRESENT	azukeru	azukenai
	PAST	azuketa	azukenakatta
MASU FORM:	PRESENT	azukemasu	azukemasen
	PAST	azukemashita	azukemasen deshita
IMPERATIVE		azukero	azukeru na
TE FORM		azukete	azukenakute
CONDITIONAL:	PLAIN	azukereba	azukenakereba
		azuketa ra	azukenakatta ra
	FORMAL	azukemashita ra	azukemasen deshita ra
PRESUMPTIVE:	PLAIN	azukeru daroo	azukenai daroo
	FORMAL	azukeru deshoo	azukenai deshoo
VOLITIONAL:	PLAIN	azukeyoo	
	FORMAL	azukemashoo	

	Affirmative		*Affirmative*
POTENTIAL	azukerareru	HONORIFIC	oazuke ni naru
	azukereru		oazuke nasaru
PASSIVE	azukerareru	HUMBLE	oazuke suru
			oazuke itasu
CAUSATIVE	azukesaseru		
CAUS. PASSIVE	azukesaserareru		

Examples:

1. *Nimotsu o uketsuke ni azukemashita.*
   I left my luggage at the reception desk.
2. *Nimotsu o azukeru tokoro wa doko desu ka.*
   Where can I leave my luggage?
   Asoko ni azukete kudasai.
   You can leave it over there.
3. *Karera wa kodomo o hoikuen ni azukete hatarakimasu.*
   They work, leaving their child in the care of a nursery school.
4. *Suzuki-san wa ginkoo ni hyaku-man en o azukete iru.*
   Mr. Suzuki has one million yen deposited in the bank.

butsukaru

ぶつかる to hit, face (difficulties), fall on (dates): (intrans.)

		Affirmative	*Negative*
PLAIN FORM:	PRESENT	butsukaru	butsukaranai
	PAST	butsukatta	butsukaranakatta
MASU FORM:	PRESENT	butsukarimasu	butsukarimasen
	PAST	butsukarimashita	butsukarimasen deshita
IMPERATIVE		butsukare	butsukaru na
TE FORM		butsukatte	butsukaranakute
CONDITIONAL:	PLAIN	butsukareba	butsukaranakereba
		butsukatta ra	butsukaranakatta ra
	FORMAL	butsukarimashita ra	butsukarimasen deshita ra
PRESUMPTIVE:	PLAIN	butsukaru daroo	butsukaranai daroo
	FORMAL	butsukaru deshoo	butsukaranai deshoo
VOLITIONAL:	PLAIN	butsukaroo	
	FORMAL	butsukarimashoo	

	Affirmative		*Affirmative*
POTENTIAL	(butsukareru)	HONORIFIC	obutsukari ni naru
			obutsukari nasaru
PASSIVE	(butsukarareru)	HUMBLE	(obutsukari suru)
			(obutsukari itasu)
CAUSATIVE	butsukaraseru		
CAUS. PASSIVE	butsukaraserareru		
	butsukarasareru		

Examples:

1. *Kata ga doa ni butsukarimashita.*
   My shoulder struck the door.
2. *Kuruma to baiku ga butsukatta.*
   A car and a motorcycle ran into each other.
3. *Iroiro na mondai ni butsukatte kimashita.*
   I have faced various difficulties.
4. *Karera wa ima ooki na kabe ni butsukatte iru.*
   They are now deadlocked. (*lit.*, They have hit a big wall.)
5. *Kyonen wa Kurisumasu to Nichiyoobi ga butsukatta.*
   Christmas fell on a Sunday last year.

ぶつける to hit against, strike, throw: (trans.)

		Affirmative	*Negative*
PLAIN FORM:	PRESENT	butsukeru	butsukenai
	PAST	butsuketa	butsukenakatta
MASU FORM:	PRESENT	butsukemasu	butsukemasen
	PAST	butsukemashita	butsukemasen deshita
IMPERATIVE		butsukero	butsukeru na
TE FORM:		butsukete	butsukenakute
CONDITIONAL:	PLAIN	butsukereba	butsukenakereba
		butsuketa ra	butsukenakatta ra
	FORMAL	butsukemashita ra	butsukemasen deshita ra
PRESUMPTIVE:	PLAIN	butsukeru daroo	butsukenai daroo
	FORMAL	butsukeru deshoo	butsukenai deshoo
VOLITIONAL:	PLAIN	butsukeyoo	
	FORMAL	butsukemashoo	

	Affirmative		*Affirmative*
POTENTIAL	butsukerareru	HONORIFIC	obutsuke ni naru
	butsukereru		obutsuke nasaru
PASSIVE	butsukerareru	HUMBLE	(obutsuke suru)
			(obutsuke itasu)
CAUSATIVE	butsukesaseru		
CAUS. PASSIVE	butsukesaserareru		

Examples:

1. *Kare wa kata o doa ni butsukemashita.*
   He hit his shoulder against the door.
2. *Kanojo wa kuruma o gaadoreeru ni butsukemashita.*
   She hit her car against the guardrail.
3. *Kodomo wa inu ni ishi o butsuketa.*
   The child threw a stone at the dog.
4. *Kuruma o butsukerareta'n desu ka.*
   Did your car get hit?
   Ee, demo sukoshi shika butsukerarete imasen.
   Yes, but it was only nicked a little.

違う to differ, be wrong: (intrans.)

		Affirmative	*Negative*
PLAIN FORM:	PRESENT	chigau	chigawanai
	PAST	chigatta	chigawanakatta
MASU FORM:	PRESENT	chigaimasu	chigaimasen
	PAST	chigaimashita	chigaimasen deshita
IMPERATIVE		(chigae)	(chigau na)
TE FORM		chigatte	chigawanakute
CONDITIONAL:	PLAIN	chigaeba	chigawanakereba
		chigatta ra	chigawanakatta ra
	FORMAL	chigaimashita ra	chigaimasen deshita ra
PRESUMPTIVE:	PLAIN	chigau daroo	chigawanai daroo
	FORMAL	chigau deshoo	chigawanai deshoo
VOLITIONAL:	PLAIN	(chigaoo)	
	FORMAL	(chigaimashoo)	

	Affirmative		*Affirmative*
POTENTIAL	(chigaeru)	HONORIFIC	(ochigai ni naru)
			(ochigai nasaru)
PASSIVE	(chigawareru)	HUMBLE	(ochigai suru)
			(ochigai itasu)
CAUSATIVE	chigawaseru		
CAUS. PASSIVE	chigawaserareru		
	chigawasareru		

Examples:

1. *Ano hito wa Nihon-jin desu ka.*
   Is that person Japanese?
   Iie, chigaimasu.
   No, he isn't.
2. *Kono heya to ano heya wa ookisa ga chigaimasu.*
   This room is different from that room in size.
3. *Watashi wa tomodachi to konomi ga chigau.*
   I have different tastes than my friend.
4. *Denwa-bangoo ga chigaimasu yo.*
   You have the wrong telephone number.

近づける to bring a thing close, allow a person to approach: (trans.)

		Affirmative	*Negative*
PLAIN FORM:	PRESENT	chikazukeru	chikazukenai
	PAST	chikazuketa	chikazukenakatta
MASU FORM:	PRESENT	chikazukemasu	chikazukemasen
	PAST	chikazukemashita	chikazukemasen deshita
IMPERATIVE		chikazukero	chikazukeru na
TE FORM		chikazukete	chikazukenakute
CONDITIONAL:	PLAIN	chikazukereba	chikazukenakereba
		chikazuketa ra	chikazukenakatta ra
	FORMAL	chikazukemashita ra	chikazukemasen deshita ra
PRESUMPTIVE:	PLAIN	chikazukeru daroo	chikazukenai daroo
	FORMAL	chikazukeru deshoo	chikazukenai deshoo
VOLITIONAL:	PLAIN	chikazukeyoo	
	FORMAL	chikazukemashoo	

	Affirmative		*Affirmative*
POTENTIAL	chikazukerareru	HONORIFIC	ochikazuke ni naru
	chikazukereru		ochikazuke nasaru
PASSIVE	chikazukerareru	HUMBLE	ochikazuke suru
			ochikazuke itasu
CAUSATIVE	chikazukesaseru		
CAUS. PASSIVE	chikazukesaserareru		

Examples:

1. *Isu o tsukue ni chikazukete kudasai.*
   Please draw your chair up to the desk.
2. *Suzuki-san wa shigoto-chuu hito o chikazukenai.*
   Mr. Suzuki keeps away from people while he is working.
3. *Kare wa kao o mado ni chikazukete, soto o mita.*
   He moved close to the window and looked outside.
4. *Kodomo o sutoobu ni chikazukenaide kudasai.*
   Please keep children away from the stove.
5. *Warui yuujin o chikazukenai yoo ni shinasai.*
   Keep a fair distance from bad friends.

chikazuku

近づく to approach, get near, associate with: (intrans.)

		Affirmative	*Negative*
PLAIN FORM:	PRESENT	chikazuku	chikazukanai
	PAST	chikazuita	chikazukanakatta
MASU FORM:	PRESENT	chikazukimasu	chikazukimasen
	PAST	chikazukimashita	chikazukimasen deshita
IMPERATIVE		chikazuke	chikazuku na
TE FORM		chikazuite	chikazukanakute
CONDITIONAL:	PLAIN	chikazukeba	chikazukanakereba
		chikazuita ra	chikazukanakatta ra
	FORMAL	chikazukimashita ra	chikazukimasen deshita ra
PRESUMPTIVE:	PLAIN	chikazuku daroo	chikazukanai daroo
	FORMAL	chikazuku deshoo	chikazukanai deshoo
VOLITIONAL:	PLAIN	chikazukoo	
	FORMAL	chikazukimashoo	

	Affirmative		*Affirmative*
POTENTIAL	chikazukeru	HONORIFIC	ochikazuki ni naru
			ochikazuki nasaru
PASSIVE	chikazukareru	HUMBLE	ochikazuki suru
			ochikazuki itasu
CAUSATIVE	chikazukaseru		
CAUS. PASSIVE	chikazukaserareru		
	chikazukasareru		

Examples:

1. *Densha wa eki ni chikazuita.*
   The train is nearing the station.
2. *Koinu ga kare ni chikazuite kimashita.*
   A puppy came up to him.
3. *Natsu-yasumi ga chikazuita.*
   Summer vacation is approaching.
4. *Kanojo wa mado ni chikazuite, soto o mita.*
   She approached the window and looked out.
5. *Aa iu hito ni wa chikazukanai hoo ga ii.*
   You should stay away from that kind of person.

抱く to hug: (trans.)

		Affirmative	*Negative*
PLAIN FORM:	PRESENT	daku	dakanai
	PAST	daita	dakanakatta
MASU FORM:	PRESENT	dakimasu	dakimasen
	PAST	dakimashita	dakimasen deshita
IMPERATIVE		dake	daku na
TE FORM		daite	dakanakute
CONDITIONAL:	PLAIN	dakeba	dakanakereba
		daita ra	dakanakatta ra
	FORMAL	dakimashita ra	dakimasen deshita ra
PRESUMPTIVE:	PLAIN	daku daroo	dakanai daroo
	FORMAL	daku deshoo	dakanai deshoo
VOLITIONAL:	PLAIN	dakoo	
	FORMAL	dakimashoo	

	Affirmative		*Affirmative*
POTENTIAL	dakeru	HONORIFIC	odaki ni naru
			odaki nasaru
PASSIVE	dakareru	HUMBLE	odaki suru
			odaki itasu
CAUSATIVE	dakaseru		
CAUS. PASSIVE	dakaserareru		
	dakasareru		

Examples:

1. *Kodomo wa kuma no nuigurumi o daite iru.*
   The child is hugging a stuffed teddy bear.
2. *Kare wa musuko o ryooude ni shikkari daita.*
   He held his son firmly in his arms.
3. *Kare wa ooki na yume o daite, kuni o deta.*
   He left his home town with a big dream.
4. *Genjuumin ni henken o dakanaide hoshii.*
   I don't want you to have prejudices against the natives.
5. *Niwatori ga tamago o daite iru.*
   A hen is sitting on her eggs.

だます to deceive, cheat: (trans.)

		Affirmative	*Negative*
PLAIN FORM:	PRESENT	damasu	damasanai
	PAST	damashita	damasanakatta
MASU FORM:	PRESENT	damashimasu	damashimasen
	PAST	damashimashita	damashimasen deshita
IMPERATIVE		damase	damasu na
TE FORM		damashite	damasanakute
CONDITIONAL:	PLAIN	damaseba	damasanakereba
		damashita ra	damasanakatta ra
	FORMAL	damashimashita ra	damashimasen deshita ra
PRESUMPTIVE:	PLAIN	damasu daroo	damasanai daroo
	FORMAL	damasu deshoo	damasanai deshoo
VOLITIONAL:	PLAIN	damasoo	
	FORMAL	damashimashoo	

	Affirmative		*Affirmative*
POTENTIAL	damaseru	HONORIFIC	odamashi ni naru
			odamashi nasaru
PASSIVE	damasareru	HUMBLE	odamashi suru
			odamashi itasu
CAUSATIVE	damasaseru		
CAUS. PASSIVE	damasaserareru		

Examples:
1. *Sono otoko wa takusan no hito o damashita.*
   That man deceived many people.
2. *Karera wa kankoo-kyaku o damashite, takai mono o kawaseta.*
   They cheated tourists into buying expensive things.
3. *Anata wa damasareta'n desu yo.*
   You were fooled.
4. *Kare wa damasare-yasui.*
   He is easily deceived.
5. *Kanojo o damasu tsumori wa nakatta.*
   I didn't mean to deceive her.

出す to put out, send, pay, submit: (trans.); begin doing: (intrans.)

		Affirmative	*Negative*
PLAIN FORM:	PRESENT	dasu	dasanai
	PAST	dashita	dasanakatta
MASU FORM:	PRESENT	dashimasu	dashimasen
	PAST	dashimashita	dashimasen deshita
IMPERATIVE		dase	dasu na
TE FORM		dashite	dasanakute
CONDITIONAL:	PLAIN	daseba	dasanakereba
		dashita ra	dasanakatta ra
	FORMAL	dashimashita ra	dashimasen deshita ra
PRESUMPTIVE:	PLAIN	dasu daroo	dasanai daroo
	FORMAL	dasu deshoo	dasanai deshoo
VOLITIONAL:	PLAIN	dasoo	
	FORMAL	dashimashoo	

	Affirmative		*Affirmative*
POTENTIAL	daseru	HONORIFIC	odashi ni naru
			odashi nasaru
PASSIVE	dasareru	HUMBLE	odashi suru
			odashi itasu
CAUSATIVE	dasaseru		
CAUS. PASSIVE	dasaserareru		
	dasasareru		

Examples:
1. *Watashi-tachi no kenkyuu ni seifu ga okane o dashimasu.*
   The government financially supports our research.
2. *Kaban kara saifu o dashimashita.*
   I took the wallet out of the bag.
3. *Ototoi tegami o dashimashita.*
   I sent the letter the day before yesterday.
4. *Kono repooto wa nan-nichi made ni dasanakereba narimasen ka.*
   By what date do I have to submit this report?
5. *Ame ga furi-dashimashita.*
   It started raining.

出かける to go out, set off (to): (intrans.)

		Affirmative	*Negative*
PLAIN FORM:	PRESENT	dekakeru	dekakenai
	PAST	dekaketa	dekakenakatta
MASU FORM:	PRESENT	dekakemasu	dekakemasen
	PAST	dekakemashita	dekakemasen deshita
IMPERATIVE		dekakero	dekakeru na
TE FORM		dekakete	dekakenakute
CONDITIONAL:	PLAIN	dekakereba	dekakenakereba
		dekaketa ra	dekakenakatta ra
	FORMAL	dekakemashita ra	dekakemasen deshita ra
PRESUMPTIVE:	PLAIN	dekakeru daroo	dekakenai daroo
	FORMAL	dekakeru deshoo	dekakenai deshoo
VOLITIONAL:	PLAIN	dekakeyoo	
	FORMAL	dekakemashoo	

	Affirmative		*Affirmative*
POTENTIAL	dekakerareru	HONORIFIC	odekake ni naru
	dekakereru		odekake nasaru
PASSIVE	dekakerareru	HUMBLE	odekake suru
			odekake itasu
CAUSATIVE	dekakesaseru		
CAUS. PASSIVE	dekakesaserareru		

Examples:

1. *Dekakemashoo.*
   Let's go out.
2. *Saitoo-san wa kaimono ni dekaketa.*
   Mr. Saito went shopping.
3. *Moshi moshi, Shachoo-san wa irasshaimasu ka.*
   Hello, may I speak to the president of your company?
   Shachoo wa ima dekakete orimasu.
   He is now out.
4. *Sensei wa roku-ji goro odekake ni narimashita.*
   The teacher went out at around six o'clock.

出来る to be completed, can, be made of: (intrans.)

		Affirmative	*Negative*
PLAIN FORM:	PRESENT	dekiru	dekinai
	PAST	dekita	dekinakatta
MASU FORM:	PRESENT	dekimasu	dekimasen
	PAST	dekimashita	dekimasen deshita
IMPERATIVE		(dekiro)	(dekiru na)
TE FORM		dekite	dekinakute
CONDITIONAL:	PLAIN	dekireba	dekinakereba
		dekita ra	dekinakatta ra
	FORMAL	dekimashita ra	dekimasen deshita ra
PRESUMPTIVE:	PLAIN	dekiru daroo	dekinai daroo
	FORMAL	dekiru deshoo	dekinai deshoo
VOLITIONAL:	PLAIN	(dekiyoo)	
	FORMAL	(dekimashoo)	

	Affirmative		*Affirmative*
POTENTIAL	(dekirareru)	HONORIFIC	odeki ni naru
			(odeki nasaru)
PASSIVE	(dekirareru)	HUMBLE	(odeki suru)
CAUSATIVE	(dekisaseru)		(odeki itasu)
CAUS. PASSIVE	(dekisaserareru)		

Examples:

1. *Shokuji no yooi ga dekita.*
   Dinner is ready.
2. *Nihon-go ga dekimasu ka.*
   Can you speak Japanese?
3. *Dekireba, mainichi Nihon-go no kurasu ni de-tai desu.*
   If possible, I'd like to attend Japanese lessons everyday.
4. *Mooshikomi-sho wa dekiru dake hayaku dashite kudasai.*
   Please submit the application form as soon as possible.
5. *Kono butsuzoo wa ki de dekite imasu.*
   This statue of Buddha is made of wood.

出る to come out, leave, attend, be published: (intrans.)*

		Affirmative	Negative
PLAIN FORM:	PRESENT	deru	denai
	PAST	deta	denakatta
MASU FORM:	PRESENT	demasu	demasen
	PAST	demashita	demasen deshita
IMPERATIVE		dero	deru na
TE FORM		dete	denakute
CONDITIONAL:	PLAIN	dereba	denakereba
		deta ra	denakatta ra
	FORMAL	demashita ra	demasen deshita ra
PRESUMPTIVE:	PLAIN	deru daroo	denai daroo
	FORMAL	deru deshoo	denai deshoo
VOLITIONAL:	PLAIN	deyoo	
	FORMAL	demashoo	

	Affirmative		Affirmative
POTENTIAL	derareru dereru	HONORIFIC	ode ni naru ode nasaru
PASSIVE	derareru	HUMBLE	(ode suru) (ode itasu)
CAUSATIVE	desaseru		
CAUS. PASSIVE	desaserareru		

Examples:

1. *Watashi-tachi no kenkyuu ni seifu kara okane ga demasu.*
   Our research is supported financially by the government.
2. *San-ji ni kaigi ni denakereba naranai node, shitsurei shimasu.*
   Excuse me, but I have to attend a meeting at three o'clock.
3. *Shinbun ni jishin no kiji ga dete imasu.*
   An article on the earthquake appeared in the newspaper.
4. *Nihon-go no sankoosho ga moo sugu shuppansha kara deru.*
   The Japanese reference book will be released soon by a publisher.
5. *Kesa nan-ji ni ie o deta'n desu ka.*
   What time did you leave the house this morning?

* As with other verbs indicating motion, *deru* may take a direct object, thus giving an idea of "going through a defined area." (*See* example 5.)

選ぶ to choose, decide on, elect: (trans.)

		Affirmative	Negative
PLAIN FORM:	PRESENT	erabu	erabanai
	PAST	eranda	erabanakatta
MASU FORM:	PRESENT	erabimasu	erabimasen
	PAST	erabimashita	erabimasen deshita
IMPERATIVE		erabe	erabu na
TE FORM		erande	erabanakute
CONDITIONAL:	PLAIN	erabeba	erabanakereba
		eranda ra	erabanakatta ra
	FORMAL	erabimashita ra	erabimasen deshita ra
PRESUMPTIVE:	PLAIN	erabu daroo	erabanai daroo
	FORMAL	erabu deshoo	erabanai deshoo
VOLITIONAL:	PLAIN	eraboo	
	FORMAL	erabimashoo	

	Affirmative		Affirmative
POTENTIAL	eraberu	HONORIFIC	oerabi ni naru
			oerabi nasaru
PASSIVE	erabareru	HUMBLE	oerabi suru
			oerabi itasu
CAUSATIVE	erabaseru		
CAUS. PASSIVE	erabaserareru		
	erabasareru		

Examples:

1. *Yoi tomodachi o erande kudasai.*
   Please choose good friends.
2. *Dooshite sono shigoto o erabimashita ka.*
   Why did you choose that job?
3. *Kore to are to dotchi o erabimasu ka.*
   Which would you prefer, this one or that one?
4. *Doozo o-suki na no o oerabi kudasai.*
   Please choose any one you like.
5. *Tanaka-san wa gichoo ni erabaremashita.*
   Mr. Tanaka was elected as chairman.

増える to increase: (intrans.)

		Affirmative	*Negative*
PLAIN FORM:	PRESENT	fueru	fuenai
	PAST	fueta	fuenakatta
MASU FORM:	PRESENT	fuemasu	fuemasen
	PAST	fuemashita	fuemasen deshita
IMPERATIVE		(fuero)	(fueru na)
TE FORM		fuete	fuenakute
CONDITIONAL:	PLAIN	fuereba	fuenakereba
		fueta ra	fuenakatta ra
	FORMAL	fuemashita ra	fuemasen deshita ra
PRESUMPTIVE:	PLAIN	fueru daroo	fuenai daroo
	FORMAL	fueru deshoo	fuenai deshoo
VOLITIONAL:	PLAIN	(fueyoo)	
	FORMAL	(fuemashoo)	

	Affirmative		*Affirmative*
POTENTIAL	(fuerareru)	HONORIFIC	ofue ni naru
			ofue nasaru
PASSIVE	(fuerareru)	HUMBLE	(ofue suru)
CAUSATIVE	fuesaseru		(ofue itasu)
CAUS. PASSIVE	fuesaserareru		

Examples:

1. *Nihon-go no goi ga fueta.*
   My Japanese vocabulary has increased.
2. *Taijuu ga go kiro fuemashita.*
   I have gained five kilos.
3. *Sekai no jinkoo wa fue-tsuzukete iru.*
   The population of the world keeps on increasing.
4. *Daitoshi de no hanzai-ritsu ga fuete iru.*
   The crime rate in big cities is increasing.
5. *Tenshoku shite kara shuunyuu ga fueta.*
   My income increased after I changed jobs.

拭く to wipe; 吹く to blow, play an instrument:* (both trans.)

		Affirmative	*Negative*
PLAIN FORM:	PRESENT	fuku	fukanai
	PAST	fuita	fukanakatta
MASU FORM:	PRESENT	fukimasu	fukimasen
	PAST	fukimashita	fukimasen deshita
IMPERATIVE		fuke	fuku na
TE FORM		fuite	fukanakute
CONDITIONAL:	PLAIN	fukeba	fukanakereba
		fuita ra	fukanakatta ra
	FORMAL	fukimashita ra	fukimasen deshita ra
PRESUMPTIVE:	PLAIN	fuku daroo	fukanai daroo
	FORMAL	fuku deshoo	fukanai deshoo
VOLITIONAL:	PLAIN	fukoo	
	FORMAL	fukimashoo	

	Affirmative		*Affirmative*
POTENTIAL	fukeru	HONORIFIC	ofuki ni naru
			ofuki nasaru
PASSIVE	fukareru	HUMBLE	ofuki suru
			ofuki itasu
CAUSATIVE	fukaseru		
CAUS. PASSIVE	fukaserareru		
	fukasareru		

Examples:

1. *Tsukue no ue o fukimasu.*
   I'll wipe the top of the desk.
2. *Soto wa tsuyoi kaze ga fuite iru.*
   It's blowing hard outside.
3. *Tanaka-san wa furuuto ga fukemasu.*
   Mr. Tanaka can play the flute.
4. *Kare wa tabako no kemuri o fuite imasu.*
   He is blowing smoke from his cigarette.
5. *Kanojo wa yoku hora o fuku kara, ki o tsukete.*
   Be careful, because she often exaggerates.

* play the flute/clarinet/trumpet → *furuuto/kurarinetto/toranpetto o fuku*
play the piano/guitar/violin → *piano/gitaa/baiorin o hiku*

fukumeru Group 2

含める to include, to convince: (trans.)

		Affirmative	*Negative*
PLAIN FORM:	PRESENT	fukumeru	fukumenai
	PAST	fukumeta	fukumenakatta
MASU FORM:	PRESENT	fukumemasu	fukumemasen
	PAST	fukumemashita	fukumemasen deshita
IMPERATIVE		fukumero	fukumeru na
TE FORM		fukumete	fukumenakute
CONDITIONAL:	PLAIN	fukumereba	fukumenakereba
		fukumeta ra	fukumenakatta ra
	FORMAL	fukumemashita ra	fukumemasen deshita ra
PRESUMPTIVE:	PLAIN	fukumeru daroo	fukumenai daroo
	FORMAL	fukumeru deshoo	fukumenai deshoo
VOLITIONAL:	PLAIN	fukumeyoo	
	FORMAL	fukumemashoo	

	Affirmative		*Affirmative*
POTENTIAL	fukumerareru fukumereru	HONORFIC	ofukume ni naru ofukume nasaru
PASSIVE	fukumerareru	HUMBLE	ofukume suru ofukume itasu
CAUSATIVE	fukumesaseru		
CAUS. PASSIVE	fukumesaserareru		

Examples:

1. *Zeikin o fukumete, san-man go-sen en desu.*
   The total is ¥35,000, including tax.
2. *Suzuki-san o fukumeru to, zenbu de juu nin ni narimasu.*
   Including Mr. Suzuki, there are ten people in all.
3. *Ryooshuusho ni kono hon no daikin wa fukumenaide kudasai.*
   Please don't include the price of this book in the receipt.
4. *Heya-dai o fukumezu ni, ichinichi wa go-sen en gurai deshita.*
   Excluding the cost of the room, one day costs about ¥5,000 yen.
5. *Kanojo wa kare ni ii-fukumerareta.*
   He made her understand completely.

含む to contain, include, hold something in the mouth: (trans. or intrans.)

		Affirmative	*Negative*
PLAIN FORM:	PRESENT	fukumu	fukumanai
	PAST	fukunda	fukumanakatta
MASU FORM:	PRESENT	fukumimasu	fukumimasen
	PAST	fukumimashita	fukumimasen deshita
IMPERATIVE		fukume	fukumu na
TE FORM		fukunde	fukumanakute
CONDITIONAL:	PLAIN	fukumeba	fukumanakereba
		fukunda ra	fukumanakatta ra
	FORMAL	fukumimashita ra	fukumimasen deshita ra
PRESUMPTIVE:	PLAIN	fukumu daroo	fukumanai daroo
	FORMAL	fukumu deshoo	fukumanai deshoo
VOLITIONAL:	PLAIN	fukumoo	
	FORMAL	fukumimashoo	

	Affirmative		*Affirmative*
POTENTIAL	(fukumeru)	HONORIFIC	ofukumi ni naru
			ofukumi nasaru
PASSIVE	fukumareru	HUMBLE	ofukumi suru
			ofukumi itasu
CAUSATIVE	fukumaseru		
CAUS. PASSIVE	fukumaserareru		
	fukumasareru		

Examples:

1. *Kore wa zeikin o fukunde imasu ka.*
   Does this include tax?
2. *Kore ni wa satoo wa fukumarete imasen.*
   There's no sugar in this.
3. *Sono jiken wa fukuzatsu na mondai o fukunde iru yoo da.*
   The incident seems to have caused complex problems.
4. *Shikke o fukunda kuuki ga amari suki ja nai.*
   I don't like damp air too much.
5. *Kare wa kuchi ni ippai mizu o fukunda.*
   He held a lot of water in his mouth.

触れる to touch, mention; ふれる (気が～) to go mad: (both intrans.)*

		Affirmative	*Negative*
PLAIN FORM:	PRESENT	fureru	furenai
	PAST	fureta	furenakatta
MASU FORM:	PRESENT	furemasu	furemasen
	PAST	furemashita	furemasen deshita
IMPERATIVE		furero	fureru na
TE FORM		furete	furenakute
CONDITIONAL:	PLAIN	furereba	furenakereba
		fureta ra	furenakatta ra
	FORMAL	furemashita ra	furemasen deshita ra
PRESUMPTIVE:	PLAIN	fureru daroo	furenai daroo
	FORMAL	fureru deshoo	furenai deshoo
VOLITIONAL:	PLAIN	fureyoo	
	FORMAL	furemashoo	

	Affirmative		*Affirmative*
POTENTIAL	furerareru	HONORIFIC	ofure ni naru
			ofure nasaru
PASSIVE	furerareru	HUMBLE	ofure suru
			ofure itasu
CAUSATIVE	furesaseru		
CAUS. PASSIVE	furesaserareru		

Examples:

1. *Kabe ni te o fureta.*
   I touched the wall.
2. *Sore wa hoo ni fureta kooi de aru.*
   That is breaking the law.
3. *Sono wadai ni wa furenai yoo ni.*
   Don't mention that subject.
4. *Michi de sono kanban ga me ni furemashita.*
   I was attracted by the sign on the street.
5. *Ano otoko wa ki ga furete iru.*
   That man is mad.

* The phrase *ki ga fureru* 気がふれる meaning "to go mad" generally has no imperative, volitional, potential, or humble forms.

降る to fall: (intrans.);* 振る to wave, to reject, to attach: (trans.)

		Affirmative	*Negative*
PLAIN FORM:	PRESENT	furu	furanai
	PAST	futta	furanakatta
MASU FORM:	PRESENT	furimasu	furimasen
	PAST	furimashita	furimasen deshita
IMPERATIVE		fure	furu na
TE FORM		futte	furanakute
CONDITIONAL:	PLAIN	fureba	furanakereba
		futta ra	furanakatta ra
	FORMAL	furimashita ra	furimasen deshita ra
PRESUMPTIVE:	PLAIN	furu daroo	furanai daroo
	FORMAL	furu deshoo	furanai deshoo
VOLITIONAL:	PLAIN	furoo	
	FORMAL	furimashoo	

	Affirmative		*Affirmative*
POTENTIAL	fureru	HONORIFIC	ofuri ni naru
			ofuri nasaru
PASSIVE	furareru	HUMBLE	ofuri suru
			ofuri itasu
CAUSATIVE	furaseru		
CAUS. PASSIVE	furaserareru		
	furasareru		

Examples:

1. *Yuki ga futte imasu.*
   It's snowing.
2. *Ame ni furarete bishonure desu.*
   I was caught in the rain and got soaked.
3. *Tooku de kodomo-tachi ga te o futte iru no ga mieta.*
   I could see children waving their hands in the distance.
4. *Kare wa kanojo ni furarete, ochikonde imasu.*
   Because he was rejected by her, he is depressed.
5. *Kanji ni kana o futte kuremasen ka.*
   Would you attach *kana* to the characters?

* In general, the intransitive *furu* 降る meaning "to fall" does not use the volitional, potential, honorific, humble, or causative passive forms.

太る to put on weight: (intrans.)

		Affirmative	*Negative*
PLAIN FORM:	PRESENT	futoru	futoranai
	PAST	futotta	futoranakatta
MASU FORM:	PRESENT	futorimasu	futorimasen
	PAST	futorimashita	futorimasen deshita
IMPERATIVE		futore	futoru na
TE FORM		futotte	futoranakute
CONDITIONAL:	PLAIN	futoreba	futoranakereba
		futotta ra	futoranakatta ra
	FORMAL	futorimashita ra	futorimasen deshita ra
PRESUMPTIVE:	PLAIN	futoru daroo	futoranai daroo
	FORMAL	futoru deshoo	futoranai deshoo
VOLITIONAL:	PLAIN	futoroo	
	FORMAL	futorimashoo	

	Affirmative		*Affirmative*
POTENTIAL	futoreru	HONORIFIC	ofutori ni naru
			ofutori nasaru
PASSIVE	futorareru	HUMBLE	(ofutori suru)
			(ofutori itasu)
CAUSATIVE	futoraseru		
CAUS. PASSIVE	futoraserareru		
	futorasareru		

Examples:

1. *Chotto futorimashita ne.*
   You've put on a little bit of weight.
2. *Tanaka-san wa futotte imasu.*
   Mr. Tanaka is fat.
3. *Futori-sugi wa karada ni warui.*
   It's bad for your health to be too fat.
4. *Moo sukoshi futotta hoo ga ii desu yo.*
   You should put on a little more weight.
5. *Kanojo wa futotta neko ga suki ja nai.*
   She doesn't like fat cats.

増やす to increase: (trans.)

		Affirmative	*Negative*
PLAIN FORM:	PRESENT	fuyasu	fuyasanai
	PAST	fuyashita	fuyasanakatta
MASU FORM:	PRESENT	fuyashimasu	fuyashimasen
	PAST	fuyashimashita	fuyashimasen deshita
IMPERATIVE		fuyase	fuyasu na
TE FORM		fuyashite	fuyasanakute
CONDITIONAL:	PLAIN	fuyaseba	fuyasanakereba
		fuyashita ra	fuyasanakatta ra
	FORMAL	fuyashimashita ra	fuyashimasen deshita ra
PRESUMPTIVE:	PLAIN	fuyasu daroo	fuyasanai daroo
	FORMAL	fuyasu deshoo	fuyasanai deshoo
VOLITIONAL:	PLAIN	fuyasoo	
	FORMAL	fuyashimashoo	

	Affirmative		*Affirmative*
POTENTIAL	fuyaseru	HONORIFIC	ofuyashi ni naru
			ofuyashi nasaru
PASSIVE	fuyasareru	HUMBLE	ofuyashi suru
			ofuyashi itasu
CAUSATIVE	fuyasaseru		
CAUS. PASSIVE	fuyasaserareru		

Examples:

1. *Motto Nihon-go no goi o fuyashi-tai.*
   I want to increase my Japanese vocabulary even more.
2. *Gakkoo wa Nihon-go no kurasu o moo hitotsu fuyashimashita.*
   The school added one more Japanese class.
3. *Kore ijoo shigoto o fuyasanaide kudasai.*
   Don't give me any more work, please.
4. *Kaisha wa hito o fuyasu soo desu.*
   I heard the company is going to hire more people.
5. *Kare wa kabu de zaisan o fuyashita rashii.*
   He seems to have made a lot of money in the stock market.

頑張る to hold out: (intrans.)

		Affirmative	*Negative*
PLAIN FORM:	PRESENT	ganbaru	ganbaranai
	PAST	ganbatta	ganbaranakatta
MASU FORM:	PRESENT	ganbarimasu	ganbarimasen
	PAST	ganbarimashita	ganbarimasen deshita
IMPERATIVE		ganbare	ganbaru na
TE FORM		ganbatte	ganbaranakute
CONDITIONAL:	PLAIN	ganbareba	ganbaranakereba
		ganbatta ra	ganbaranakatta ra
	FORMAL	ganbarimashita ra	ganbarimasen deshita ra
PRESUMPTIVE:	PLAIN	ganbaru daroo	ganbaranai daroo
	FORMAL	ganbaru deshoo	ganbaranai deshoo
VOLITIONAL:	PLAIN	ganbaroo	
	FORMAL	ganbarimashoo	

	Affirmative		*Affirmative*
POTENTIAL	ganbareru	HONORIFIC	(oganbari ni naru)
			(oganbari nasaru)
PASSIVE	ganbarareru	HUMBLE	(oganbari suru)
			(oganbari itasu)
CAUSATIVE	ganbaraseru		
CAUS. PASSIVE	ganbaraserareru		
	ganbarasareru		

Examples:

1. *Ganbatte kudasai.*
   Do your best./Cheer up.
2. *Ganbare!*
   Hold out!
3. *Karera wa saigo made ganbatte oyoida.*
   Without giving up, they kept on swimming to the end.
4. *Shigoto wa taihen desu ga, ganbari-tai to omoimasu.*
   The job is hard, but I'll do my best.
5. *Donna ni ganbatte mo, dame na toki ga aru.*
   No matter how hard you try, sometimes it's useless.

御座る to be:* (intrans.)

		Affirmative	*Negative*
PLAIN FORM:	PRESENT	(gozaru)	(gozaranai)
	PAST	(gozatta)	(gozaranakatta)
MASU FORM:	PRESENT	gozaimasu**	gozaimasen
	PAST	gozaimashita	gozaimasen deshita
IMPERATIVE		(gozare)	(gozaru na)
TE FORM		(gozatte)	(gozaranakute)
CONDITIONAL:	PLAIN	(gozareba)	(gozaranakereba)
		(gozatta ra)	(gozaranakatta)
	FORMAL	gozaimashita ra	gozaimasen deshita ra
PRESUMPTIVE:	PLAIN	(gozaru daroo)	(gozaranai daroo)
	FORMAL	(gozaru deshoo)	(gozaranai deshoo)
VOLITIONAL:	PLAIN	(gozaroo)	
	FORMAL	gozaimashoo	

	Affirmative		*Affirmative*
POTENTIAL	(gozareru)	HONORIFIC	–
PASSIVE	(gozarareru)	HUMBLE	–
CAUSATIVE	(gozaraseru)		
CAUS. PASSIVE	(gozarasareru)		

Examples:

1. *Denwa wa doko ni gozaimasu ka.*
   Where is a telephone?
   Nikai ni gozaimasu.
   On the second floor.
2. *Shitsurei desu ga, Yamada Sensei de wa gozaimasen ka.*
   Excuse me, but would you be Professor Yamada?
   Hai, Yamada de gozaimasu ga, dochira-sama desu ka.
   Yes, I am Yamada. And may I ask who you are?
3. *Arigatoo gozaimasu.*
   Thank you.

*In modern day Japanese, *gozaru* most often is used as the humble equivalent of *aru* and *de aru*, but occasionally it is used as the humble equivalent of *iru, kuru,* and *iku.*
**For euphonic reasons, *gozaimasu* is used rather than *gozarimasu.*

入る to enter, join, contain, accommodate: (intrans.)

		Affirmative	*Negative*
PLAIN FORM:	PRESENT	hairu	hairanai
	PAST	haitta	hairanakatta
MASU FORM:	PRESENT	hairimasu	hairimasen
	PAST	hairimashita	hairimasen deshita
IMPERATIVE		haire	hairu na
TE FORM		haitte	hairanakute
CONDITIONAL:	PLAIN	haireba	hairanakereba
		haitta ra	hairanakatta ra
	FORMAL	hairimashita ra	hairimasen deshita ra
PRESUMPTIVE:	PLAIN	hairu daroo	hairanai daroo
	FORMAL	hairu deshoo	hairanai deshoo
VOLITIONAL:	PLAIN	hairoo	
	FORMAL	hairimashoo	

	Affirmative		*Affirmative*
POTENTIAL	haireru	HONORIFIC	ohairi ni naru
			ohairi nasaru
PASSIVE	hairareru	HUMBLE	ohairi suru
			ohairi itasu
CAUSATIVE	hairaseru		
CAUS. PASSIVE	hairaserareru		
	hairasareru		

Examples:

1. *Doozo ohairi kudasai.*
   Come in, please.
2. *Yuube tonari no uchi ni doroboo ga haitta.*
   A burglar broke into our neighbor's house last night.
3. *Jikan ga areba, supootsu kurabu ni hairi-tai.*
   If I have time, I'd like to join a sports club.
4. *Kono hako ni nani ga haitte iru no?*
   What's in this box?
5. *Kono yakyuujoo wa san-man nin hairemasu.*
   This ballpark can accommodate thirty thousand people.

始まる to begin, start, break out: (intrans.)

		Affirmative	*Negative*
PLAIN FORM:	PRESENT	hajimaru	hajimaranai
	PAST	hajimatta	hajimaranakatta
MASU FORM:	PRESENT	hajimarimasu	hajimarimasen
	PAST	hajimarimashita	hajimarimasen deshita
IMPERATIVE		(hajimare)	(hajimaru na)
TE FORM		hajimatte	hajimaranakute
CONDITIONAL:	PLAIN	hajimareba	hajimaranakereba
		hajimatta ra	hajimaranakatta ra
	FORMAL	hajimarimashita ra	hajimarimasen deshita ra
PRESUMPTIVE:	PLAIN	hajimaru daroo	hajimaranai daroo
	FORMAL	hajimaru deshoo	hajimaranai deshoo
VOLITIONAL:	PLAIN	(hajimaroo)	
	FORMAL	(hajimarimashoo)	

	Affirmative		*Affirmative*
POTENTIAL	(hajimareru)	HONORIFIC	(ohajimari ni naru)
			(ohajimari nasaru)
PASSIVE	(hajimarareru)	HUMBLE	(ohajimari suru)
			(ohajimari itasu)
CAUSATIVE	(hajimaraseru)		
CAUS. PASSIVE	(hajimaraserareru)		

Examples:

1. *Eiga wa nan-ji ni hajimarimasu ka.*
   What time does the movie start?
2. *Kaigi wa moo hajimatte imasu.*
   The meeting has begun already.
3. *Sadoo ga hajimatta no wa Muromachi jidai da to iwarete imasu.*
   It's said the tea ceremony dates back to the Muromachi period.
4. *Sunde shimatta koto o kookai shite mo hajimaranai.*
   "It's no use crying over spilt milk."
5. *Sen kyuu-hyaku yon-juu nen ni sensoo ga hajimatta.*
   The war broke out in 1940.

始める to begin, open: (trans.)

		Affirmative	*Negative*
PLAIN FORM:	PRESENT	hajimeru	hajimenai
	PAST	hajimeta	hajimenakatta
MASU FORM:	PRESENT	hajimemasu	hajimemasen
	PAST	hajimemashita	hajimemasen deshita
IMPERATIVE		hajimero	hajimeru na
TE FORM		hajimete	hajimenakute
CONDITIONAL:	PLAIN	hajimereba	hajimenakereba
		hajimeta ra	hajimenakatta ra
	FORMAL	hajimemashita ra	hajimemasen deshita ra
PRESUMPTIVE:	PLAIN	hajimeru daroo	hajimenai daroo
	FORMAL	hajimeru deshoo	hajimenai deshoo
VOLITIONAL:	PLAIN	hajimeyoo	
	FORMAL	hajimemashoo	

	Affirmative		*Affirmative*
POTENTIAL	hajimerareru hajimereru	HONORIFIC	ohajime ni naru ohajime nasaru
PASSIVE	hajimerareru	HUMBLE	ohajime suru ohajime itasu
CAUSATIVE	hajimesaseru		
CAUS. PASSIVE	hajimesaserareru		

Examples:

1. *Benkyoo o hajimemashoo.*
   Let's start studying.
2. *Juu-ji ni kaigi o hajimemasu.*
   We'll have a meeting at ten o'clock.
3. *Nani kara hajimemashoo ka.*
   What shall we begin with?
4. *Kare wa booeki no shigoto o hajimeru tsumori da.*
   He intends to begin a trading business.
5. *Heya ni modotte, kanojo wa mata tegami o kaki-hajimemashita.*
   Returning to her room, she started writing a letter again.

計る to measure, weigh; 図る to attempt, deceive: (both trans.)

		Affirmative	*Negative*
PLAIN FORM:	PRESENT	hakaru	hakaranai
	PAST	hakatta	hakaranakatta
MASU FORM:	PRESENT	hakarimasu	hakarimasen
	PAST	hakarimashita	hakarimasen deshita
IMPERATIVE		hakare	hakaru na
TE FORM		hakatte	hakaranakute
CONDITIONAL:	PLAIN	hakareba	hakaranakereba
		hakatta ra	hakaranakatta ra
	FORMAL	hakarimashita ra	hakarimasen deshita ra
PRESUMPTIVE:	PLAIN	hakaru daroo	hakaranai daroo
	FORMAL	hakaru deshoo	hakaranai deshoo
VOLITIONAL:	PLAIN	hakaroo	
	FORMAL	hakarimashoo	

	Affirmative		*Affirmative*
POTENTIAL	hakareru	HONORIFIC	ohakari ni naru
			ohakari nasaru
PASSIVE	hakarareru	HUMBLE	ohakari suru
			ohakari itasu
CAUSATIVE	hakaraseru		
CAUS. PASSIVE	hakaraserareru		
	hakarasareru		

Examples:

1. *Taijuu o hakarimashita.*
   I weighed myself.
2. *Netsu o hakatte mite kudasai.*
   Please try to take your temperature.
3. *Kozutsumi no omosa o hakatte itadakemasu ka.*
   Would you weigh this parcel?
4. *Kare wa jisatsu o hakatta ga, kekkyoku shinenakatta.*
   He attempted suicide, but failed.
5. *Karera ni hakarareta no kamo-shirenai.*
   Perhaps I was deceived by them.

運ぶ to carry: (trans.)

		Affirmative	*Negative*
PLAIN FORM:	PRESENT	hakobu	hakobanai
	PAST	hakonda	hakobanakatta
MASU FORM:	PRESENT	hakobimasu	hakobimasen
	PAST	hakobimashita	hakobimasen deshita
IMPERATIVE		hakobe	hakobu na
TE FORM		hakonde	hakobanakute
CONDITIONAL:	PLAIN	hakobeba	hakobanakereba
		hakonda ra	hakobanakatta ra
	FORMAL	hakobimashita ra	hakobimasen deshita ra
PRESUMPTIVE:	PLAIN	hakobu daroo	hakobanai daroo
	FORMAL	hakobu deshoo	hakobanai deshoo
VOLITIONAL:	PLAIN	hakoboo	
	FORMAL	hakobimashoo	

	Affirmative		*Affirmative*
POTENTIAL	hakoberu	HONORIFIC	ohakobi ni naru
			ohakobi nasaru
PASSIVE	hakobareru	HUMBLE	ohakobi suru
			ohakobi itasu
CAUSATIVE	hakobaseru		
CAUS. PASSIVE	hakobaserareru		
	hakobasareru		

Examples:

1. *Kaban o hakobimashita.*
   I carried the bag.
2. *Nimotsu o heya ni hakonde kudasai.*
   Please carry the luggage to the room.
3. *Kagu o zenbu soto ni hakobi-dashimashita.*
   I carried all the furniture out of the house.
4. *Iroiro na koto ga umaku hakonde iru.*
   Things keep going well.
5. *Kuyakusho ni nan-do mo ashi o hakobanakereba narimasen.*
   I have to go to the ward office many, many times.

履く to put on (footwear); 吐く to vomit, breathe out; 掃く to sweep: (all trans.)

		Affirmative	Negative
PLAIN FORM:	PRESENT	haku	hakanai
	PAST	haita	hakanakatta
MASU FORM:	PRESENT	hakimasu	hakimasen
	PAST	hakimashita	hakimasen deshita
IMPERATIVE		hake	haku na
TE FORM		haite	hakanakute
CONDITIONAL:	PLAIN	hakeba	hakanakereba
		haita ra	hakanakatta ra
	FORMAL	hakimashita ra	hakimasen deshita ra
PRESUMPTIVE:	PLAIN	haku daroo	hakanai daroo
	FORMAL	haku deshoo	hakanai deshoo
VOLITIONAL:	PLAIN	hakoo	
	FORMAL	hakimashoo	

	Affirmative		Affirmative
POTENTIAL	hakeru	HONORIFIC	ohaki ni naru
			ohaki nasaru
PASSIVE	hakareru	HUMBLE	ohaki suru
			ohaki itasu
CAUSATIVE	hakaseru		
CAUS. PASSIVE	hakaserareru		
	hakasareru		

Examples:

1. *Kutsu o haite kudasai.*
   Please put on your shoes.
2. *Kutsu-shita o haite imasu ka.*
   Do you have socks on?
3. *Kibun ga warukute, hakimashita.*
   I felt sick and threw up.
4. *Iki o sutte, yukkuri haite kudasai.*
   Please breathe in and out slowly.
5. *Yuka o haita bakari desu.*
   I've just swept the floor.

話す to speak; 離す to keep away; 放す to set free, let go: (all trans.)

		Affirmative	*Negative*
PLAIN FORM:	PRESENT	hanasu	hanasanai
	PAST	hanashita	hanasanakatta
MASU FORM:	PRESENT	hanashimasu	hanashimasen
	PAST	hanashimashita	hanashimasen deshita
IMPERATIVE		hanase	hanasu na
TE FORM		hanashite	hanasanakute
CONDITIONAL:	PLAIN	hanaseba	hanasanakereba
		hanashita ra	hanasanakatta ra
	FORMAL	hanashimashita ra	hanashimasen deshita ra
PRESUMPTIVE:	PLAIN	hanasu daroo	hanasanai daroo
	FORMAL	hanasu deshoo	hanasanai deshoo
VOLITIONAL:	PLAIN	hanasoo	
	FORMAL	hanashimashoo	

	Affirmative		*Affirmative*
POTENTIAL	hanaseru	HONORIFIC	ohanashi ni naru
			ohanashi nasaru
PASSIVE	hanasareru	HUMBLE	ohanashi suru
			ohanashi itasu
CAUSATIVE	hanasaseru		
CAUS. PASSIVE	hanasaserareru		

Examples:

1. *Jon wa Nihon-go ga hanasemasu.*
   John can speak Japanese.
2. *Sensei ga anata ni ohanashi ni nari-tai soo desu.*
   It seems that the teacher wants to talk with you.
3. *Tanaka-san wa akanboo kara me ga hanasenai.*
   Mr. Tanaka cannot take his eyes off the baby.
4. *Gomen nasai. Ima shigoto de te ga hanasemasen.*
   I'm sorry. Right now, I'm too busy to do it. (*lit.*, can't free my hands)
5. *Sono otoko no ko wa inu o kusari kara hanashite yatta.*
   That boy set the dog free from the chain.

払う to pay, sweep, wipe, pay attention: (trans.)

		Affirmative	*Negative*
PLAIN FORM:	PRESENT	harau	harawanai
	PAST	haratta	harawanakatta
MASU FORM:	PRESENT	haraimasu	haraimasen
	PAST	haraimashita	haraimasen deshita
IMPERATIVE		harae	harau na
TE FORM		haratte	harawanakute
CONDITIONAL:	PLAIN	haraeba	harawanakereba
		haratta ra	harawanakatta ra
	FORMAL	haraimashita ra	haraimasen deshita ra
PRESUMPTIVE:	PLAIN	harau daroo	harawanai daroo
	FORMAL	harau deshoo	harawanai deshoo
VOLITIONAL:	PLAIN	haraoo	
	FORMAL	haraimashoo	

	Affirmative		*Affirmative*
POTENTIAL	haraeru	HONORIFIC	oharai ni naru
			oharai nasaru
PASSIVE	harawareru	HUMBLE	oharai suru
			oharai itasu
CAUSATIVE	harawaseru		
CAUS. PASSIVE	harawaserareru		
	harawasareru		

Examples:

1. *Yachin o haraimasu.*
   I'll pay the house rent.
2. *Watashi ni harawasete kudasai.*
   Please let me pay.
3. *Tana no hokori o harawanakereba narimasen.*
   I must dust the shelf.
4. *Aitsura o oi-harae.*
   Drive those guys away.
5. *Unten suru toki, hokoosha ni chuui o harau yoo ni.*
   When you drive a car, pay attention to the pedestrians.

晴れる to clear up, be dispelled;* 腫れる to swell: (both intrans.)

		Affirmative	*Negative*
PLAIN FORM:	PRESENT	hareru	harenai
	PAST	hareta	harenakatta
MASU FORM:	PRESENT	haremasu	haremasen
	PAST	haremashita	haremasen deshita
IMPERATIVE		harero	hareru na
TE FORM		harete	harenakute
CONDITIONAL:	PLAIN	harereba	harenakereba
		hareta ra	harenakatta ra
	FORMAL	haremashita ra	haremasen deshita ra
PRESUMPTIVE:	PLAIN	hareru daroo	harenai daroo
	FORMAL	hareru deshoo	harenai deshoo
VOLITIONAL:	PLAIN	(hareyoo)	
	FORMAL	(haremashoo)	

	Affirmative		*Affirmative*
POTENTIAL	(harerareru)	HONORIFIC	ohare ni naru
			ohare nasaru
PASSIVE	(harerareru)	HUMBLE	(ohare suru)
			(ohare itasu)
CAUSATIVE	haresaseru		
CAUS. PASSIVE	haresaserareru		

Examples:

1. *Ashita wa hareru deshoo.*
   It will probably be nice weather tomorrow.
2. *Gogo wa hareta-ri kumotta-ri deshita.*
   It was alternately fair and cloudy in the afternoon.
3. *Kiri ga hare-soo desu.*
   The fog seems to be lifting.
4. *Kare wa satsujin no yoogi ga hareta.*
   He was cleared of the murder charge.
5. *Kega o shita yubi ga harete iru.*
   My injured finger is swollen.

* Besides those forms listed above, the verb *hareru* 晴れる meaning "to clear up" generally has no honorific, causative, or causative passive forms.

貼る to stick; 張る to pitch, stretch, extend: (both trans.)

		Affirmative	*Negative*
PLAIN FORM:	PRESENT	haru	haranai
	PAST	hatta	haranakatta
MASU FORM:	PRESENT	harimasu	harimasen
	PAST	harimashita	harimasen deshita
IMPERATIVE		hare	haru na
TE FORM		hatte	haranakute
CONDITIONAL:	PLAIN	hareba	haranakereba
		hatta ra	haranakatta ra
	FORMAL	harimashita ra	harimasen deshita ra
PRESUMPTIVE:	PLAIN	haru daroo	haranai daroo
	FORMAL	haru deshoo	haranai deshoo
VOLITIONAL:	PLAIN	haroo	
	FORMAL	harimashoo	

	Affirmative		*Affirmative*
POTENTIAL	hareru	HONORIFIC	ohari ni naru
			ohari nasaru
PASSIVE	harareru	HUMBLE	ohari suru
			ohari itasu
CAUSATIVE	haraseru		
CAUS. PASSIVE	haraserareru		
	harasareru		

Examples:

1. *Fuutoo ni kitte o hatta.*
   I stuck a stamp on the envelope.
2. *Kabe ni posutaa ga hatte aru.*
   A poster has been posted on the wall.
3. *Watashi-tachi wa kawara de tento o hatta.*
   We pitched a tent by the riverside.
4. *Mukashi, sono atari wa bukkyoo ga seiryoku o hatte ita.*
   Long ago, Buddhism extended it's influence in that area.
5. *Ano hito wa yoku mie o haru.*
   That person shows off a lot.

走る to run: (intrans.)*

		Affirmative	*Negative*
PLAIN FORM:	PRESENT	hashiru	hashiranai
	PAST	hashitta	hashiranakatta
MASU FORM:	PRESENT	hashirimasu	hashirimasen
	PAST	hashirimashita	hashirimasen deshita
IMPERATIVE		hashire	hashiru na
TE FORM		hashitte	hashiranakute
CONDITIONAL:	PLAIN	hashireba	hashiranakereba
		hashitta ra	hashiranakatta ra
	FORMAL	hashirimashita ra	hashirimasen deshita ra
PRESUMPTIVE:	PLAIN	hashiru daroo	hashiranai daroo
	FORMAL	hashiru deshoo	hashiranai deshoo
VOLITIONAL:	PLAIN	hashiroo	
	FORMAL	hashirimashoo	

	Affirmative		*Affirmative*
POTENTIAL	hashireru	HONORIFIC	ohashiri ni naru
			ohashiri nasaru
PASSIVE	hashirareru	HUMBLE	(ohashiri suru)
			(ohashiri itasu)
CAUSATIVE	hashiraseru		
CAUS. PASSIVE	hashiraserareru		
	hashirasareru		

Examples:

1. *Eki made hashirimashita.*
   I ran to the station.
2. *Rooka o hashiru na.*
   Don't run in the corridor.
3. *Shinkansen ga hashitte iru.*
   The bullet train is running.
4. *Kono machi o nanboku ni hashiru kawa ga arimasu.*
   There is a river that runs from south to north through this town.
5. *Kare no hidari ashi ni hageshii itami ga hashitta.*
   He felt an acute pain run through his left leg.

* As with other verbs indicating movement, *hashiru* may take a direct object, thus giving an idea of "going through a defined area." (*See* examples 2 and 4.)

働く to work, operate by: (intrans.); commit a crime: (trans.)

		Affirmative	*Negative*
PLAIN FORM:	PRESENT	hataraku	hatarakanai
	PAST	hataraita	hatarakanakatta
MASU FORM:	PRESENT	hatarakimasu	hatarakimasen
	PAST	hatarakimashita	hatarakimasen deshita
IMPERATIVE		hatarake	hataraku na
TE FORM		hataraite	hatarakanakute
CONDITIONAL:	PLAIN	hatarakeba	hatarakanakereba
		hataraita ra	hatarakanakatta ra
	FORMAL	hatarakimashita ra	hatarakimasen deshita ra
PRESUMPTIVE:	PLAIN	hataraku daroo	hatarakanai daroo
	FORMAL	hataraku deshoo	hatarakanai deshoo
VOLITIONAL:	PLAIN	hatarakoo	
	FORMAL	hatarakimashoo	

	Affirmative		*Affirmative*
POTENTIAL	hatarakeru	HONORIFIC	ohataraki ni naru
			ohataraki nasaru
PASSIVE	hatarakareru	HUMBLE	ohataraki suru
			ohataraki itasu
CAUSATIVE	hatarakaseru		
CAUS. PASSIVE	hatarakaserareru		
	hatarakasareru		

Examples:

1. *Tanaka-san wa ku-ji kara go-ji made hatarakimasu.*
   Mr. Tanaka works from nine to five.
2. *Suzuki-san wa booeki-gaisha de hataraite imasu.*
   Mr. Suzuki works at a trading company.
3. *Kyoo wa doomo atama ga hatarakanai.*
   Somehow my brain doesn't seem to function today.
4. *Enshinryoku ga hataraite iru.*
   (This is) operating by centrifugal force.
5. *Ano ko wa suupaa-maaketto de nusumi o hataraita soo da.*
   They say that child stole something at the supermarket.

はやる to be in fashion, popular, prevail: (intrans.)

		Affirmative	*Negative*
PLAIN FORM:	PRESENT	hayaru	hayaranai
	PAST	hayatta	hayaranakatta
MASU FORM:	PRESENT	hayarimasu	hayarimasen
	PAST	hayarimashita	hayarimasen deshita
IMPERATIVE		(hayare)	(hayaru na)
TE FORM		hayatte	hayaranakute
CONDITIONAL:	PLAIN	hayareba	hayaranakereba
		hayatta ra	hayaranakatta ra
	FORMAL	hayarimashita ra	hayarimasen deshita ra
PRESUMPTIVE:	PLAIN	hayaru daroo	hayaranai daroo
	FORMAL	hayaru deshoo	hayaranai deshoo
VOLITIONAL:	PLAIN	(hayaroo)	
	FORMAL	(hayarimashoo)	

	Affirmative		*Affirmative*
POTENTIAL	(hayareru)	HONORIFIC	(ohayari ni naru)
			(ohayari nasaru)
PASSIVE	(hayarareru)	HUMBLE	(ohayari suru)
			(ohayari itasu)
CAUSATIVE	hayaraseru		
CAUS. PASSIVE	(hayaraserareru)		

Examples:

1. *Ima donna fasshon ga hayatte imasu ka.*
   What kind of fashion is popular now?
2. *Kuroi fuku ga hayatte imasu.*
   Black clothes are in fashion.
3. *Sono uta wa ni-juu nen gurai mae totemo hayatta.*
   That song was very popular about twenty years ago.
4. *Uyoku shisoo ga wakai hito no aida de hayatte iru.*
   Right-wing views are popular among young people.
5. *Ano resutoran wa yoku hayatte imasu.*
   That restaurant is very popular.

減らす to decrease, reduce: (trans.)

		Affirmative	*Negative*
PLAIN FORM:	PRESENT	herasu	herasanai
	PAST	herashita	herasanakatta
MASU FORM:	PRESENT	herashimasu	herashimasen
	PAST	herashimashita	herashimasen deshita
IMPERATIVE		herase	herasu na
TE FORM		herashite	herasanakute
CONDITIONAL:	PLAIN	heraseba	herasanakereba
		herashita ra	herasanakatta ra
	FORMAL	herashimashita ra	herashimasen deshita ra
PRESUMPTIVE:	PLAIN	herasu daroo	herasanai daroo
	FORMAL	herasu deshoo	herasanai deshoo
VOLITIONAL:	PLAIN	herasoo	
	FORMAL	herashimashoo	

	Affirmative		*Affirmative*
POTENTIAL	heraseru	HONORIFIC	oherashi ni naru
			oherashi nasaru
PASSIVE	herasareru	HUMBLE	oherashi suru
			oherashi itasu
CAUSATIVE	herasaseru		
CAUS. PASSIVE	herasaserareru		

Examples:

1. *Shachoo wa shain o herashita.*
   The company president reduced the number of employees.
2. *Keiei-fushin de kyuuryoo ga herasaremashita.*
   Because of financial difficulties, salaries were reduced.
3. *Shoku-hi o herasu no wa muzukashii.*
   It's difficult to cut down on food expenses.
4. *Moo sukoshi taijuu o herase to isha ni iwaremashita.*
   I was told by the doctor to lose a little more weight.
5. *Onaka o herashita kodomo-tachi ga takusan iru.*
   There are many children who are starving.

減る   to decrease: (intrans.)

		Affirmative	*Negative*
PLAIN FORM:	PRESENT	heru	heranai
	PAST	hetta	heranakatta
MASU FORM:	PRESENT	herimasu	herimasen
	PAST	herimashita	herimasen deshita
IMPERATIVE		(here)	(heru na)
TE FORM		hette	heranakute
CONDITIONAL:	PLAIN	hereba	heranakereba
		hetta ra	heranakatta ra
	FORMAL	herimashita ra	herimasen deshita ra
PRESUMPTIVE:	PLAIN	heru daroo	heranai daroo
	FORMAL	heru deshoo	heranai deshoo
VOLITIONAL:	PLAIN	(heroo)	
	FORMAL	(herimashoo)	

	Affirmative		*Affirmative*
POTENTIAL	(hereru)	HONORIFIC	oheri ni naru
			oheri nasaru
PASSIVE	(herareru)	HUMBLE	(oheri suru)
			(oheri itasu)
CAUSATIVE	(heraseru)		
CAUS. PASSIVE	heraserareru		
	herasareru		

Examples:

1. *Shussei-ritsu ga hette iru.*
   The birth rate is decreasing.
2. *Yushutsu ga hette, shigoto mo hetta.*
   Our exports have diminished and our work also has decreased.
3. *Kanojo wa taijuu ga go kiro herimashita.*
   She lost five kilos in weight.
4. *Supootsu kurabu no kaiin-suu ga oohaba ni hette kita.*
   The membership of the sports club has decreased sharply.
5. *Onaka ga hetta.*
   I'm hungry.

引く to pull, draw (a line), catch (a cold), consult (a dictionary);
弾く to play (string instruments): (both trans.)

		Affirmative	*Negative*
PLAIN FORM:	PRESENT	hiku	hikanai
	PAST	hiita	hikanakatta
MASU FORM:	PRESENT	hikimasu	hikimasen
	PAST	hikimashita	hikimasen deshita
IMPERATIVE		hike	hiku na
TE FORM		hiite	hikanakute
CONDITIONAL:	PLAIN	hikeba	hikanakereba
		hiita ra	hikanakatta ra
	FORMAL	hikimashita ra	hikimasen deshita ra
PRESUMPTIVE:	PLAIN	hiku daroo	hikanai daroo
	FORMAL	hiku deshoo	hikanai deshoo
VOLITIONAL:	PLAIN	hikoo	
	FORMAL	hikimashoo	

	Affirmative		*Affirmative*
POTENTIAL	hikeru	HONORIFIC	ohiki ni naru
			ohiki nasaru
PASSIVE	hikareru	HUMBLE	ohiki suru
			ohiki itasu
CAUSATIVE	hikaseru		
CAUS. PASSIVE	hikaserareru		
	hikasareru		

Examples:

1. *Tsuna o hiite kudasai.*
   Pull the rope, please.
2. *Ji no shita ni sen o hikimashita.*
   I drew a line under the letters.
3. *Ima kaze o hiite imasu.*
   I have a cold now.
4. *Imi ga wakaranakereba, jisho o hiki-nasai.*
   If you don't know the meaning, look it up in a dictionary.
5. *Piano mo gitaa mo sukoshi hikemasu.*
   I can play both the piano and the guitar a little.

拾う to pick up, find: (trans.)

		Affirmative	*Negative*
PLAIN FORM:	PRESENT	hirou	hirowanai
	PAST	hirotta	hirowanakatta
MASU FORM:	PRESENT	hiroimasu	hiroimasen
	PAST	hiroimashita	hiroimasen deshita
IMPERATIVE		hiroe	hirou na
TE FORM		hirotte	hirowanakute
CONDITIONAL:	PLAIN	hiroeba	hirowanakereba
		hirotta ra	hirowanakatta ra
	FORMAL	hiroimashita ra	hiroimasen deshita ra
PRESUMPTIVE:	PLAIN	hirou daroo	hirowanai daroo
	FORMAL	hirou deshoo	hirowanai deshoo
VOLITIONAL:	PLAIN	hirooo	
	FORMAL	hiroimashoo	

	Affirmative		*Affirmative*
POTENTIAL	hiroeru	HONORIFIC	ohiroi ni naru
			ohiroi nasaru
PASSIVE	hirowareru	HUMBLE	ohiroi suru
			ohiroi itasu
CAUSATIVE	hirowaseru		
CAUS. PASSIVE	hirowaserareru		
	hirowasareru		

Examples:

1. *Gomi o hirotte kudasai.*
   Please pick up the rubbish.
2. *Otoko no ko wa michi de saifu o hirotta.*
   The boy found a wallet on the street.
3. *Doko ka de takushii o hirotte kaeroo.*
   Let's pick up a taxi somewhere and go home.
4. *Ano hito no saabu wa hiroi-nikui.*
   That player's serves are difficult to return.
5. *Shitsugyoo-chuu ni, shachoo ni hirowareta.*
   When I was unemployed, I was given work by the company president.

誉める to praise, commend: (trans.)

		Affirmative	Negative
PLAIN FORM:	PRESENT	homeru	homenai
	PAST	hometa	homenakatta
MASU FORM:	PRESENT	homemasu	homemasen
	PAST	homemashita	homemasen deshita
IMPERATIVE		homero	homeru na
TE FORM		homete	homenakute
CONDITIONAL:	PLAIN	homereba	homenakereba
		hometa ra	homenakatta ra
	FORMAL	homemashita ra	homemasen deshita ra
PRESUMPTIVE:	PLAIN	homeru daroo	homenai daroo
	FORMAL	homeru deshoo	homenai deshoo
VOLITIONAL:	PLAIN	homeyoo	
	FORMAL	homemashoo	

	Affirmative		Affirmative
POTENTIAL	homerareru	HONORIFIC	ohome ni naru
	homereru		ohome nasaru
PASSIVE	homerareru	HUMBLE	ohome suru
			ohome itasu
CAUSATIVE	homesaseru		
CAUS. PASSIVE	homesaserareru		

Examples:

1. *Sensei wa seito-tachi o hometa.*
   The teacher praised the students.
2. *Kare no doryoku o homete age-tai.*
   I'd like to commend him for his efforts.
3. *Yoku benkyoo shita node, chichi wa watashi o homete kureta.*
   Since I studied very hard, my father praised me.
4. *Kanojo wa yoku anata no yasashisa o homete imasu.*
   She often speaks well of your kindness.
5. *Sore wa amari homerareta koto ja nai.*
   Not too much can be said for that.

ikiru

生きる to live, become alive: (intrans.)

		Affirmative	*Negative*
PLAIN FORM:	PRESENT	ikiru	ikinai
	PAST	ikita	ikinakatta
MASU FORM:	PRESENT	ikimasu	ikimasen
	PAST	ikimashita	ikimasen deshita
IMPERATIVE		ikiro	ikiru na
TE FORM		ikite	ikinakute
CONDITIONAL:	PLAIN	ikireba	ikinakereba
		ikita ra	ikinakatta ra
	FORMAL	ikimashita ra	ikimasen deshita ra
PRESUMPTIVE:	PLAIN	ikiru daroo	ikinai daroo
	FORMAL	ikiru deshoo	ikinai deshoo
VOLITIONAL:	PLAIN	ikiyoo	
	FORMAL	ikimashoo	

	Affirmative		*Affirmative*
POTENTIAL	ikirareru	HONORIFIC	oiki ni naru
			oiki nasaru
PASSIVE	ikirareru	HUMBLE	(oiki suru)
			(oiki itasu)
CAUSATIVE	ikisaseru		
CAUS. PASSIVE	ikisaserareru		

Examples:

1. *Sofu wa kyuu-juu-ni sai made ikita.*
   My grandfather lived to be ninety-two.
2. *Kono sakana wa mada ikite imasu.*
   This fish is still alive.
3. *Kani o ikita mama nabe ni irete nimasu.*
   Put live crabs into the pot and boil them.
4. *Isshoo shigoto ni ikiru tsumori desu ka.*
   Do you intend to devote your whole life to your job?
5. *Akai bara o oku to, kono heya wa ikite kuru.*
   Placing red roses in this room will make it come to life.

行く to go: (intrans.)

		Affirmative	*Negative*
PLAIN FORM:	PRESENT	iku	ikanai
	PAST	itta	ikanakatta
MASU FORM:	PRESENT	ikimasu	ikimasen
	PAST	ikimashita	ikimasen deshita
IMPERATIVE		ike	iku na
TE FORM		itte	ikanakute
CONDITIONAL:	PLAIN	ikeba	ikanakereba
		itta ra	ikanakatta ra
	FORMAL	ikimashita ra	ikimasen deshita ra
PRESUMPTIVE:	PLAIN	iku daroo	ikanai daroo
	FORMAL	iku deshoo	ikanai deshoo
VOLITIONAL:	PLAIN	ikoo	
	FORMAL	ikimashoo	

	Affirmative		*Affirmative*
POTENTIAL	ikeru	HONORIFIC	irassharu
PASSIVE	ikareru	HUMBLE	mairu
CAUSATIVE	ikaseru		
CAUS. PASSIVE	ikaserareru		
	ikasareru		

Examples:

1. *Ashita ku-ji ni gakkoo e ikimasu.*
   I'm going to school at nine o'clock tomorrow.
2. *Kyooto e itta koto ga arimasu ka.*
   Have you been to Kyoto?
3. *Kono michi o massugu itte kudasai.*
   Please go straight down this road.
4. *Iroiro na koto ga umaku itte iru.*
   Everything is going well.
5. *Chotto eki made kaimono ni itte kimasu.*
   I'm going shopping near the station, but I'll be right back.

祈る to pray, hope: (trans.)

		Affirmative	*Negative*
PLAIN FORM:	PRESENT	inoru	inoranai
	PAST	inotta	inoranakatta
MASU FORM:	PRESENT	inorimasu	inorimasen
	PAST	inorimashita	inorimasen deshita
IMPERATIVE		inore	inoru na
TE FORM		inotte	inoranakute
CONDITIONAL:	PLAIN	inoreba	inoranakereba
		inotta ra	inoranakatta ra
	FORMAL	inorimashita ra	inorimasen deshita ra
PRESUMPTIVE:	PLAIN	inoru daroo	inoranai daroo
	FORMAL	inoru deshoo	inoranai deshoo
VOLITIONAL:	PLAIN	inoroo	
	FORMAL	inorimashoo	

	Affirmative		*Affirmative*
POTENTIAL	inoreru	HONORIFIC	oinori ni naru
			oinori nasaru
PASSIVE	inorareru	HUMBLE	oinori suru
			oinori itasu
CAUSATIVE	inoraseru		
CAUS. PASSIVE	inoraserareru		
	inorasareru		

Examples:

1. *Ano hito wa mainichi kami ni inorimasu.*
   That person prays to God everyday.
2. *Haha wa kodomo no byooki no kaifuku o inotta.*
   The mother prayed for the child's recovery.
3. *Gookaku o inoru.*
   I hope you pass the exam.
4. *Inotte mo muda desu.*
   Even praying is useless.
5. *O-shigoto no seikoo o oinori mooshi-agemasu.*
   I hope you are successful in your work.

いらっしゃる to go, come, to be:* (intrans.)

		Affirmative	*Negative*
PLAIN FORM:	PRESENT	irassharu	irassharanai
	PAST	irasshatta	irassharanakatta
MASU FORM:	PRESENT	irasshaimasu**	irasshaimasen
	PAST	irasshaimashita	irasshaimasen deshita
IMPERATIVE		(irasshare)	(irassharu na)
TE FORM		irasshatte	irassharanakute
CONDITIONAL:	PLAIN	irasshareba	irassharanakereba
		irasshatta ra	irassharanakatta ra
	FORMAL	irasshaimashita ra	irasshaimasen deshita ra
PRESUMPTIVE:	PLAIN	irassharu daroo	irassharanai daroo
	FORMAL	irassharu deshoo	irassharanai deshoo
VOLITIONAL:	PLAIN	irassharoo	
	FORMAL	irasshaimashoo	

	Affirmative		*Affirmative*
POTENTIAL	irasshareru	HONORIFIC	——
PASSIVE	irassharareru	HUMBLE	——
CAUSATIVE	irassharaseru		
CAUS. PASSIVE	irassharasareru		

Examples:

1. *Sensei ga irasshattara, kore o watashite itadakemasen ka.*
   When the teacher comes, could you hand this to him?
2. *Shachoo wa raishuu Rondon e irassharu deshoo.*
   The company president probably is going to London next week.
3. *Yamada-san, irasshaimasu ka.*
   Is Miss Yamada there?
   Hai, watashi desu ga . . .
   Yes, speaking . . .
4. *Takeshita Soori wa gotaboo de irasshaimasu.*
   Prime Minister Takeshita is very busy.

*Irassharu is the honorific equivalent of *iku, kuru, iru,* and *aru.*
**For euphonic reasons, *irasshaimasu* is used rather than *irassharimasu.*

入れる to put in, include, pour in: (trans.)

		Affirmative	*Negative*
PLAIN FORM:	PRESENT	ireru	irenai
	PAST	ireta	irenakatta
MASU FORM:	PRESENT	iremasu	iremasen
	PAST	iremashita	iremasen deshita
IMPERATIVE		irero	ireru na
TE FORM		irete	irenakute
CONDITIONAL:	PLAIN	irereba	irenakereba
		ireta ra	irenakatta ra
	FORMAL	iremashita ra	iremasen deshita ra
PRESUMPTIVE:	PLAIN	ireru daroo	irenai daroo
	FORMAL	ireru deshoo	irenai deshoo
VOLITIONAL:	PLAIN	ireyoo	
	FORMAL	iremashoo	

	Affirmative		*Affirmative*
POTENTIAL	irerareru	HONORIFIC	oire ni naru
			oire nasaru
PASSIVE	irerareru	HUMBLE	oire suru
			oire itasu
CAUSATIVE	iresaseru		
CAUS. PASSIVE	iresaserareru		

Examples:

1. *Poketto ni te o ireta.*
   I put my hand in my pocket.
2. *Kare wa musuko o sono gakkoo ni ireta.*
   He placed his son in that school.
3. *Shain wa watashi o irete, ni-juu-go nin desu.*
   There are twenty-five people, including me, on the staff of this company.
4. *Ocha o oire shimashoo ka.*
   Shall I make tea for you?
5. *Kono shorui ni namae o kaki-irete kudasai.*
   Please fill in your name on this paper.

居る to be, stay; いる to keep, be doing:* (both intrans.)

		Affirmative	*Negative*
PLAIN FORM:	PRESENT	iru	inai
	PAST	ita	inakatta
MASU FORM:	PRESENT	imasu	imasen
	PAST	imashita	imasen deshita
IMPERATIVE		iro	iru na
TE FORM		ite	inakute
CONDITIONAL:	PLAIN	ireba	inakereba
		ita ra	inakatta ra
	FORMAL	imashita ra	imasen deshita ra
PRESUMPTIVE:	PLAIN	iru daroo	inai daroo
	FORMAL	iru deshoo	inai deshoo
VOLITIONAL:	PLAIN	iyoo	
	FORMAL	imashoo	

	Affirmative		*Affirmative*
POTENTIAL	irareru ireru	HONORIFIC	irassharu
PASSIVE	irareru	HUMBLE	oru
CAUSATIVE	isaseru		
CAUS. PASSIVE	isaserareru		

Examples:

1. *Asoko ni Junko-san ga imasu.*
   Junko is over there.
2. *Tookyoo ni dono gurai iru tsumori desu ka.*
   How long do you plan to stay in Tokyo?
3. *Moshi moshi. Jon-san, irasshaimasu ka.*
   Hello. May I speak to John? (*lit.*, Is John there?)
4. *Kanojo wa zutto damatte ita.*
   She kept silent.
5. *Ame ga futte imasu.*
   It's raining.

* Used in conjunction with other verbs to form the present and past progressive tenses. (*See* examples 4 and 5.)

要る to need: (intrans.)

		Affirmative	*Negative*
PLAIN FORM:	PRESENT	iru	iranai
	PAST	itta	iranakatta
MASU FORM:	PRESENT	irimasu	irimasen
	PAST	irimashita	irimasen deshita
IMPERATIVE		(ire)	(iru na)
TE FORM		itte	iranakute
CONDITIONAL:	PLAIN	ireba	iranakereba
		itta ra	iranakatta ra
	FORMAL	irimashita ra	irimasen deshita ra
PRESUMPTIVE:	PLAIN	iru daroo	iranai daroo
	FORMAL	iru deshoo	iranai deshoo
VOLITIONAL:	PLAIN	(iroo)	
	FORMAL	(irimashoo)	

	Affirmative		*Affirmative*
POTENTIAL	(ireru)	HONORIFIC	oiri ni naru
			oiri nasaru
PASSIVE	(irareru)	HUMBLE	(oiri suru)
			(oiri itasu)
CAUSATIVE	(iraseru)		
CAUS. PASSIVE	(iraserareru)		

Examples:

1. *Atarashii kutsu ga irimasu.*
   I need new shoes.
2. *Sore o jikkoo suru no ni yuuki ga iru.*
   It takes courage to put that into practice.
3. *Hoka ni nani ka iru mono ga arimasu ka.*
   Is there anything else you need?
   Iie, moo nani mo irimasen.
   No, I don't need anything else.
4. *Sono hon ga iranakereba, watashi ni kuremasu ka.*
   If you don't need that book, would you give it to me?

急ぐ to hurry: (intrans. and trans.)

		Affirmative	*Negative*
PLAIN FORM:	PRESENT	isogu	isoganai
	PAST	isoida	isoganakatta
MASU FORM:	PRESENT	isogimasu	isogimasen
	PAST	isogimashita	isogimasen deshita
IMPERATIVE		isoge	isogu na
TE FORM		isoide	isoganakute
CONDITIONAL:	PLAIN	isogeba	isoganakereba
		isoida ra	isoganakatta ra
	FORMAL	isogimashita ra	isogimasen deshita ra
PRESUMPTIVE:	PLAIN	isogu daroo	isoganai daroo
	FORMAL	isogu deshoo	isoganai deshoo
VOLITIONAL:	PLAIN	isogoo	
	FORMAL	isogimashoo	

	Affirmative		*Affirmative*
POTENTIAL	isogeru	HONORIFIC	oisogi ni naru
			oisogi nasaru
PASSIVE	isogareru	HUMBLE	oisogi suru
			oisogi itasu
CAUSATIVE	isogaseru		
CAUS. PASSIVE	isogaserareru		
	isogasareru		

Examples:

1. *Eki e isogoo.*
   Let's hurry to the station.
2. *Isoganai to maniawanai.*
   If we don't hurry, we won't be on time.
3. *Kanojo wa isoide, uchi ni kaetta.*
   She rushed back to her house.
4. *Shigoto o isoida hoo ga ii desu.*
   We should speed up our work.
5. *Isogeba maware.*
   Haste makes waste.

致す to do, cause:* (trans.)

		Affirmative	*Negative*
PLAIN FORM:	PRESENT	itasu	itasanai
	PAST	itashita	itasanakatta
MASU FORM:	PRESENT	itashimasu	itashimasen
	PAST	itashimashita	itashimasen deshita
IMPERATIVE		itase	itasu na
TE FORM		itashite	itasanakute
CONDITIONAL:	PLAIN	itaseba	itasanakereba
		itashita ra	itasanakatta ra
	FORMAL	itashimashita ra	itashimasen deshita ra
PRESUMPTIVE:	PLAIN	itasu daroo	itasanai daroo
	FORMAL	itasu deshoo	itasanai deshoo
VOLITIONAL:	PLAIN	itasoo	
	FORMAL	itashimashoo	

	Affirmative		*Affirmative*
POTENTIAL	itaseru	HONORIFIC	—
PASSIVE	itasareru	HUMBLE	—
CAUSATIVE	itasaseru		
CAUS. PASSIVE	itasaserareru		

Examples:

1. *Ikaga itashimashoo ka.*
   What shall I do?
2. *Tegami o okutte kurete, arigatoo.*
   Thanks for mailing the letter for me.
   Doo itashimashite.
   You're welcome.
3. *Hon o omochi itashimashoo.*
   I'll carry the books.
4. *Sore wa watashi no futoku no itasu tokoro desu.*
   That's all my fault.

*Itasu is the humble equivalent of *suru*.

言う to say, tell: (trans.)

		Affirmative	*Negative*
PLAIN FORM:	PRESENT	iu	iwanai
	PAST	itta	iwanakatta
MASU FORM:	PRESENT	iimasu	iimasen
	PAST	iimashita	iimasen deshita
IMPERATIVE		ie	iu na
TE FORM		itte	iwanakute
CONDITIONAL:	PLAIN	ieba	iwanakereba
		itta ra	iwanakatta ra
	FORMAL	iimashita ra	iimasen deshita ra
PRESUMPTIVE:	PLAIN	iu daroo	iwanai daroo
	FORMAL	iu deshoo	iwanai deshoo
VOLITIONAL:	PLAIN	ioo	
	FORMAL	iimashoo	

	Affirmative		*Affirmative*
POTENTIAL	ieru	HONORIFIC	ossharu
PASSIVE	iwareru	HUMBLE	moosu
CAUSATIVE	iwaseru		
CAUS. PASSIVE	iwaserareru		
	iwasareru		

Examples:

1. *Suzuki-san wa yoku joodan o iimasu.*
   Mr. Suzuki often tells jokes.
2. *Watashi wa Satoo to mooshimasu. Doozo yoroshiku.*
   My name is Mr. Sato. It is nice to meet you.
3. *Sensei wa nan to osshaimashita ka.*
   What did the teacher say?
   Ashita anata ni denwa suru to osshaimashita.
   He said that he would call you tomorrow.
4. *Watashi no iu koto o kiite kudasai.*
   Please listen to what I have to say.

祝う to congratulate, celebrate: (trans.)

		Affirmative	*Negative*
PLAIN FORM:	PRESENT	iwau	iwawanai
	PAST	iwatta	iwawanakatta
MASU FORM:	PRESENT	iwaimasu	iwaimasen
	PAST	iwaimashita	iwaimasen deshita
IMPERATIVE		iwae	iwau na
TE FORM		iwatte	iwawanakute
CONDITIONAL:	PLAIN	iwaeba	iwawanakereba
		iwatta ra	iwawanakatta ra
	FORMAL	iwaimashita ra	iwaimasen deshita ra
PRESUMPTIVE:	PLAIN	iwau daroo	iwawanai daroo
	FORMAL	iwau deshoo	iwawanai deshoo
VOLITIONAL:	PLAIN	iwaoo	
	FORMAL	iwaimashoo	

	Affirmative		*Affirmative*
POTENTIAL	iwaeru	HONORIFIC	oiwai ni naru
			oiwai nasaru
PASSIVE	iwawareru	HUMBLE	oiwai suru
			oiwai itasu
CAUSATIVE	iwawaseru		
CAUS. PASSIVE	iwawaserareru		
	iwawasareru		

Examples:

1. *Watashi-tachi wa tomodachi no tanjoobi o iwaimashita.*
   We celebrated a friend's birthday.
2. *Go-kekkon o oiwai mooshi-agemasu.*
   I congratulate you on your wedding.
3. *Kaisha no sooritsu ni-juu-go shuunen o iwau yotei desu.*
   They plan to celebrate the twenty-fifth anniversary of the founding of the company.
4. *Minna wa watashi no byooki no kaifuku o iwatte kuremashita.*
   Everybody congratulated me on my recovery from being ill.
5. *Kare no yuushoo o iwau tame ni tomodachi ga minna atsumarimashita.*
   All his friends gathered to congratulate him for winning.

帰る to go home; 返る to return: (both intrans.)

		Affirmative	*Negative*
PLAIN FORM:	PRESENT	kaeru	kaeranai
	PAST	kaetta	kaeranakatta
MASU FORM:	PRESENT	kaerimasu	kaerimasen
	PAST	kaerimashita	kaerimasen deshita
IMPERATIVE		kaere	kaeru na
TE FORM		kaette	kaeranakute
CONDITIONAL:	PLAIN	kaereba	kaeranakereba
		kaetta ra	kaeranakatta ra
	FORMAL	kaerimashita ra	kaerimasen deshita ra
PRESUMPTIVE:	PLAIN	kaeru daroo	kaeranai daroo
	FORMAL	kaeru deshoo	kaeranai deshoo
VOLITIONAL:	PLAIN	kaeroo	
	FORMAL	kaerimashoo	

	Affirmative		*Affirmative*
POTENTIAL	kaereru	HONORIFIC	okaeri ni naru
			okaeri nasaru
PASSIVE	kaerareru	HUMBLE	(okaeri suru)
			(okaeri itasu)
CAUSATIVE	kaeraseru		
CAUS. PASSIVE	kaeraserareru		
	kaerasareru		

Examples:

1. *Go-ji ni uchi ni/e kaerimashita.*
   I went home at five o'clock.
2. *Suzuki-san wa raigetsu Amerika kara kaerimasu.*
   Mr. Suzuki will come back from the U.S. next month.
3. *Okaeri ni narimashita ra go-renraku kudasai.*
   When you come back, please contact me.
4. *Okaeri-nasai.*
   Welcome home.
5. *Nakushita okane ga kaetta'n desu.*
   The money I lost was returned to me.

kaeru

変える，替える，換える，代える to change: (trans.)

		Affirmative	*Negative*
PLAIN FORM:	PRESENT	kaeru	kaenai
	PAST	kaeta	kaenakatta
MASU FORM:	PRESENT	kaemasu	kaemasen
	PAST	kaemashita	kaemasen deshita
IMPERATIVE		kaero	kaeru na
TE FORM		kaete	kaenakute
CONDITIONAL:	PLAIN	kaereba	kaenakereba
		kaeta ra	kaenakatta ra
	FORMAL	kaemashita ra	kaemasen deshita ra
PRESUMPTIVE:	PLAIN	kaeru daroo	kaenai daroo
	FORMAL	kaeru deshoo	kaenai deshoo
VOLITIONAL:	PLAIN	kaeyoo	
	FORMAL	kaemashoo	

	Affirmative		*Affirmative*
POTENTIAL	kaerareru kaereru	HONORIFIC	okae ni naru okae nasaru
PASSIVE	kaerareru	HUMBLE	okae suru okae itasu
CAUSATIVE	kaesaseru		
CAUS. PASSIVE	kaesaserareru		

Examples:

1. *Heya no kaaten o kaemasu.*
   I'll change the curtains in the room.
2. *Apaato o kaeyoo to omou.*
   I think I'll change apartments.
3. *Sen-en satsu o hyaku-en dama ni kaete moratta.*
   I had a 1,000-yen note changed into 100-yen coins.
4. *Shinjuku de densha o nori-kaeyoo.*
   Let's change trains at Shinjuku.
5. *Kare wa shigoto o kaeru kamo-shirenai.*
   He might change his job.

返す to return, restore: (trans.)

		Affirmative	*Negative*
PLAIN FORM:	PRESENT	kaesu	kaesanai
	PAST	kaeshita	kaesanakatta
MASU FORM:	PRESENT	kaeshimasu	kaeshimasen
	PAST	kaeshimashita	kaeshimasen deshita
IMPERATIVE		kaese	kaesu na
TE FORM		kaeshite	kaesanakute
CONDITIONAL:	PLAIN	kaeseba	kaesanakereba
		kaeshita ra	kaesanakatta ra
	FORMAL	kaeshimashita ra	kaeshimasen deshita ra
PRESUMPTIVE:	PLAIN	kaesu daroo	kaesanai daroo
	FORMAL	kaesu deshoo	kaesanai deshoo
VOLITIONAL:	PLAIN	kaesoo	
	FORMAL	kaeshimashoo	

	Affirmative		*Affirmative*
POTENTIAL	kaeseru	HONORIFIC	okaeshi ni naru
			okaeshi nasaru
PASSIVE	kaesareru	HUMBLE	okaeshi suru
			okaeshi itasu
CAUSATIVE	kaesaseru		
CAUS. PASSIVE	kaesaserareru		

Examples:

1. *Ashita kasa o kaeshimasu.*
   I'll return the umbrella tomorrow.
2. *Teepu wa itsu okaeshi sureba ii desu ka.*
   When should I return the tape?
   Raishuu kaeshite kudasai.
   Please return it next week.
3. *Yonda hon wa moto no tokoro ni kaeshite kudasai.*
   Please return the books to their original places.
4. *Boku no jitensha o kaeshite hoshii'n desu ga.*
   I'd like you to give my bicycle back to me.

kakaru

懸かる *or* 掛かる to take, hang; 係る depend on; かかる be taken ill: (all intrans.)

		Affirmative	*Negative*
PLAIN FORM:	PRESENT	kakaru	kakaranai
	PAST	kakatta	kakaranakatta
MASU FORM:	PRESENT	kakarimasu	kakarimasen
	PAST	kakarimashita	kakarimasen deshita
IMPERATIVE		(kakare)	(kakaru na)
TE FORM		kakatte	kakaranakute
CONDITIONAL:	PLAIN	kakareba	kakaranakereba
		kakatta ra	kakaranakatta ra
	FORMAL	kakarimashita ra	kakarimasen deshita ra
PRESUMPTIVE:	PLAIN	kakaru daroo	kakaranai daroo
	FORMAL	kakaru deshoo	kakaranai deshoo
VOLITIONAL:	PLAIN	(kakaroo)	
	FORMAL	(kakarimashoo)	

	Affirmative		*Affirmative*
POTENTIAL	(kakareru)	HONORIFIC	okakari ni naru
			okakari nasaru
PASSIVE	(kakarareru)	HUMBLE	(okakari suru)
			(okakari itasu)
CAUSATIVE	(kakaraseru)		
CAUS. PASSIVE	(kakaraserareru)		

Examples:

1. *Kono shigoto ni wa jikan ga kakarimasu.*
   It will take time to do this work.
2. *Kabe ni e ga kakatte iru.*
   There is a picture hanging on the wall.
3. *Sono mondai no sekinin wa kare ni kakatte iru.*
   The responsibility for the problem rests with him.
4. *Korera no shoohin ni wa zeikin ga kakarimasen.*
   These goods are tax-free.
5. *Kare wa gan ni kakatte imasu.*
   He suffers from cancer.

掛ける to spend, hang, telephone, lock, sit; かける to bet: (both trans.)

		Affirmative	*Negative*
PLAIN FORM:	PRESENT	kakeru	kakenai
	PAST	kaketa	kakenakatta
MASU FORM:	PRESENT	kakemasu	kakemasen
	PAST	kakemashita	kakemasen deshita
IMPERATIVE		kakero	kakeru na
TE FORM		kakete	kakenakute
CONDITIONAL:	PLAIN	kakereba	kakenakereba
		kaketa ra	kakenakatta ra
	FORMAL	kakemashita ra	kakemasen deshita ra
PRESUMPTIVE:	PLAIN	kakeru daroo	kakenai daroo
	FORMAL	kakeru deshoo	kakenai deshoo
VOLITIONAL:	PLAIN	kakeyoo	
	FORMAL	kakemashoo	

	Affirmative		*Affirmative*
POTENTIAL	kakerareru kakereru	HONORIFIC	okake ni naru okake nasaru
PASSIVE	kakerareru	HUMBLE	okake suru okake itasu
CAUSATIVE	kakesaseru		
CAUS. PASSIVE	kakesaserareru		

Examples:

1. *Kare wa atarashii jigyoo ni takusan okane to jikan o kaketa.*
   He spent much time and money on the new business.
2. *Kabe ni e o kakemasu.*
   I'll hang a picture on the wall.
3. *Tanaka-san ni denwa o kakemashita.*
   I telephoned Mr. Tanaka.
4. *Doa ni kagi o kakeru no o wasurenaide.*
   Don't forget to lock the door.
5. *Kare wa sono uma ni ichi-man en o kaketa.*
   He bet 10,000 yen on that horse.

kaku

書く to write; 描く* to draw, paint: (both trans.)

		Affirmative	*Negative*
PLAIN FORM:	PRESENT	kaku	kakanai
	PAST	kaita	kakanakatta
MASU FORM:	PRESENT	kakimasu	kakimasen
	PAST	kakimashita	kakimasen deshita
IMPERATIVE		kake	kaku na
TE FORM		kaite	kakanakute
CONDITIONAL:	PLAIN	kakeba	kakanakereba
		kaita ra	kakanakatta ra
	FORMAL	kakimashita ra	kakimasen deshita ra
PRESUMPTIVE:	PLAIN	kaku daroo	kakanai daroo
	FORMAL	kaku deshoo	kakanai deshoo
VOLITIONAL:	PLAIN	kakoo	
	FORMAL	kakimashoo	

	Affirmative		*Affirmative*
POTENTIAL	kakeru	HONORIFIC	okaki ni naru
			okaki nasaru
PASSIVE	kakareru	HUMBLE	okaki suru
			okaki itasu
CAUSATIVE	kakaseru		
CAUS. PASSIVE	kakaserareru		
	kakasareru		

Examples:

1. *Igirisu no tomodachi ni tegami o kakimashita.*
   I wrote a letter to my English friend.
2. *Kanji ga ikutsu gurai kakemasu ka.*
   How many characters can you write?
3. *Ano kanban ni wa nan to kaite arimasu ka.*
   What is written on that sign?
4. *Kare wa Shinjuku no chizu o kaite kureta.*
   He drew a map of Shinjuku for me.
5. *Kanojo no shumi wa e o kaku koto desu.*
   Her hobby is drawing.

* Also read *egaku*.

隠れる to hide, conceal: (intrans.)

		Affirmative	*Negative*
PLAIN FORM:	PRESENT	kakureru	kakurenai
	PAST	kakureta	kakurenakatta
MASU FORM:	PRESENT	kakuremasu	kakuremasen
	PAST	kakuremashita	kakuremasen deshita
IMPERATIVE		kakurero	kakureru na
TE FORM		kakurete	kakurenakute
CONDITIONAL:	PLAIN	kakurereba	kakurenakereba
		kakureta ra	kakurenakatta ra
	FORMAL	kakuremashita ra	kakuremasen deshita ra
PRESUMPTIVE:	PLAIN	kakureru daroo	kakurenai daroo
	FORMAL	kakureru deshoo	kakurenai deshoo
VOLITIONAL:	PLAIN	kakureyoo	
	FORMAL	kakuremashoo	

	Affirmative		*Affirmative*
POTENTIAL	kakurerareru	HONORIFIC	(okakure ni naru)
			(okakure nasaru)
PASSIVE	kakurerareru	HUMBLE	(okakure suru)
			(okakure itasu)
CAUSATIVE	kakuresaseru		
CAUS. PASSIVE	kakuresaserareru		

Examples:

1. *Kare wa kokage ni kakureta.*
   He hid in the shade of a tree.
2. *Kodomo-tachi no kakureta sainoo o hiki-dashi-tai.*
   I'd like to draw out the children's latent talents.
3. *Oya ni kakurete, akuji o hataraite wa ikenai.*
   You must not do wrong behind your parent's back.
4. *Tsuki ga kumo ni kakurete iru.*
   The moon is hidden by clouds.
5. *Sore wa jizen no na ni kakureta kyooaku hanzai de aru.*
   That's a terrible crime hidden under the name of charity.

kakusu

隠す to hide, cover: (trans.)

		Affirmative	*Negative*
PLAIN FORM:	PRESENT	kakusu	kakusanai
	PAST	kakushita	kakusanakatta
MASU FORM:	PRESENT	kakushimasu	kakushimasen
	PAST	kakushimashita	kakushimasen deshita
IMPERATIVE		kakuse	kakusu na
TE FORM		kakushite	kakusanakute
CONDITIONAL:	PLAIN	kakuseba	kakusanakereba
		kakushita ra	kakusanakatta ra
	FORMAL	kakushimashita ra	kakushimasen deshita ra
PRESUMPTIVE:	PLAIN	kakusu daroo	kakusanai daroo
	FORMAL	kakusu deshoo	kakusanai deshoo
VOLITIONAL:	PLAIN	kakusoo	
	FORMAL	kakushimashoo	

	Affirmative		*Affirmative*
POTENTIAL	kakuseru	HONORIFIC	okakushi ni naru
			okakushi nasaru
PASSIVE	kakusareru	HUMBLE	okakushi suru
			okakushi itasu
CAUSATIVE	kakusaseru		
CAUS. PASSIVE	kakusaserareru		

Examples:

1. *Kare wa kokage ni mi o kakushita.*
   He hid himself in the shade of a tree.
2. *Watashi wa toowaku o kakusenakatta.*
   I could not hide my confusion.
3. *Hannin ga kakushita kyooki ga mitsukarimashita.*
   The weapon the criminal had hidden was found.
4. *Karera wa jijitsu o kakusoo to shita.*
   They tried to keep the truth secret.
5. *Kakusanaide hontoo no koto o itte hoshii.*
   I'd like you to tell me the truth without hiding anything.

構う to mind, care: (trans.)

		Affirmative	*Negative*
PLAIN FORM:	PRESENT	kamau	kamawanai
	PAST	kamatta	kamawanakatta
MASU FORM:	PRESENT	kamaimasu	kamaimasen
	PAST	kamaimashita	kamaimasen deshita
IMPERATIVE		kamae	kamau na
TE FORM		kamatte	kamawanakute
CONDITIONAL:	PLAIN	kamaeba	kamawanakereba
		kamatta ra	kamawanakatta ra
	FORMAL	kamaimashita ra	kamaimasen deshita ra
PRESUMPTIVE:	PLAIN	kamau daroo	kamawanai daroo
	FORMAL	kamau deshoo	kamawanai deshoo
VOLITIONAL:	PLAIN	kamaoo	
	FORMAL	kamaimashoo	

	Affirmative		*Affirmative*
POTENTIAL	kamaeru	HONORIFIC	okamai ni naru
			okamai nasaru
PASSIVE	kamawareru	HUMBLE	okamai suru
			okamai itasu
CAUSATIVE	kamawaseru		
CAUS. PASSIVE	kamawaserareru		
	kamawasareru		

Examples:

1. *Watashi ni kamawanaide kudasai.*
   Please leave me alone.
2. *Ashita o-ukagai shite mo kamaimasen ka.*
   Would you mind if I visit you tomorrow?
   Ee, kamaimasen.
   No, that would be fine.
3. *Haha wa minari ni kamawanai.*
   My mother is indifferent about her looks.
4. *Nani ga okoroo to kamaimasen.*
   No matter what happens, I won't care.

考える to think of, consider: (trans.)

		Affirmative	*Negative*
PLAIN FORM:	PRESENT	kangaeru	kangaenai
	PAST	kangaeta	kangaenakatta
MASU FORM:	PRESENT	kangaemasu	kangaemasen
	PAST	kangaemashita	kangaemasen deshita
IMPERATIVE		kangaero	kangaeru na
TE FORM		kangaete	kangaenakute
CONDITIONAL:	PLAIN	kangaereba	kangaenakereba
		kangaeta ra	kangaenakatta ra
	FORMAL	kangaemashita ra	kangaemasen deshita ra
PRESUMPTIVE:	PLAIN	kangaeru daroo	kangaenai daroo
	FORMAL	kangaeru deshoo	kangaenai deshoo
VOLITIONAL:	PLAIN	kangaeyoo	
	FORMAL	kangaemashoo	

	Affirmative		*Affirmative*
POTENTIAL	kangaerareru	HONORIFIC	okangae ni naru
	kangaereru		okangae nasaru
PASSIVE	kangaerareru	HUMBLE	(okangae suru)
			(okangae itasu)
CAUSATIVE	kangaesaseru		
CAUS. PASSIVE	kangaesaserareru		

Examples:

1. *Moo ichido kangaete mimasu.*
   I'll try to think about it again.
2. *Kono mondai ni tsuite doo okangae ni narimasu ka.*
   What do you think about this problem?
3. *Kare ga uso o tsuita to wa kangaerarenai.*
   It's unthinkable that he told a lie.
4. *Jon wa Nihon de hataraku koto o kangaete iru.*
   John is thinking of working in Japan.
5. *Sono koto wa moo sukoshi kangaesasete kuremasen ka.*
   Please let me think over that matter a little more.

感じる to feel: (intrans. and trans.)

		Affirmative	*Negative*
PLAIN FORM:	PRESENT	kanjiru	kanjinai
	PAST	kanjita	kanjinakatta
MASU FORM:	PRESENT	kanjimasu	kanjimasen
	PAST	kanjimashita	kanjimasen deshita
IMPERATIVE		kanjiro	kanjiru na
TE FORM		kanjite	kanjinakute
CONDITIONAL:	PLAIN	kanjireba	kanjinakereba
		kanjita ra	kanjinakatta ra
	FORMAL	kanjimashita ra	kanjimasen deshita ra
PRESUMPTIVE:	PLAIN	kanjiru daroo	kanjinai daroo
	FORMAL	kanjiru deshoo	kanjinai deshoo
VOLITIONAL:	PLAIN	kanjiyoo	
	FORMAL	kanjimashoo	

	Affirmative		*Affirmative*
POTENTIAL	kanjirareru kanjireru	HONORIFIC	okanji ni naru okanji nasaru
PASSIVE	kanjirareru	HUMBLE	(okanji suru) (okanji itasu)
CAUSATIVE	kanjisaseru		
CAUS. PASSIVE	kanjisaserareru		

Examples:

1. *Shiken wa muzukashiku kanjita.*
   I felt the exam was difficult.
2. *Kare wa kata ni hageshii itami o kanjimashita.*
   He felt a sharp pain in his shoulder.
3. *Kanjita mama ni iken o itte kudasai.*
   Please feel free to express your feelings.
4. *Karera wa otagai ni tekii o kanjite iru yoo da.*
   They seem to feel hostile toward each other.
5. *Karera no atatakai motenashi ni kanjinai hito wa inai.*
   There is no one who doesn't respond to their warm hospitality.

借りる to borrow, rent: (trans.)

		Affirmative	*Negative*
PLAIN FORM:	PRESENT	kariru	karinai
	PAST	karita	karinakatta
MASU FORM:	PRESENT	karimasu	karimasen
	PAST	karimashita	karimasen deshita
IMPERATIVE		kariro	kariru na
TE FORM		karite	karinakute
CONDITIONAL:	PLAIN	karireba	karinakereba
		karita ra	karinakatta ra
	FORMAL	karimashita ra	karimasen deshita ra
PRESUMPTIVE:	PLAIN	kariru daroo	karinai daroo
	FORMAL	kariru deshoo	karinai deshoo
VOLITIONAL:	PLAIN	kariyoo	
	FORMAL	karimashoo	

	Affirmative		*Affirmative*
POTENTIAL	karirareru	HONORIFIC	okari ni naru
	karireru		okari nasaru
PASSIVE	karirareru	HUMBLE	okari suru
			okari itasu
CAUSATIVE	karisaseru		
CAUS. PASSIVE	karisaserareru		

Examples:

1. *Tomodachi ni/kara okane o karimashita.*
   I borrowed money from a friend.
2. *Sensei ni chikara o okari shiyoo.*
   Let's ask for the teacher's help.
3. *Denwa o karite mo ii desu ka.*
   May I use the phone?
4. *Kare wa Tookyoo de apaato o karite iru.*
   He rents an apartment in Tokyo.
5. *Neko no te mo kari-tai.*
   I wish I had three hands. (*lit.*, I'd like to borrow even a cat's paw.)

貸す to lend, give a hand: (trans.)

		Affirmative	*Negative*
PLAIN FORM:	PRESENT	kasu	kasanai
	PAST	kashita	kasanakatta
MASU FORM:	PRESENT	kashimasu	kashimasen
	PAST	kashimashita	kashimasen deshita
IMPERATIVE		kase	kasu na
TE FORM		kashite	kasanakute
CONDITIONAL:	PLAIN	kaseba	kasanakereba
		kashita ra	kasanakatta ra
	FORMAL	kashimashita ra	kashimasen deshita ra
PRESUMPTIVE:	PLAIN	kasu daroo	kasanai daroo
	FORMAL	kasu deshoo	kasanai deshoo
VOLITIONAL:	PLAIN	kasoo	
	FORMAL	kashimashoo	

	Affirmative		*Affirmative*
POTENTIAL	kaseru	HONORIFIC	okashi ni naru
			okashi nasaru
PASSIVE	kasareru	HUMBLE	okashi suru
			okashi itasu
CAUSATIVE	kasaseru		
CAUS. PASSIVE	kasaserareru		
	kasasareru		

Examples:

1. *Tomodachi ni okane o kashimashita.*
   I lent some money to a friend.
2. *Enpitsu o kashite itadakemasen ka.*
   Would you kindly lend me a pencil?
3. *Chotto te o kashite kurenai ka.*
   Could you please give me a hand?
4. *Kanojo wa oya no iu koto ni mimi o kasanakatta.*
   She didn't listen to her parents. (*lit.*, lend an ear)
5. *Yoroshikatta ra, kono jisho o okashi shimasu yo.*
   If you like, I'll lend you this dictionary.

片付ける to put in order, tidy up, finish: (trans.)

		Affirmative	*Negative*
PLAIN FORM:	PRESENT	katazukeru	katazukenai
	PAST	katazuketa	katazukenakatta
MASU FORM:	PRESENT	katazukemasu	katazukemasen
	PAST	katazukemashita	katazukemasen deshita
IMPERATIVE		katazukero	katazukeru na
TE FORM		katazukete	katazukenakute
CONDITIONAL:	PLAIN	katazukereba	katazukenakereba
		katazuketa ra	katazukenakatta ra
	FORMAL	katazukemashita ra	katazukemasen deshita ra
PRESUMPTIVE:	PLAIN	katazukeru daroo	katazukenai daroo
	FORMAL	katazukeru deshoo	katazukenai deshoo
VOLITIONAL:	PLAIN	katazukeyoo	
	FORMAL	katazukemashoo	

	Affirmative		*Affirmative*
POTENTIAL	katazukerareru	HONORIFIC	okatazuke ni naru
	katazukereru		okatazuke nasaru
PASSIVE	katazukerareru	HUMBLE	okatazuke suru
			okatazuke itasu
CAUSATIVE	katazukesaseru		
CAUS. PASSIVE	katazukesaserareru		

Examples:

1. *Tsukue no ue o katazukemasu.*
   I'll tidy up the top of the desk.
2. *Koppu ya sara o katazukete.*
   Clear away the cups and plates.
3. *Kono mondai o dekiru dake hayaku katazuke-tai.*
   We want to settle this problem as soon as possible.
4. *Go-ji made ni shigoto o katazukenakereba narimasen.*
   I have to finish my work by five o'clock.
5. *Karera wa musume-tachi o zenbu katazuketa.*
   They married off all their daughters.

勝つ to win: (intrans.)

		Affirmative	*Negative*
PLAIN FORM:	PRESENT	katsu	katanai
	PAST	katta	katanakatta
MASU FORM:	PRESENT	kachimasu	kachimasen
	PAST	kachimashita	kachimasen deshita
IMPERATIVE		kate	katsu na
TE FORM		katte	katanakute
CONDITIONAL:	PLAIN	kateba	katanakereba
		katta ra	katanakatta ra
	FORMAL	kachimashita ra	kachimasen deshita ra
PRESUMPTIVE:	PLAIN	katsu daroo	katanai daroo
	FORMAL	katsu deshoo	katanai deshoo
VOLITIONAL:	PLAIN	katoo	
	FORMAL	kachimashoo	

	Affirmative		*Affirmative*
POTENTIAL	kateru	HONORIFIC	okachi ni naru
			okachi nasaru
PASSIVE	katareru	HUMBLE	(okachi suru)
			(okachi itasu)
CAUSATIVE	kataseru		
CAUS. PASSIVE	kataserareru		
	katasareru		

Examples:

1. *Kare wa tenisu no shiai ni katta.*
   He won his tennis match.
2. *Yon tai san de karera no chiimu ga kachimashita.*
   Their team won by a score of four to three.
3. *Ima, dotchi ga katte imasu ka.*
   Which side is now winning?
4. *Jibun jishin ni katanakereba narimasen.*
   You must control yourself.
5. *Toshi ni wa katenai.*
   He is beginning to show his age.

買う to buy, incur, appreciate; 飼う to keep animals: (both trans.)

		Affirmative	*Negative*
PLAIN FORM:	PRESENT	kau	kawanai
	PAST	katta	kawanakatta
MASU FORM:	PRESENT	kaimasu	kaimasen
	PAST	kaimashita	kaimasen deshita
IMPERATIVE		kae	kau na
TE FORM		katte	kawanakute
CONDITIONAL:	PLAIN	kaeba	kawanakereba
		katta ra	kawanakatta ra
	FORMAL	kaimashita ra	kaimasen deshita ra
PRESUMPTIVE:	PLAIN	kau daroo	kawanai daroo
	FORMAL	kau deshoo	kawanai deshoo
VOLITIONAL:	PLAIN	kaoo	
	FORMAL	kaimashoo	

	Affirmative		*Affirmative*
POTENTIAL	kaeru	HONORIFIC	okai ni naru
			okai nasaru
PASSIVE	kawareru	HUMBLE	okai suru
			okai itasu
CAUSATIVE	kawaseru		
CAUS. PASSIVE	kawaserareru		
	kawasareru		

Examples:

1. *Ano mise de uooku-man o kaimasu.*
   I'll buy a Walkman from that shop.
2. *Tomodachi ni chuukosha o go-juu-man en de katte moratta.*
   I had my friend buy my secondhand car for 500,000 yen.
3. *Kare no kotoba wa chichioya no ikari o katta.*
   His words incurred his father's anger.
4. *Kanojo wa jooshi ni nooryoku o kawarete iru.*
   Her boss thinks highly of her ability.
5. *Kodomo-tachi wa usagi o katte iru.*
   The children raise rabbits.

乾かす to dry: (trans.)

		Affirmative	*Negative*
PLAIN FORM:	PRESENT	kawakasu	kawakasanai
	PAST	kawakashita	kawakasanakatta
MASU FORM:	PRESENT	kawakashimasu	kawakashimasen
	PAST	kawakashimashita	kawakashimasen deshita
IMPERATIVE		kawakase	kawakasu na
TE FORM		kawakashite	kawakasanakute
CONDITIONAL:	PLAIN	kawakaseba	kawakasanakereba
		kawakashita ra	kawakasanakatta ra
	FORMAL	kawakashimashita ra	kawakashimasen deshita ra
PRESUMPTIVE:	PLAIN	kawakasu daroo	kawakasanai daroo
	FORMAL	kawakasu deshoo	kawakasanai deshoo
VOLITIONAL:	PLAIN	kawakasoo	
	FORMAL	kawakashimashoo	

	Affirmative		*Affirmative*
POTENTIAL	kawakaseru	HONORIFIC	okawakashi ni naru
			okawakashi nasaru
PASSIVE	kawakasareru	HUMBLE	okawakashi suru
			okawakashi itasu
CAUSATIVE	kawakasaseru		
CAUS. PASSIVE	kawakasaserareru		

Examples:

1. *Nureta shatsu o kawakashimashita.*
   I dried my wet shirt.
2. *Itsumo doraiyaa de kami o kawakashimasu.*
   I always dry my hair with a blow-dryer.
3. *Koko de kutsu o kawakashite mo ii desu.*
   You can dry your shoes here.
4. *Narubeku hayaku sono fuku o kawakashita hoo ga ii desu yo.*
   You should dry those clothes as soon as possible.
5. *Futon o mainichi hi ni atete kawakashimasu.*
   I air my futon in the sun everyday.

kawaku

乾く to get dry; 渇く to get dry, be thirsty: (both intrans.)

		Affirmative	*Negative*
PLAIN FORM:	PRESENT	kawaku	kawakanai
	PAST	kawaita	kawakanakatta
MASU FORM:	PRESENT	kawakimasu	kawakimasen
	PAST	kawakimashita	kawakimasen deshita
IMPERATIVE		(kawake)	(kawaku na)
TE FORM		kawaite	kawakanakute
CONDITIONAL:	PLAIN	kawakeba	kawakanakereba
		kawaita ra	kawakanakatta ra
	FORMAL	kawakimashita ra	kawakimasen deshita ra
PRESUMPTIVE:	PLAIN	kawaku daroo	kawakanai daroo
	FORMAL	kawaku deshoo	kawakanai deshoo
VOLITIONAL:	PLAIN	(kawakoo)	
	FORMAL	(kawakimashoo)	

	Affirmative		*Affirmative*
POTENTIAL	(kawakeru)	HONORIFIC	okawaki ni naru
			okawaki nasaru
PASSIVE	(kawakareru)	HUMBLE	(okawaki suru)
			(okawaki itasu)
CAUSATIVE	(kawakaseru)		
CAUS. PASSIVE	(kawakaserareru)		

Examples:

1. *Sentaku-mono wa kawakimashita ka.*
   Has the laundry dried?
   Iie, mada kawaite imasen.
   No, not yet.
2. *Kuuki ga kawaite iru.*
   The air is dry.
3. *Tsukue wa kawaita nuno de fuite kudasai.*
   Wipe the desk with a dry cloth, please.
4. *Nodo ga kawaita.*
   I'm thirsty. (*lit.,* My throat is dry.)

変わる to change, be different; 代わる to replace: (both trans.)

		Affirmative	*Negative*
PLAIN FORM:	PRESENT	kawaru	kawaranai
	PAST	kawatta	kawaranakatta
MASU FORM:	PRESENT	kawarimasu	kawarimasen
	PAST	kawarimashita	kawarimasen deshita
IMPERATIVE		kaware	kawaru na
TE FORM		kawatte	kawaranakute
CONDITIONAL:	PLAIN	kawareba	kawaranakereba
		kawatta ra	kawaranakatta ra
	FORMAL	kawarimashita ra	kawarimasen deshita ra
PRESUMPTIVE:	PLAIN	kawaru daroo	kawaranai daroo
	FORMAL	kawaru deshoo	kawaranai deshoo
VOLITIONAL:	PLAIN	kawaroo	
	FORMAL	kawarimashoo	

	Affirmative		*Affirmative*
POTENTIAL	kawareru	HONORIFIC	okawari ni naru
			okawari nasaru
PASSIVE	kawarareru	HUMBLE	okawari suru
			okawari itasu
CAUSATIVE	kawaraseru		
CAUS. PASSIVE	kawaraserareru		
	kawarasareru		

Examples:

1. *Kono atari wa totemo kawatta.*
   This area has changed greatly.
2. *Suzuki-san wa apaato o kawarimashita.*
   Ms. Suzuki changed her apartment.
3. *Seki o kawatte kuremasu ka.*
   Would you please change seats?
4. *Ano hito wa kawatte iru.*
   That person is strange.
5. *Ashita isogashii node, watashi to kawatte kudasai.*
   Because I'm busy tomorrow, please take my place.

kazoeru

数える to count: (trans.)

		Affirmative	*Negative*
PLAIN FORM:	PRESENT	kazoeru	kazoenai
	PAST	kazoeta	kazoenakatta
MASU FORM:	PRESENT	kazoemasu	kazoemasen
	PAST	kazoemashita	kazoemasen deshita
IMPERATIVE		kazoero	kazoeru na
TE FORM		kazoete	kazoenakute
CONDITIONAL:	PLAIN	kazoereba	kazoenakereba
		kazoeta ra	kazoenakatta ra
	FORMAL	kazoemashita ra	kazoemasen deshita ra
PRESUMPTIVE:	PLAIN	kazoeru daroo	kazoenai daroo
	FORMAL	kazoeru deshoo	kazoenai deshoo
VOLITIONAL:	PLAIN	kazoeyoo	
	FORMAL	kazoemashoo	

	Affirmative		*Affirmative*
POTENTIAL	kazoerareru	HONORIFIC	okazoe ni naru
	kazoereru		okazoe nasaru
PASSIVE	kazoerareru	HUMBLE	okazoe suru
			okazoe itasu
CAUSATIVE	kazoesaseru		
CAUS. PASSIVE	kazoesaserareru		

Examples:

1. *Okane o kazoemashita.*
   I counted my money.
2. *Ichi kara juu made kazoete mita.*
   I tried to count from one to ten.
3. *Kazoe-kirenai hodo oozei hito ga imashita.*
   There were too many people to count.
4. *Kore mo kare no sakuhin no hitotsu ni kazoerarete iru.*
   This is also counted among one of his works.
5. *Mono ni yotte kazoe-kata ga chigaimasu.*
   There are different ways to count different things.

消す to extinguish, turn off, erase, disappear: (trans.)

		Affirmative	*Negative*
PLAIN FORM:	PRESENT	kesu	kesanai
	PAST	keshita	kesanakatta
MASU FORM:	PRESENT	keshimasu	keshimasen
	PAST	keshimashita	keshimasen deshita
IMPERATIVE		kese	kesu na
TE FORM		keshite	kesanakute
CONDITIONAL:	PLAIN	keseba	kesanakereba
		keshita ra	kesanakatta ra
	FORMAL	keshimashita ra	keshimasen deshita ra
PRESUMPTIVE:	PLAIN	kesu daroo	kesanai dəroo
	FORMAL	kesu deshoo	kesanai deshoo
VOLITIONAL:	PLAIN	kesoo	
	FORMAL	keshimashoo	

	Affirmative		*Affirmative*
POTENTIAL	keseru	HONORIFIC	okeshi ni naru
			okeshi nasaru
PASSIVE	kesareru	HUMBLE	okeshi suru
			okeshi itasu
CAUSATIVE	kesaseru		
CAUS. PASSIVE	kesaserareru		

Examples:

1. *Shooboosha wa kaji o keshimashita.*
   Fire engines extinguished the fire.
2. *Denki o kesanaide.*
   Don't turn off the light.
3. *Kore wa keshigomu de kesemasen.*
   This cannot be erased by an eraser.
4. *Sono otoko wa kono atari de sugata o keshita.*
   The man disappeared around here.
5. *Hannin ni shooko o kesareta.*
   The evidence was destroyed by the criminal.

kieru

消える to go out, disappear, vanish: (intrans.)

		Affirmative	*Negative*
PLAIN FORM:	PRESENT	kieru	kienai
	PAST	kieta	kienakatta
MASU FORM:	PRESENT	kiemasu	kiemasen
	PAST	kiemashita	kiemasen deshita
IMPERATIVE		kiero	kieru na
TE FORM		kiete	kienakute
CONDITIONAL:	PLAIN	kiereba	kienakereba
		kieta ra	kienakatta ra
	FORMAL	kiemashita ra	kiemasen deshita ra
PRESUMPTIVE:	PLAIN	kieru daroo	kienai daroo
	FORMAL	kieru deshoo	kienai deshoo
VOLITIONAL:	PLAIN	kieyoo	
	FORMAL	kiemashoo	

	Affirmative		*Affirmative*
POTENTIAL	(kierareru)	HONORIFIC	(okie ni naru)
			(okie nasaru)
PASSIVE	(kierareru)	HUMBLE	(okie suru)
			(okie itasu)
CAUSATIVE	(kiesaseru)		
CAUS. PASSIVE	(kiesaserareru)		

Examples:

1. *Kaji ga kiemashita.*
   The fire went out.
2. *Tsukue no ue ni atta okane ga kieta.*
   The money on the desk disappeared.
3. *Yama no yuki ga dandan kiete kimashita.*
   The snow on the mountain disappeared little by little.
4. *Watashi no yume ga kiete shimatta.*
   My dream has vanished.
5. *Furui shuukan ga kie-tsutsu arimasu.*
   Traditional customs continue to die out.

聞こえる to hear, sound, be known: (intrans.)

		Affirmative	*Negative*
PLAIN FORM:	PRESENT	kikoeru	kikoenai
	PAST	kikoeta	kikoenakatta
MASU FORM:	PRESENT	kikoemasu	kikoemasen
	PAST	kikoemashita	kikoemasen deshita
IMPERATIVE		(kikoero)	(kikoeru na)
TE FORM		kikoete	kikoenakute
CONDITIONAL:	PLAIN	kikoereba	kikoenakereba
		kikoeta ra	kikoenakatta ra
	FORMAL	kikoemashita ra	kikoemasen deshita ra
PRESUMPTIVE:	PLAIN	kikoeru daroo	kikoenai daroo
	FORMAL	kikoeru deshoo	kikoenai deshoo
VOLITIONAL:	PLAIN	(kikoeyoo)	
	FORMAL	(kikoemashoo)	

	Affirmative		*Affirmative*
POTENTIAL	(kikoerareru)	HONORIFIC	(okikoe ni naru)
			(okikoe nasaru)
PASSIVE	(kikoerareru)	HUMBLE	(okikoe suru)
			(okikoe itasu)
CAUSATIVE	(kikoesaseru)		
CAUS. PASSIVE	(kikoesaserareru)		

Examples:

1. *Moshi moshi, kikoemasu ka.*
   Hello, can you hear me?
2. *Kuruma no oto ga kikoemasu.*
   I can hear the sound of a car.
3. *Kodomo-tachi ga asonde iru no ga kikoeta.*
   I heard the children playing.
4. *Hen ni kikoeru kamo-shirenai keredo, hontoo no hanashi desu.*
   It may sound strange, but it's true.
5. *Kanojo no na wa seken ni kikoete iru.*
   Her name is known by everyone.

聞く to hear, listen, ask: (trans.); 利く to be effective: (in-trans.)*

		Affirmative	*Negative*
PLAIN FORM:	PRESENT	kiku	kikanai
	PAST	kiita	kikanakatta
MASU FORM:	PRESENT	kikimasu	kikimasen
	PAST	kikimashita	kikimasen deshita
IMPERATIVE		kike	kiku na
TE FORM		kiite	kikanakute
CONDITIONAL:	PLAIN	kikeba	kikanakereba
		kiita ra	kikanakatta ra
	FORMAL	kikimashita ra	kikimasen deshita ra
PRESUMPTIVE:	PLAIN	kiku daroo	kikanai daroo
	FORMAL	kiku deshoo	kikanai deshoo
VOLITIONAL:	PLAIN	kikoo	
	FORMAL	kikimashoo	

	Affirmative		*Affirmative*
POTENTIAL	kikeru	HONORIFIC	okiki ni naru
			okiki nasaru
PASSIVE	kikareru	HUMBLE	okiki suru
			okiki itasu
CAUSATIVE	kikaseru		
CAUS. PASSIVE	kikaserareru		
	kikasareru		

Examples:
1. *Heya de rajio o kikimashita.*
   I listened to the radio in the room.
2. *Watashi no hanashi o kiite kudasai.*
   Please listen to me.
3. *Sensei no iu koto o kiita hoo ga ii.*
   You should listen to your teacher.
4. *Omawari-san ni michi o kikimashita.*
   I asked the policeman for directions.
5. *Kono kusuri wa kaze ni kiku.*
   This medicine works well on colds.

* The intransitive *kiku* 利く meaning "to be effective" generally has no imperative, volitional, potential, or passive forms.

決まる to be decided, fixed, certain: (intrans.)

		Affirmative	*Negative*
PLAIN FORM:	PRESENT	kimaru	kimaranai
	PAST	kimatta	kimaranakatta
MASU FORM:	PRESENT	kimarimasu	kimarimasen
	PAST	kimarimashita	kimarimasen deshita
IMPERATIVE		(kimare)	(kimaru na)
TE FORM		kimatte	kimaranakute
CONDITIONAL:	PLAIN	kimareba	kimaranakereba
		kimatta ra	kimaranakatta ra
	FORMAL	kimarimashita ra	kimarimasen deshita ra
PRESUMPTIVE:	PLAIN	kimaru daroo	kimaranai daroo
	FORMAL	kimaru deshoo	kimaranai deshoo
VOLITIONAL:	PLAIN	(kimaroo)	
	FORMAL	(kimarimashoo)	

	Affirmative		*Affirmative*
POTENTIAL	(kimareru)	HONORIFIC	okimari ni naru
			okimari nasaru
PASSIVE	(kimarareru)	HUMBLE	(okimari suru)
			(okimari itasu)
CAUSATIVE	(kimaraseru)		
CAUS. PASSIVE	(kimaraserareru)		

Examples:

1. *Ryokoo no nittei ga kimarimashita.*
   The travel itinerary has been set.
2. *Shigoto no keiyaku ga kimarimashita.*
   An agreement to the business contract has been reached.
3. *Kanojo ga gichoo ni kimatta.*
   It was decided that she be the chairman.
4. *Kare wa kuru ni kimatte iru yo.*
   He is certain to come.
5. *Kare wa shigoto ga owaru to, kimatte kono nomiya ni yoru.*
   He always drops in this bar after he finishes his work.

決める to decide, fix, choose: (trans.)

		Affirmative	*Negative*
PLAIN FORM:	PRESENT	kimeru	kimenai
	PAST	kimeta	kimenakatta
MASU FORM:	PRESENT	kimemasu	kimemasen
	PAST	kimemashita	kimemasen deshita
IMPERATIVE		kimero	kimeru na
TE FORM		kimete	kimenakute
CONDITIONAL:	PLAIN	kimereba	kimenakereba
		kimeta ra	kimenakatta ra
	FORMAL	kimemashita ra	kimemasen deshita ra
PRESUMPTIVE:	PLAIN	kimeru daroo	kimenai daroo
	FORMAL	kimeru deshoo	kimenai deshoo
VOLITIONAL:	PLAIN	kimeyoo	
	FORMAL	kimemashoo	

	Affirmative		*Affirmative*
POTENTIAL	kimerareru	HONORIFIC	okime ni naru
			okime nasaru
PASSIVE	kimerareru	HUMBLE	okime suru
			okime itasu
CAUSATIVE	kimesaseru		
CAUS. PASSIVE	kimesaserareru		

Examples:

1. *Ryokoo no nittei o kimemashita.*
   We decided on the travel itinerary.
2. *Dono daigaku ni iku ka kimenakereba narimasen.*
   I have to choose which university to enter.
3. *Kare wa jibun de nani mo kimerarenai.*
   He cannot decide anything by himself.
4. *Kanojo wa rainen Igirisu de benkyoo suru koto ni kimete iru.*
   She has decided to study in England next year.
5. *Kimerareta kisoku o mamotte kudasai.*
   Observe the rules, please.

切れる to cut off, expire, be sharp: (intrans.)

		Affirmative	*Negative*
PLAIN FORM:	PRESENT	kireru	kirenai
	PAST	kireta	kirenakatta
MASU FORM:	PRESENT	kiremasu	kiremasen
	PAST	kiremashita	kiremasen deshita
IMPERATIVE		(kirero)	(kireru na)
TE FORM		kirete	kirenakute
CONDITIONAL:	PLAIN	kirereba	kirenakereba
		kireta ra	kirenakatta ra
	FORMAL	kiremashita ra	kiremasen deshita ra
PRESUMPTIVE:	PLAIN	kireru daroo	kirenai daroo
	FORMAL	kireru deshoo	kirenai deshoo
VOLITIONAL:	PLAIN	(kireyoo)	
	FORMAL	(kiremashoo)	

	Affirmative		*Affirmative*
POTENTIAL	(kirerareru)	HONORIFIC	(okire ni naru)
			(okire nasaru)
PASSIVE	(kirerareru)	HUMBLE	(okire suru)
			(okire itasu)
CAUSATIVE	kiresaseru		
CAUS. PASSIVE	kiresaserareru		

Examples:

1. *Himo ga kirete shimaimashita.*
   The strings were cut.
2. *Hanashi-chuu ni denwa ga kireta.*
   I was cut off while talking on the phone.
3. *Pasupooto no kigen ga moo sugu kiremasu.*
   My passport will expire soon.
4. *Kono naifu wa yoku kireru.*
   This knife cuts well.
5. *Ano ko wa atama ga kireru.*
   That child is very smart.

切る to cut, (attached to a verb) to do completely: (trans.)

		Affirmative	*Negative*
PLAIN FORM:	PRESENT	kiru	kiranai
	PAST	kitta	kiranakatta
MASU FORM:	PRESENT	kirimasu	kirimasen
	PAST	kirimashita	kirimasen deshita
IMPERATIVE		kire	kiru na
TE FORM		kitte	kiranakute
CONDITIONAL:	PLAIN	kireba	kiranakereba
		kitta ra	kiranakatta ra
	FORMAL	kirimashita ra	kirimasen deshita ra
PRESUMPTIVE:	PLAIN	kiru daroo	kiranai daroo
	FORMAL	kiru deshoo	kiranai deshoo
VOLITIONAL:	PLAIN	kiroo	
	FORMAL	kirimashoo	

	Affirmative		*Affirmative*
POTENTIAL	kireru	HONORIFIC	okiri ni naru
			okiri nasaru
PASSIVE	kirareru	HUMBLE	okiri suru
			okiri itasu
CAUSATIVE	kiraseru		
CAUS. PASSIVE	kiraserareru		
	kirasareru		

Examples:

1. *Hasami de himo o kirimashita.*
   I cut the string with scissors.
2. *Naifu de yubi o kitte shimaimashita.*
   I cut my finger with a knife.
3. *Karera wa kaze o kitte aruita.*
   They walked through the wind.
4. *Kare to wa moo te o kirimashita.*
   I have nothing to do with him any longer.
5. *Minna tsukare-kitte imasu.*
   Everybody is completely worn out.

着る to wear, put on, take the blame for: (trans.)

		Affirmative	*Negative*
PLAIN FORM:	PRESENT	kiru	kinai
	PAST	kita	kinakatta
MASU FORM:	PRESENT	kimasu	kimasen
	PAST	kimashita	kimasen deshita
IMPERATIVE		kiro	kiru na
TE FORM:		kite	kinakute
CONDITIONAL:	PLAIN	kireba	kinakereba
		kitara	kinakatta ra
	FORMAL	kimashita ra	kimasen deshita ra
PRESUMPTIVE:	PLAIN	kiru daroo	kinai daroo
	FORMAL	kiru deshoo	kinai deshoo
VOLITIONAL:	PLAIN	kiyoo	
	FORMAL	kimashoo	

	Affirmative		*Affirmative*
POTENTIAL	kirareru	HONORIFIC	omeshi nasaru
	kireru		omeshi ni naru
PASSIVE	kirareru	HUMBLE	(omeshi suru)
			(omeshi itasu)
CAUSATIVE	kisaseru		
CAUS. PASSIVE	kisaserareru		

Examples:

1. *Kooto o kimashita.*
   I put on a coat.
2. *Ano kuroi fuku o kita hito ga Tanaka-san desu.*
   The man wearing black clothes is Mr. Tanaka.
3. *Kare wa otooto no tsumi o kita.*
   He took the blame for his younger brother's wrongdoing.
4. *Omeshi ni natte mite kudasai.*
   Please try this on.
5. *Futotta no de, kono waishatsu wa moo kirenaku natta.*
   Because I gained weight, I can no longer wear this shirt.

Note: *megane o kakeru* → to wear a pair of glasses
     booshi o kaburu → to put on a hat/cap
     shatsu/burausu o kiru → to put on a shirt/blouse
     zubon/sukaato o haku → to put on pants/a skirt
     tebukuro o suru → to put on gloves

koeru

越える to go over, pass, surpass;* 肥える to be fertile, fat: (both intrans.)

		Affirmative	*Negative*
PLAIN FORM:	PRESENT	koeru	koenai
	PAST	koeta	koenakatta
MASU FORM:	PRESENT	koemasu	koemasen
	PAST	koemashita	koemasen deshita
IMPERATIVE		koero	koeru na
TE FORM		koete	koenakute
CONDITIONAL:	PLAIN	koereba	koenakereba
		koeta ra	koenakatta ra
	FORMAL	koemashita ra	koemasen deshita ra
PRESUMPTIVE:	PLAIN	koeru daroo	koenai daroo
	FORMAL	koeru deshoo	koenai deshoo
VOLITIONAL:	PLAIN	koeyoo	
	FORMAL	koemashoo	

	Affirmative		*Affirmative*
POTENTIAL	koerareru	HONORIFIC	okoe ni naru
	koereru		okoe nasaru
PASSIVE	koerareru	HUMBLE	(okoe suru)
			(okoe itasu)
CAUSATIVE	koesaseru		
CAUS. PASSIVE	koesaserareru		

Examples:

1. *Ato ni-hyaku meetoru de kokkyoo o koeru.*
   After two hundred more meters, we'll cross the national border.
2. *Oobosha wa sen nin o koemashita.*
   There were over one thousand applicants.
3. *Kare wa moo hachi-jussai o koeta roojin de aru.*
   He is an old man over eighty years old.
4. *Kono kawa o koenakereba narimasen.*
   You must cross this river.
5. *Kono atari no tochi wa koete iru.*
   The earth around here is fertile.

* Technically classified as an intransitive verb, but nearly always used as a transitive verb.

困る to be in trouble, in a fix, at a loss: (intrans.)

		Affirmative	*Negative*
PLAIN FORM:	PRESENT	komaru	komaranai
	PAST	komatta	komaranakatta
MASU FORM:	PRESENT	komarimasu	komarimasen
	PAST	komarimashita	komarimasen deshita
IMPERATIVE		(komare)	(komaru na)
TE FORM		komatte	komaranakute
CONDITIONAL:	PLAIN	komareba	komaranakereba
		komatta ra	komaranakatta ra
	FORMAL	komarimashita ra	komarimasen deshita ra
PRESUMPTIVE:	PLAIN	komaru daroo	komaranai daroo
	FORMAL	komaru deshoo	komaranai deshoo
VOLITIONAL:	PLAIN	(komaroo)	
	FORMAL	(komarimashoo)	

	Affirmative		*Affirmative*
POTENTIAL	(komareru)	HONORIFIC	okomari ni naru
			okomari nasaru
PASSIVE	komarareru	HUMBLE	(okomari suru)
			(okomari itasu)
CAUSATIVE	komaraseru		
CAUS. PASSIVE	komaraserareru		

Examples:

1. *Taiya ga panku shite komatte imasu.*
   I'm in a fix because I have a flat tire.
2. *Kare wa keizaiteki ni komatte imasu.*
   He has financial difficulties.
3. *Hidoi ame ni furarete, komarimashita.*
   We had trouble because we were caught in heavy rain.
4. *Doo kotaeta ra ii ka wakaranakute komarimashita.*
   I was at a loss for an answer.
5. *Komaraseru yoo na shitsumon o shinaide kudasai.*
   Please don't ask embarrassing questions.

komu

込む to be crowded, (attached to a verb) to come in, put in: (intrans.)

		Affirmative	*Negative*
PLAIN FORM:	PRESENT	komu	komanai
	PAST	konda	komanakatta
MASU FORM:	PRESENT	komimasu	komimasen
	PAST	komimashita	komimasen deshita
IMPERATIVE		(kome)	(komu na)
TE FORM		konde	komanakute
CONDITIONAL:	PLAIN	komeba	komanakereba
		konda ra	komanakatta ra
	FORMAL	komimashita ra	komimasen deshita ra
PRESUMPTIVE:	PLAIN	komu daroo	komanai daroo
	FORMAL	komu deshoo	komanai deshoo
VOLITIONAL:	PLAIN	(komoo)	
	FORMAL	(komimashoo)	

	Affirmative		*Affirmative*
POTENTIAL	(komeru)	HONORIFIC	(okomi ni naru)
			(okomi nasaru)
PASSIVE	(komareru)	HUMBLE	(okomi suru)
			(okomi itasu)
CAUSATIVE	komaseru		
CAUS. PASSIVE	komaserareru		
	komasareru		

Examples:

1. *Tookyoo no densha wa itsumo konde imasu ne.*
   Trains are always crowded in Tokyo, aren't they?
2. *Nichiyoobi na node eigakan wa taihen konde imashita.*
   The movie theater was very crowded because it was Sunday.
3. *Kono ran ni namae o kaki-konde kudasai.*
   Please fill in your name in this blank.
4. *Kare wa shibaraku no aida kangae-konde imashita.*
   For a while, he was deep in his thoughts.
5. *Ima wa choodo komi-au jikan desu.*
   It's rush hour right now.

殺す to kill, murder: (trans.)

		Affirmative	*Negative*
PLAIN FORM:	PRESENT	korosu	korosanai
	PAST	koroshita	korosanakatta
MASU FORM:	PRESENT	koroshimasu	koroshimasen
	PAST	koroshimashita	koroshimasen deshita
IMPERATIVE		korose	korosu na
TE FORM		koroshite	korosanakute
CONDITIONAL:	PLAIN	koroseba	korosanakereba
		koroshita ra	korosanakatta ra
	FORMAL	koroshimashita ra	koroshimasen deshita ra
PRESUMPTIVE:	PLAIN	korosu daroo	korosanai daroo
	FORMAL	korosu deshoo	korosanai deshoo
VOLITIONAL:	PLAIN	korosoo	
	FORMAL	koroshimashoo	

	Affirmative		*Affirmative*
POTENTIAL	koroseru	HONORIFIC	okoroshi ni naru
			okoroshi nasaru
PASSIVE	korosareru	HUMBLE	okoroshi suru
			okoroshi itasu
CAUSATIVE	korosaseru		
CAUS. PASSIVE	korosaserareru		

Examples:

1. *Ano hito o koroshita.*
   He killed that person.
2. *Yamada-san ga heya de korosarete iru no ga hakken sareta.*
   Mr. Yamada was found murdered in the room.
3. *Kare wa ni-rui de korosaremashita.*
   He was put out at second base.
4. *Roojin wa kane o nerawarete korosaremashita.*
   The old man was killed for his money.
5. *Kare wa mushi mo korosanai hodo yasashii hito desu.*
   He is so gentle that he couldn't hurt a fly.

kosu

越す *or* 超す to cross, go over, go through: (intrans.)*

		Affirmative	*Negative*
PLAIN FORM:	PRESENT	kosu	kosanai
	PAST	koshita	kosanakatta
MASU FORM:	PRESENT	koshimasu	koshimasen
	PAST	koshimashita	koshimasen deshita
IMPERATIVE		kose	kosu na
TE FORM		koshite	kosanakute
CONDITIONAL:	PLAIN	koseba	kosanakereba
		koshita ra	kosanakatta ra
	FORMAL	koshimashita ra	koshimasen deshita ra
PRESUMPTIVE:	PLAIN	kosu daroo	kosanai daroo
	FORMAL	kosu deshoo	kosanai deshoo
VOLITIONAL:	PLAIN	kosoo	
	FORMAL	koshimashoo	

	Affirmative		*Affirmative*
POTENTIAL	koseru	HONORIFIC	okoshi ni naru
			okoshi nasaru
PASSIVE	kosareru	HUMBLE	(okoshi suru)
			(okoshi itasu)
CAUSATIVE	kosaseru		
CAUS. PASSIVE	kosaserareru		

Examples:

1. *Watashi-tachi wa kokkyoo o koshita.*
   We crossed the national border.
2. *Seiseki de tomodachi ni saki o kosareta.*
   I was surpassed by my friend in grades.
3. *Kibishii fuyu o kosanakereba narimasen.*
   We have to make it through the severe winter.
4. *Kion wa yon-juu do o koshimashita.*
   The temperature went up over forty degrees.
5. *Byooki wa tooge o koshita yoo desu.*
   His sickness seems to have passed its worst stage. (*lit.*, go over the peak)

* Technically classified as an intransitive verb, but nearly always used as a transitive verb.

答える to answer, respond; 応える have an effect on: (both intrans.)

		Affirmative	*Negative*
PLAIN FORM:	PRESENT	kotaeru	kotaenai
	PAST	kotaeta	kotaenakatta
MASU FORM:	PRESENT	kotaemasu	kotaemasen
	PAST	kotaemashita	kotaemasen deshita
IMPERATIVE		kotaero	kotaeru na
TE FORM		kotaete	kotaenakute
CONDITIONAL:	PLAIN	kotaereba	kotaenakereba
		kotaeta ra	kotaenakatta ra
	FORMAL	kotaemashita ra	kotaemasen deshita ra
PRESUMPTIVE:	PLAIN	kotaeru daroo	kotaenai daroo
	FORMAL	kotaeru deshoo	kotaenai deshoo
VOLITIONAL:	PLAIN	kotaeyoo	
	FORMAL	kotaemashoo	

	Affirmative		*Affirmative*
POTENTIAL	kotaerareru kotaereru	HONORIFIC	okotae ni naru okotae nasaru
PASSIVE	kotaerareru	HUMBLE	okotae suru okotae itasu
CAUSATIVE	kotaesaseru		
CAUS. PASSIVE	kotaesaserareru		

Examples:

1. *Nihon-go de kotaete kudasai.*
   Please answer in Japanese.
2. *Ano shitsumon ni kotaerarenakatta.*
   I couldn't answer that question.
3. *Doa o nokku shita'n desu ga, dare mo kotaemasen deshita.*
   I knocked on the door, but no one answered.
4. *Namae o yobareta ra, "hai" to kotaemashoo.*
   If your name is called, respond by saying "yes."
5. *Kono samusa wa kotaemasu ne.*
   This cold weather really is hard to take, isn't it?

断る to refuse, decline, ask permission, warn: (trans.)

		Affirmative	*Negative*
PLAIN FORM:	PRESENT	kotowaru	kotowaranai
	PAST	kotowatta	kotowaranakatta
MASU FORM:	PRESENT	kotowarimasu	kotowarimasen
	PAST	kotowarimashita	kotowarimasen deshita
IMPERATIVE		kotoware	kotowaru na
TE FORM		kotowatte	kotowaranakute
CONDITIONAL:	PLAIN	kotowareba	kotowaranakereba
		kotowatta ra	kotowaranakatta ra
	FORMAL	kotowarimashita ra	kotowarimasen deshita ra
PRESUMPTIVE:	PLAIN	kotowaru daroo	kotowaranai daroo
	FORMAL	kotowaru deshoo	kotowaranai deshoo
VOLITIONAL:	PLAIN	kotowaroo	
	FORMAL	kotowarimashoo	

	Affirmative		*Affirmative*
POTENTIAL	kotowareru	HONORIFIC	okotowari ni naru
			okotowari nasaru
PASSIVE	kotowarareru	HUMBLE	okotowari suru
			okotowari itasu
CAUSATIVE	kotowaraseru		
CAUS. PASSIVE	kotowaraserareru		
	kotowarasareru		

Examples:

1. *Kanojo ni deeto o kotowararemashita.*
   She refused to go on a date with me.
2. *Haha ga byooki na node, zangyoo o kotowarimashita.*
   Since my mother is sick, I refused to do overtime.
3. *Yameru toki wa ikka-getsu mae ni kotowatte kudasai.*
   Please ask a month in advance if you want to quit.
4. *Shachoo ni kotowatte, yatta no desu ka.*
   Did the president give you permission to do it?
5. *Kotowatte oku ga, moo ichido yatta ra kubi da.*
   I'm warning you! You'll be fired if you do it again.

壊れる to be broken, damaged, out of order: (intra

		Affirmative	*Negative*
PLAIN FORM:	PRESENT	kowareru	kowarenai
	PAST	kowareta	kowarenakatta
MASU FORM:	PRESENT	kowaremasu	kowaremasen
	PAST	kowaremashita	kowaremasen deshita
IMPERATIVE		(kowarero)	(kowareru na)
TE FORM		kowarete	kowarenakute
CONDITIONAL:	PLAIN	kowarereba	kowarenakereba
		kowareta ra	kowarenakatta ra
	FORMAL	kowaremashita ra	kowaremasen deshita ra
PRESUMPTIVE:	PLAIN	kowareru daroo	kowarenai daroo
	FORMAL	kowareru deshoo	kowarenai deshoo
VOLITIONAL:	PLAIN	(kowareyoo)	
	FORMAL	(kowaremashoo)	

	Affirmative		*Affirmative*
POTENTIAL	(kowarerareru)	HONORIFIC	okoware ni naru
			okoware nasaru
PASSIVE	(kowarerareru)	HUMBLE	(okoware suru)
			(okoware itasu)
CAUSATIVE	(kowaresaseru)		
CAUS. PASSIVE	(kowaresaserareru)		

Examples:

1. *Tokei ga kowaremashita.*
   The watch is broken.
2. *Jishin de uchi ga takusan kowaremashita.*
   Many houses were destroyed by the earthquake.
3. *Kikai ga kowarete naose-soo mo arimasen.*
   The machine is damaged beyond all hopes of repair.
4. *Sono keikaku wa kowareta.*
   That plan fell through.
5. *Kon'yaku wa ryooshin no hantai de kowaremashita.*
   The engagement was broken off because their parents opposed it.

壊す to break, destroy, injure: (trans.)

		Affirmative	*Negative*
PLAIN FORM:	PRESENT	kowasu	kowasanai
	PAST	kowashita	kowasanakatta
MASU FORM:	PRESENT	kowashimasu	kowashimasen
	PAST	kowashimashita	kowashimasen deshita
IMPERATIVE		kowase	kowasu na
TE FORM		kowashite	kowasanakute
CONDITIONAL:	PLAIN	kowaseba	kowasanakereba
		kowashita ra	kowasanakatta ra
	FORMAL	kowashimashita ra	kowashimasen deshita ra
PRESUMPTIVE:	PLAIN	kowasu daroo	kowasanai daroo
	FORMAL	kowasu deshoo	kowasanai deshoo
VOLITIONAL:	PLAIN	kowasoo	
	FORMAL	kowashimashoo	

	Affirmative		*Affirmative*
POTENTIAL	kowaseru	HONORIFIC	okowashi ni naru
			okowashi nasaru
PASSIVE	kowasareru	HUMBLE	okowashi suru
			okowashi itasu
CAUSATIVE	kowasaseru		
CAUS. PASSIVE	kowasaserareru		

Examples:

1. *Kono isu o kowashita no wa dare desu ka.*
   Who broke this chair?
2. *Tomodachi ni conpyuutaa o kowasaremashita.*
   My friend broke the computer.
3. *Hanashi o kowasanaide kudasai.*
   Please don't spoil the conversation.
4. *Hataraki-sugite, karada o kowashite shimaimashita.*
   I ruined my health by working too much.
5. *Tabe-sugita node, onaka o kowashite shimaimashita.*
   Since I ate too much, I had stomach trouble.

曇る to become cloudy, be gloomy: (intrans.)

		Affirmative	*Negative*
PLAIN FORM:	PRESENT	kumoru	kumoranai
	PAST	kumotta	kumoranakatta
MASU FORM:	PRESENT	kumorimasu	kumorimasen
	PAST	kumorimashita	kumorimasen deshita
IMPERATIVE		(kumore)	(kumoru na)
TE FORM		kumotte	kumoranakute
CONDITIONAL:	PLAIN	kumoreba	kumoranakereba
		kumotta ra	kumoranakatta ra
	FORMAL	kumorimashita ra	kumorimasen deshita ra
PRESUMPTIVE:	PLAIN	kumoru daroo	kumoranai daroo
	FORMAL	kumoru deshoo	kumoranai deshoo
VOLITIONAL:	PLAIN	(kumoroo)	
	FORMAL	(kumorimashoo)	

	Affirmative		*Affirmative*
POTENTIAL	(kumoreru)	HONORIFIC	okumori ni naru
			okumori nasaru
PASSIVE	(komorareru)	HUMBLE	(okumori suru)
			(okumori itasu)
CAUSATIVE	kumoraseru		
CAUS. PASSIVE	kumoraserareru		

Examples:

1. *Ichinichi-juu kumotte imashita.*
   It was cloudy all day.
2. *Totsuzen sora ga kumorimashita.*
   Suddenly the sky became overcast.
3. *Densha ni notta ra, megane ga kumotte shimaimashita.*
   When I got on the train, my glasses fogged up.
4. *Kare wa kao ga kumotte iru ne.*
   He looks gloomy doesn't he?
   Hontoo ni kumotte iru ne.
   He sure does look gloomy.

比べる to compare (trans.)

		Affirmative	*Negative*
PLAIN FORM:	PRESENT	kuraberu	kurabenai
	PAST	kurabeta	kurabenakatta
MASU FORM:	PRESENT	kurabemasu	kurabemasen
	PAST	kurabemashita	kurabemasen deshita
IMPERATIVE		kurabero	kuraberu na
TE FORM		kurabete	kurabenakute
CONDITIONAL:	PLAIN	kurabereba	kurabenakereba
		kurabeta ra	kurabenakatta ra
	FORMAL	kurabemashita ra	kurabemasen deshita ra
PRESUMPTIVE:	PLAIN	kuraberu daroo	kurabenai daroo
	FORMAL	kuraberu deshoo	kurabenai deshoo
VOLITIONAL:	PLAIN	kurabeyoo	
	FORMAL	kurabemashoo	

	Affirmative		*Affirmative*
POTENTIAL	kuraberareru	HONORIFIC	okurabe ni naru
			okurabe nasaru
PASSIVE	kuraberareru	HUMBLE	okurabe suru
			okurabe itasu
CAUSATIVE	kurabesaseru		
CAUS. PASSIVE	kurabesaserareru		

Examples:

1. *Tookyoo to Nyuu Yooku o kuraberu to, dotchi ga abunai desu ka.*
   Which city is more dangerous, Tokyo or New York?
   Nyuu Yooku no hoo ga abunai desu.
   New York is more dangerous.
2. *Dare ga ichiban se ga takai ka kurabete mimashoo.*
   Let's see who is the tallest.
3. *Kotoshi wa kyonen ni kurabete yuki ga ooi desu.*
   There has been more snow this year than last year.
4. *Kare no hisseki o kogitte no to kurabete mita.*
   I compared his handwriting with that on the check.

くれる to give: (trans.); 暮れる to end, get dark: (intrans.)*

		Affirmative	*Negative*
PLAIN FORM:	PRESENT	kureru	kurenai
	PAST	kureta	kurenakatta
MASU FORM:	PRESENT	kuremasu	kuremasen
	PAST	kuremashita	kuremasen deshita
IMPERATIVE		kurero	kureru na
TE FORM		kurete	kurenakute
CONDITIONAL:	PLAIN	kurereba	kurenakereba
		kureta ra	kurenakatta ra
	FORMAL	kuremashita ra	kuremasen deshita ra
PRESUMPTIVE:	PLAIN	kureru daroo	kurenai daroo
	FORMAL	kureru deshoo	kurenai deshoo
VOLITIONAL:	PLAIN	kureyoo	
	FORMAL	kuremashoo	

	Affirmative		*Affirmative*
POTENTIAL	(kurerareru)	HONORIFIC	kudasaru
PASSIVE	(kurerareru)	HUMBLE	(okure suru)
			(okure itasu)
CAUSATIVE	(kuresaseru)		
CAUS. PASSIVE	(kuresaserareru)		

Examples:

1. *Haha wa watashi ni purezento o kuremashita.*
   My mother gave me a present.
2. *Sensei wa watashi ni hon o katte kuremashita.*
   My teacher bought me a book.
3. *Nihon-go o oshiete kurenai?*
   Will you teach Japanese to me?
4. *Toshi ga kureyoo to shite imasu.*
   It is getting pretty close to New Years.
5. *Hi ga kureru mae ni kaeroo.*
   Let's go home before it gets dark.

* Besides the forms shown above, the intransitive verb *kureru* 暮れる meaning "to get dark, to end" generally does not use the imperative, volitional, or honorific forms.

来る to come, arrive: (intrans.)

		Affirmative	*Negative*
PLAIN FORM:	PRESENT	kuru	konai
	PAST	kita	konakatta
MASU FORM:	PRESENT	kimasu	kimasen
	PAST	kimashita	kimasen deshita
IMPERATIVE		koi	kuru na
TE FORM		kite	konakute
CONDITIONAL:	PLAIN	kureba	konakereba
		kita ra	konakatta ra
	FORMAL	kimashita ra	kimasen deshita ra
PRESUMPTIVE:	PLAIN	kuru daroo	konai daroo
	FORMAL	kuru deshoo	konai deshoo
VOLITIONAL:	PLAIN	koyoo	
	FORMAL	kimashoo	

	Affirmative		*Affirmative*
POTENTIAL	korareru koreru	HONORIFIC	irassharu oide ni naru oide nasaru
PASSIVE	korareru	HUMBLE	mairu
CAUSATIVE	kosaseru		
CAUS. PASSIVE	kosaserareru kosasareru		

Examples:

1. *Ashita nan-ji ni irasshaimasu ka.*
   What time will you come tomorrow?
2. *Basu ga kimashita yo.*
   The bus has arrived.
3. *Tomodachi kara tegami ga konakatta node, shinpai shimashita.*
   Since I didn't receive a letter from my friend, I was worried.
4. *Konogoro futotte kita node, undoo suru tsumori desu.*
   I'm going to exercise because recently I've put on weight.
5. *Ashita kono shorui o motte kite kudasai.*
   Please bring this paper tomorrow.

加える to add, increase; くわえる to hold in mouth: (both trans.)

		Affirmative	*Negative*
PLAIN FORM:	PRESENT	kuwaeru	kuwaenai
	PAST	kuwaeta	kuwaenakatta
MASU FORM:	PRESENT	kuwaemasu	kuwaemasen
	PAST	kuwaemashita	kuwaemasen deshita
IMPERATIVE		kuwaero	kuwaeru na
TE FORM		kuwaete	kuwaenakute
CONDITIONAL:	PLAIN	kuwaereba	kuwaenakaereba
		kuwaeta ra	kuwaenakatta ra
	FORMAL	kuwaemashita ra	kuwaemasen deshita ra
PRESUMPTIVE:	PLAIN	kuwaeru daroo	kuwaenai daroo
	FORMAL	kuwaeru deshoo	kuwaenai deshoo
VOLITIONAL:	PLAIN	kuwaeyoo	
	FORMAL	kuwaemashoo	

	Affirmative		*Affirmative*
POTENTIAL	kuwaerareru kuwaereru	HONORIFIC	okuwae ni naru okuwae nasaru
PASSIVE	kuwaerareru	HUMBLE	(okuwae suru)
CAUSATIVE	kuwaesaseru		(okuwae itasu)
CAUS. PASSIVE	kuwaesaserareru		

Examples:

1. *San ni ichi o kuwaeru to yon desu.*
   Three plus one is four.
2. *Kare o nakama ni kuwaeta ra doo desu ka.*
   Why don't we let him join us?
3. *Kono ryoori ni wa moo sukoshi satoo o kuwaeta hoo ga ii desu.*
   I think you should add a little more sugar to this dish.
4. *Densha wa supiido o kuwaemashita.*
   The train gathered speed.
5. *Neko ga sakana o kuwaete nigete itta.*
   The cat ran away with the fish in its mouth.

machigaeru

間違える to make a mistake: (trans.)

		Affirmative	*Negative*
PLAIN FORM:	PRESENT	machigaeru	machigaenai
	PAST	machigaeta	machigaenakatta
MASU FORM:	PRESENT	machigaemasu	machigaemasen
	PAST	machigaemashita	machigaemasen deshita
IMPERATIVE		machigaero	machigaeru na
TE FORM		machigaete	machigaenakute
CONDITIONAL:	PLAIN	machigaereba	machigaenakereba
		machigaeta ra	machigaenakatta ra
	FORMAL	machigaemashita ra	machigaemasen deshita ra
PRESUMPTIVE:	PLAIN	machigaeru daroo	machigaenai daroo
	FORMAL	machigaeru deshoo	machigaenai deshoo
VOLITIONAL:	PLAIN	machigaeyoo	
	FORMAL	machigaemashoo	

	Affirmative		*Affirmative*
POTENTIAL	machigaerareru	HONORIFIC	omachigae ni naru
	machigaereru		omachigae nasaru
PASSIVE	machigaerareru	HUMBLE	(omachigae suru)
			(omachigae itasu)
CAUSATIVE	machigaesaseru		
CAUS. PASSIVE	machigaesaserareru		

Examples:

1. *Michi o machigaemashita.*
   I took the wrong road.
2. *Imi o machigaenaide kudasai.*
   Please don't mistake the meaning.
3. *Heya o machigaete tonari no heya ni haitte shimatta.*
   By mistake, I entered the room next door.
4. *Keisan o machigaeta.*
   I calculated wrong.
5. *Ueetaa ni machigaeraremashita.*
   I was mistaken for a waiter.

間違う to make a mistake: (intrans.)*

		Affirmative	*Negative*
PLAIN FORM:	PRESENT	machigau	machigawanai
	PAST	machigatta	machigawanakatta
MASU FORM:	PRESENT	machigaimasu	machigaimasen
	PAST	machigaimashita	machigaimasen deshita
IMPERATIVE		machigae	machigau na
TE FORM		machigatte	machigawanakute
CONDITIONAL:	PLAIN	machigaeba	machigawanakereba
		machigatta ra	machigawanakatta ra
	FORMAL	machigaimashita ra	machigaimasen deshita ra
PRESUMPTIVE:	PLAIN	machigau daroo	machigawanai daroo
	FORMAL	machigau deshoo	machigawanai deshoo
VOLITIONAL:	PLAIN	machigaoo	
	FORMAL	machigaimashoo	

	Affirmative		*Affirmative*
POTENTIAL	(machigaeru)	HONORIFIC	omachigai ni naru
			omachigai nasaru
PASSIVE	machigawareru	HUMBLE	(omachigai suru)
			(omachigai itasu)
CAUSATIVE	machigawaseru		
CAUS. PASSIVE	machigawaserareru		
	machigawasareru		

Examples:

1. *Kono tegami wa juusho ga machigatte imasu.*
   The address on this letter is wrong.
2. *Watashi wa Yamada-san ni machigawaremashita.*
   I was mistaken for Mr. Yamada.
3. *Machigatte kono hon o motte kite shimatta.*
   I brought this book by mistake.
4. *Keisan o machigatta.*
   I made a mistake in the calculation.
5. *Machigatte mo kare ni itte wa ikemasen.*
   Whatever you do, don't mention it to him.

* Also used as a transitive verb. (*See* example 4.)

曲がる to bend, curve, turn: (intrans.)

		Affirmative	*Negative*
PLAIN FORM:	PRESENT	magaru	magaranai
	PAST	magatta	magaranakatta
MASU FORM:	PRESENT	magarimasu	magarimasen
	PAST	magarimashita	magarimasen deshita
IMPERATIVE		magare	magaru na
TE FORM		magatte	magaranakute
CONDITIONAL:	PLAIN	magareba	magaranakereba
		magatta ra	magaranakatta ra
	FORMAL	magarimashita ra	magarimasen deshita ra
PRESUMPTIVE:	PLAIN	magaru daroo	magaranai daroo
	FORMAL	magaru deshoo	magaranai deshoo
VOLITIONAL:	PLAIN	magaroo	
	FORMAL	magarimashoo	

	Affirmative		*Affirmative*
POTENTIAL	magareru	HONORIFIC	omagari ni naru
			omagari nasaru
PASSIVE	magarareru	HUMBLE	(omagari suru)
			(omagari itasu)
CAUSATIVE	magaraseru		
CAUS. PASSIVE	magaraserareru		

Examples:

1. *Migi e/ni magatte kudasai.*
   Please turn right.
2. *Nekutai ga magatte imasu yo.*
   Your tie is crooked.
3. *Ano roojin wa koshi ga magatte imasu.*
   That old man's back is bent.
4. *Hidari e/ni magaru to kooen ga arimasu yo.*
   Turn left, and you'll find the park.
5. *Kokoro no magatta hito wa suki ja arimasen.*
   I don't like a dishonest man. (*lit.*, man with a crooked heart)

曲げる to bend, curve, twist: (trans.)

		Affirmative	*Negative*
PLAIN FORM:	PRESENT	mageru	magenai
	PAST	mageta	magenakatta
MASU FORM:	PRESENT	magemasu	magemasen
	PAST	magemashita	magemasen deshita
IMPERATIVE		magero	mageru na
TE FORM		magete	magenakute
CONDITIONAL:	PLAIN	magereba	magenakereba
		mageta ra	magenakatta ra
	FORMAL	magemashita ra	magemasen deshita ra
PRESUMPTIVE:	PLAIN	mageru daroo	magenai daroo
	FORMAL	mageru deshoo	magenai deshoo
VOLITIONAL:	PLAIN	mageyoo	
	FORMAL	magemashoo	

	Affirmative		*Affirmative*
POTENTIAL	magerareru	HONORIFIC	omage ni naru
	magereru		omage nasaru
PASSIVE	magerareru	HUMBLE	omage suru
			omage itasu
CAUSATIVE	magesaseru		
CAUS. PASSIVE	magesaserareru		

Examples:

1. *Kono tetsuboo o mageraremasu ka.*
   Can you bend this iron bar?
   Ee, mageraremasu.
   Yes, I can.
2. *Kega o shita node, ashi o magerarenaku natta.*
   I hurt myself and couldn't bend my leg.
3. *Dooshite mo kare wa iken o mageyoo to shinai'n desu.*
   He won't alter his opinion for anything.
4. *Sono otoko no ko wa booshi o magete, kabutte ita.*
   That boy had his cap on slightly to one side.

任す to entrust to, leave to, use freely; 負かす to defeat: (both trans.)

		Affirmative	*Negative*
PLAIN FORM:	PRESENT	makasu	makasanai
	PAST	makashita	makasanakatta
MASU FORM:	PRESENT	makashimasu	makashimasen
	PAST	makashimashita	makashimasen deshita
IMPERATIVE		makase	makasu na
TE FORM		makashite	makasanakute
CONDITIONAL:	PLAIN	makaseba	makasanakereba
		makashita ra	makasanakatta ra
	FORMAL	makashimashita ra	makashimasen deshita ra
PRESUMPTIVE:	PLAIN	makasu daroo	makasanai daroo
	FORMAL	makasu deshoo	makasanai deshoo
VOLITIONAL:	PLAIN	makasoo	
	FORMAL	makashimashoo	

	Affirmative		*Affirmative*
POTENTIAL	makaseru	HONORIFIC	omakashi ni naru
			omakashi nasaru
PASSIVE	makasareru	HUMBLE	omakashi suru
			omakashi itasu
CAUSATIVE	makasaseru		
CAUS. PASSIVE	makasaserareru		
	makasareru		

Examples:

1. *Kono shigoto wa watashi ni makashite kudasai.*
   Please leave this job up to me.
2. *Dare ni makasareta shigoto desu ka.*
   Who left this work for you to do?
   Buchoo ni makasareta shigoto desu.
   The department chief left this work with me.
3. *Hima ni makashite Nihon no shoosetsu o yomimashita.*
   With so much time at my disposal, I read Japanese novels.
4. *Watashi-tachi wa futtobooru no shiai de puro chiimu o makashita.*
   Our team beat the professional team at football.

負ける to be defeated, to lose: (intrans.); give a price reduction: (trans.)

		Affirmative	*Negative*
PLAIN FORM:	PRESENT	makeru	makenai
	PAST	maketa	makenakatta
MASU FORM:	PRESENT	makemasu	makemasen
	PAST	makemashita	makemasen deshita
IMPERATIVE		makero	makeru na
TE FORM		makete	makenakute
CONDITIONAL:	PLAIN	makereba	makenakereba
		maketa ra	makenakatta ra
	FORMAL	makemashita ra	makemasen deshita ra
PRESUMPTIVE:	PLAIN	makeru daroo	makenai daroo
	FORMAL	makeru deshoo	makenai deshoo
VOLITIONAL:	PLAIN	makeyoo	
	FORMAL	makemashoo	

	Affirmative		*Affirmative*
POTENTIAL	makerareru	HONORIFIC	omake ni naru
	makereru		omake nasaru
PASSIVE	makerareru	HUMBLE	omake suru
			omake itasu
CAUSATIVE	makesaseru		
CAUS. PASSIVE	makesaserareru		

Examples:

1. *Kyoosoo ni maketa.*
   We lost in the competition.
2. *Kaajinaruzu wa yon tai san de Tsuinzu ni makemashita.*
   The Cardinals lost the game to the Twins by four to three.
3. *Tsugi no shiai ni wa makenai yoo ni ganbaroo.*
   Let's stick in there and win the next game.
4. *Kanojo wa yuuwaku ni makete shimatta.*
   She yielded to temptation.
5. *Nedan o makete itadakemasen ka.*
   Would you make it cheaper?

巻く to bind, roll up; 撒く to sprinkle: (both trans.)

		Affirmative	*Negative*
PLAIN FORM:	PRESENT	maku	makanai
	PAST	maita	makanakatta
MASU FORM:	PRESENT	makimasu	makimasen
	PAST	makimashita	makimasen deshita
IMPERATIVE		make	maku na
TE FORM		maite	makanakute
CONDITIONAL:	PLAIN	makeba	makanakereba
		maita ra	makanakatta ra
	FORMAL	makimashita ra	makimasen deshita ra
PRESUMPTIVE:	PLAIN	maku daroo	makanai daroo
	FORMAL	maku deshoo	makanai deshoo
VOLITIONAL:	PLAIN	makoo	
	FORMAL	makimashoo	

	Affirmative		*Affirmative*
POTENTIAL	makeru	HONORIFIC	omaki ni naru
			omaki nasaru
PASSIVE	makareru	HUMBLE	omaki suru
			omaki itasu
CAUSATIVE	makaseru		
CAUS. PASSIVE	makaserareru		
	makasareru		

Examples:

1. *Ashi ni hootai o maita.*
   I bandaged my leg.
2. *Yamada-san wa atama ni hootai o maite kuremashita.*
   Mr. Yamada bound my head with a bandage.
3. *Kanojo wa sukaafu o kubi ni maite iru.*
   She has a scarf wrapped around her neck.
4. *Kare no shokuyoku ni wa shita o maita.*
   I was astounded at his appetite. (*lit.*, my tongue was bound)
5. *Mizu o makimashoo.*
   Let's sprinkle some water.

守る to protect, keep, defend: (trans.)

		Affirmative	*Negative*
PLAIN FORM:	PRESENT	mamoru	mamoranai
	PAST	mamotta	mamoranakatta
MASU FORM:	PRESENT	mamorimasu	mamorimasen
	PAST	mamorimashita	mamorimasen deshita
IMPERATIVE		mamore	mamoru na
TE FORM		mamotte	mamoranakute
CONDITIONAL:	PLAIN	mamoreba	mamoranakereba
		mamotta ra	mamoranakatta ra
	FORMAL	mamorimashita ra	mamorimasen deshita ra
PRESUMPTIVE:	PLAIN	mamoru daroo	mamoranai daroo
	FORMAL	mamoru deshoo	mamoranai deshoo
VOLITIONAL:	PLAIN	mamoroo	
	FORMAL	mamorimashoo	

	Affirmative		*Affirmative*
POTENTIAL	mamoreru	HONORIFIC	omamori ni naru
			omamori nasaru
PASSIVE	mamorareru	HUMBLE	omamori suru
			omamori itasu
CAUSATIVE	mamoraseru		
CAUS. PASSIVE	mamoraserareru		
	mamorasareru		

Examples:

1. *Kisoku wa mamoranakereba narimasen.*
   You must stick to the rules.
2. *Kare to no yakusoku wa mamoroo.*
   Let's keep our promise to him.
3. *Yamada-san wa itsumo jikan o mamoranakute, komarimasu.*
   Mr. Yamada's always being late is a problem.
4. *Kare wa chinmoku o mamotte iru.*
   He kept his silence.
5. *Kaihatsu kara shizen o mamoroo.*
   Let's protect nature from being (commercially) developed.

間に合う to be in time, be enough, be able to do without: (intrans.)

		Affirmative	*Negative*
PLAIN FORM:	PRESENT	maniau	maniawanai
	PAST	maniatta	maniawanakatta
MASU FORM:	PRESENT	maniaimasu	maniaimasen
	PAST	maniaimashita	maniaimasen deshita
IMPERATIVE		maniae	maniau na
TE FORM		maniatte	maniawanakute
CONDITIONAL:	PLAIN	maniaeba	maniawanakereba
		maniatta ra	maniawanakatta ra
	FORMAL	maniaimashita ra	maniaimasen deshita ra
PRESUMPTIVE:	PLAIN	maniau daroo	maniawanai daroo
	FORMAL	maniau deshoo	maniawanai deshoo
VOLITIONAL:	PLAIN	maniaoo	
	FORMAL	maniaimashoo	

	Affirmative		*Affirmative*
POTENTIAL	maniaeru	HONORIFIC	omaniai ni naru
			omaniai nasaru
PASSIVE	maniawareru	HUMBLE	(omaniai suru)
			(omaniai itasu)
CAUSATIVE	maniawaseru		
CAUS. PASSIVE	maniawaserareru		
	maiawasareru		

Examples:

1. *Shuuden ni maniawanakatta.*
   I missed the last train.
2. *Roku-ji no hikooki ni maniau yoo ni isogimashoo.*
   Let's hurry so we can make the six o'clock plane.
3. *Ato go-sen en areba juubun maniaimasu.*
   If I have five thousand yen more, it'll be more than enough.
4. *Bideo wa irimasen ka.*
   Do you need a video?
   Iie, maniatte imasu.
   No, I'm fine as is.

待つ to wait: (trans.)

		Affirmative	*Negative*
PLAIN FORM:	PRESENT	matsu	matanai
	PAST	matta	matanakatta
MASU FORM:	PRESENT	machimasu	machimasen
	PAST	machimashita	machimasen deshita
IMPERATIVE		mate	matsu na
TE FORM		matte	matanakute
CONDITIONAL:	PLAIN	mateba	matanakereba
		matta ra	matanakatta ra
	FORMAL	machimashita ra	machimasen deshita ra
PRESUMPTIVE:	PLAIN	matsu daroo	matanai daroo
	FORMAL	matsu deshoo	matanai deshoo
VOLITIONAL:	PLAIN	matoo	
	FORMAL	machimashoo	

	Affirmative		*Affirmative*
POTENTIAL	materu	HONORIFIC	omachi ni naru
			omachi nasaru
PASSIVE	matareru	HUMBLE	omachi suru
			omachi itasu
CAUSATIVE	mataseru		
CAUS. PASSIVE	mataserareru		
	matasareru		

Examples:

1. *Chotto omachi kudasai.*
   Please wait a moment.
2. *Getsuyoobi no go-ji ni omachi shite orimasu.*
   I look forward to seeing you at five o'clock on Monday.
3. *Isogimashoo. Takushii o matasete arimasu kara.*
   Let's hurry up. The taxi is waiting.
4. *Shichi-ji ni tomodachi to machi-awasete imasu.*
   I arranged to meet my friend at seven o'clock.
5. *Okyaku-san o matasete aru node, moo kaerimasu.*
   I should go home since I have a visitor waiting.

回る to turn around: (intrans.);* go around: (trans.)

		Affirmative	*Negative*
PLAIN FORM:	PRESENT	mawaru	mawaranai
	PAST	mawatta	mawaranakatta
MASU FORM:	PRESENT	mawarimasu	mawarimasen
	PAST	mawarimashita	mawarimasen deshita
IMPERATIVE		maware	mawaru na
TE FORM		mawatte	mawaranakute
CONDITIONAL:	PLAIN	mawareba	mawaranakereba
		mawatta ra	mawaranakatta ra
	FORMAL	mawarimashita ra	mawarimasen deshita ra
PRESUMPTIVE:	PLAIN	mawaru daroo	mawaranai daroo
	FORMAL	mawaru deshoo	mawaranai deshoo
VOLITIONAL:	PLAIN	mawaroo	
	FORMAL	mawarimashoo	

	Affirmative		*Affirmative*
POTENTIAL	mawareru	HONORIFIC	omawari ni naru
			omawari nasaru
PASSIVE	mawarareru	HUMBLE	(omawari suru)
			(omawari itasu)
CAUSATIVE	mawaraseru		
CAUS. PASSIVE	mawaraserareru		
	mawarasareru		

Examples:

1. *Tsuki wa chikyuu no mawari o mawatte imasu.*
   The moon revolves around the earth.
2. *Utau ban ga mawatte kita.*
   My turn to sing came.
3. *Kankoku kara Nihon o mawatte kaeru tsumori desu.*
   I'm going to go home from Korea via Japan.
4. *Kare wa sono shirase o ii-mawatta.*
   He went around announcing that news.
5. *Ohiru o sukoshi mawatte, kanojo ga kita.*
   She came a little after noon.

* The intransitive *mawaru* meaning "to turn around" generally does not use the potential, passive, causative passive, honorific, or humble forms.

回す to turn, pass round, send on: (trans.)

		Affirmative	*Negative*
PLAIN FORM:	PRESENT	mawasu	mawasanai
	PAST	mawashita	mawasanakatta
MASU FORM:	PRESENT	mawashimasu	mawashimasen
	PAST	mawashimashita	mawashimasen deshita
IMPERATIVE		mawase	mawasu na
TE FORM		mawashite	mawasanakute
CONDITIONAL:	PLAIN	mawaseba	mawasanakereba
		mawashita ra	mawasanakatta ra
	FORMAL	mawashimashita ra	mawashimasen deshita ra
PRESUMPTIVE:	PLAIN	mawasu daroo	mawasanai daroo
	FORMAL	mawasu deshoo	mawasanai deshoo
VOLITIONAL:	PLAIN	mawasoo	
	FORMAL	mawashimashoo	

	Affirmative		*Affirmative*
POTENTIAL	mawaseru	HONORIFIC	omawashi ni naru
			omawashi nasaru
PASSIVE	mawasareru	HUMBLE	omawashi suru
			omawashi itasu
CAUSATIVE	mawasaseru		
CAUS. PASSIVE	mawasaserareru		

Examples:

1. *Senpuuki o mawashita.*
   I turned on an electric fan.
2. *Kono hon o mawashite kudasai.*
   Please pass this book on.
3. *Satoo o mawashite kuremasen ka.*
   Would you pass me the sugar?
4. *Kare wa betsu no ka ni mawasareta.*
   He was transferred to another section.
5. *Okane ga atta ra, watashi ni mawashite kudasai.*
   If you have any money, will you lend it to me?

迷う to be lost, be in doubt, be captivated: (intrans.)

		Affirmative	*Negative*
PLAIN FORM:	PRESENT	mayou	mayowanai
	PAST	mayotta	mayowanakatta
MASU FORM:	PRESENT	mayoimasu	mayoimasen
	PAST	mayoimashita	mayoimasen deshita
IMPERATIVE		mayoe	mayou na
TE FORM		mayotte	mayowanakute
CONDITIONAL:	PLAIN	mayoeba	mayowanakereba
		mayotta ra	mayowanakatta ra
	FORMAL	mayoimashita ra	mayoimasen deshita ra
PRESUMPTIVE:	PLAIN	mayou daroo	mayowanai daroo
	FORMAL	mayou deshoo	mayowanai deshoo
VOLITIONAL:	PLAIN	mayooo	
	FORMAL	mayoimashoo	

	Affirmative		*Affirmative*
POTENTIAL	mayoeru	HONORIFIC	omayoi ni naru
			omayoi nasaru
PASSIVE	mayowareru	HUMBLE	(omayoi suru)
			(omayoi itasu)
CAUSATIVE	mayowaseru		
CAUS. PASSIVE	mayowaserareru		
	mayowasareru		

Examples:

1. *Tookyoo de michi ni mayotta.*
   I lost my way in Tokyo.
2. *Dotchi no kutsu o kaoo ka mayotte imasu.*
   I'm not sure which shoes to buy.
3. *Kotori ga heya ni mayoi-komimashita.*
   The small bird strayed around the room.
4. *Sonna ni mayou koto ja nai yo.*
   That's not something to worry so much about.
5. *Kare wa onna ni mayotta.*
   He was captivated by the woman.

目立つ to be outstanding, remarkable: (intrans.)

		Affirmative	*Negative*
PLAIN FORM:	PRESENT	medatsu	medatanai
	PAST	medatta	medatanakatta
MASU FORM:	PRESENT	medachimasu	medachimasen
	PAST	medachimashita	medachimasen deshita
IMPERATIVE		medate	medatsu na
TE FORM		medatte	medatanakute
CONDITIONAL:	PLAIN	medateba	medatanakereba
		medatta ra	medatanakatta ra
	FORMAL	medachimashita ra	medachimasen deshita ra
PRESUMPTIVE:	PLAIN	medatsu daroo	medatanai daroo
	FORMAL	medatsu deshoo	medatanai deshoo
VOLITIONAL:	PLAIN	medatoo	
	FORMAL	medachimashoo	

	Affirmative		*Affirmative*
POTENTIAL	(medateru)	HONORIFIC	(omedachi ni naru)
			(omedachi nasaru)
PASSIVE	(medatareru)	HUMBLE	(omedachi suru)
			(omedachi itasu)
CAUSATIVE	medataseru		
CAUS. PASSIVE	medataserareru		
	medatasareru		

Examples:

1. *Kare wa se ga takai node medachimasu.*
   Because he is tall, he sticks out.
2. *Sono fuku wa medachi-sugimasu.*
   Those clothes are too eye-catching.
3. *Saikin, kekkon shinai hito ga medatte imasu.*
   Recently there's been a remarkable number of unmarried people.
4. *Kanojo wa Nihon-go ga medatte, joozu ni natta.*
   She made remarkable progress in her Japanese.
5. *Kono sebiro wa sugu yogore ga medachimasu.*
   Dirt and stains show up easily on this suit.

mieru

見える to be seen, be able to see, to appear, come: (intrans.)

		Affirmative	*Negative*
PLAIN FORM:	PRESENT	mieru	mienai
	PAST	mieta	mienakatta
MASU FORM:	PRESENT	miemasu	miemasen
	PAST	miemashita	miemasen deshita
IMPERATIVE		(miero)	(mieru na)
TE FORM		miete	mienakute
CONDITIONAL:	PLAIN	miereba	mienakereba
		mieta ra	mienakatta ra
	FORMAL	miemashita ra	miemasen deshita ra
PRESUMPTIVE:	PLAIN	mieru daroo	mienai daroo
	FORMAL	mieru deshoo	mienai deshoo
VOLITIONAL:	PLAIN	(mieyoo)	
	FORMAL	(miemashoo)	

	Affirmative		*Affirmative*
POTENTIAL	(mierareru)	HONORIFIC	omie ni naru
			irrasharu
PASSIVE	(mierareru)	HUMBLE	(omie suru)
			(omie itasu)
CAUSATIVE	(miesaseru)		
CAUS. PASSIVE	(miesaserareru)		

Examples:

1. *Yama ga yoku miemasu.*
   The mountain can be seen clearly.
2. *Koko kara wa nani mo miemasen.*
   Nothing is visible from here.
3. *Mienaku naru made kare o miokutta.*
   I saw him off until he was out of sight.
4. *Yamada-san wa wakaku miemasu ne.*
   Mr. Yamada looks young, doesn't he?
5. *Sensei wa mamonaku omie ni narimasu.*
   The teacher will arrive before long.

磨く to polish, brush, improve, cultivate: (trans.)

		Affirmative	*Negative*
PLAIN FORM:	PRESENT	migaku	migakanai
	PAST	migaita	migakanakatta
MASU FORM:	PRESENT	migakimasu	migakimasen
	PAST	migakimashita	migakimasen deshita
IMPERATIVE		migake	migaku na
TE FORM		migaite	migakanakute
CONDITIONAL:	PLAIN	migakeba	migakanakereba
		migaita ra	migakanakatta ra
	FORMAL	migakimashita ra	migakimasen deshita ra
PRESUMPTIVE:	PLAIN	migaku daroo	migakanai daroo
	FORMAL	migakimashoo	migakanai deshoo
VOLITIONAL:	PLAIN	migakoo	
	FORMAL	migakimashoo	

	Affirmative		*Affirmative*
POTENTIAL	migakeru	HONORIFIC	omigaki ni naru
			omigaki nasaru
PASSIVE	migakareru	HUMBLE	omigaki suru
			omigaki itasu
CAUSATIVE	migakaseru		
CAUS. PASSIVE	migakaserareru		
	migakasareru		

Examples:

1. *Maiasa ha o migakimashoo.*
   Let's brush our teeth every morning.
2. *Dekakeru mae ni kutsu o migakimashita.*
   Before going out I shined my shoes.
3. *Kare wa megane no renzu o migaite moratta.*
   He had the lenses of his glasses polished.
4. *Juudoo no ude o migaku tame ni, Nihon ni ikimashita.*
   I went to Japan to improve my judo skills.
5. *Gorufu no ude o migaki-ageta.*
   I honed my golfing skills.

miru

見る to see, look at, watch, to try, to look after: (trans.)

		Affirmative	*Negative*
PLAIN FORM:	PRESENT	miru	minai
	PAST	mita	minakatta
MASU FORM:	PRESENT	mimasu	mimasen
	PAST	mimashita	mimasen deshita
IMPERATIVE		miro	miru na
TE FORM		mite	minakute
CONDITIONAL:	PLAIN	mireba	minakereba
		mita ra	minakatta ra
	FORMAL	mimashita ra	mimasen deshita ra
PRESUMPTIVE:	PLAIN	miru daroo	minai daroo
	FORMAL	miru deshoo	minai deshoo
VOLITIONAL:	PLAIN	miyoo	
	FORMAL	mimashoo	

	Affirmative		*Affirmative*
POTENTIAL	mirareru mireru	HONORIFIC	goran ni naru
PASSIVE	mirareru	HUMBLE	haiken suru haiken itasu
CAUSATIVE	misaseru		
CAUS. PASSIVE	misaserareru		

Examples:

1. *Yamada-san wa sono heya de terebi o mite imasu.*
   Mr. Yamada is watching TV in that room.
2. *Eiga demo mi ni ikimasen ka.*
   Shall we go to see a movie or something?
3. *Muzukashii mondai desu ne. Demo yatte mimasu.*
   That's a difficult problem, isn't it? But I'll try to do it.
4. *Kono ryoori no aji o mite itadakemasen ka.*
   Would you sample the flavor of this dish?
5. *Watashi wa ryooshin no mendoo o minakereba narimasen.*
   I have to look after my parents in their old age.

見せる to show, display: (trans.)

		Affirmative	*Negative*
PLAIN FORM:	PRESENT	miseru	misenai
	PAST	miseta	misenakatta
MASU FORM:	PRESENT	misemasu	misemasen
	PAST	misemashita	misemasen deshita
IMPERATIVE		misero	miseru na
TE FORM		misete	misenakute
CONDITIONAL:	PLAIN	misereba	misenakereba
		miseta ra	misenakatta ra
	FORMAL	misemashita ra	misemasen deshita ra
PRESUMPTIVE:	PLAIN	miseru daroo	misenai daroo
	FORMAL	miseru deshoo	misenai deshoo
VOLITIONAL:	PLAIN	miseyoo	
	FORMAL	misemashoo	

	Affirmative		*Affirmative*
POTENTIAL	miserareru misereru	HONORIFIC	omise ni naru omise nasaru
PASSIVE	miserareru	HUMBLE	omise suru omise itasu
CAUSATIVE	misesaseru		
CAUS. PASSIVE	misesaserareru		

Examples:

1. *Chotto sono hon o misete kudasai.*
   Please show me that book.
2. *Tomodachi ni Nihon no kodomo-tachi no shashin o misete moratta.*
   I had my friend show me pictures of Japanese children.
3. *Kodomo o isha ni miseta.*
   I took my child to see a doctor.
4. *Kanojo wa jibun o wakaku miseta-gatte iru.*
   She wants to make herself look young.
5. *Kanarazu yatte misemasu.*
   I'll show you I can do it.

認める to permit, admit, recognize: (trans.)

		Affirmative	*Negative*
PLAIN FORM:	PRESENT	mitomeru	mitomenai
	PAST	mitometa	mitomenakatta
MASU FORM:	PRESENT	mitomemasu	mitomemasen
	PAST	mitomemashita	mitomemasen deshita
IMPERATIVE		mitomero	mitomeru na
TE FORM		mitomete	mitomenakute
CONDITIONAL:	PLAIN	mitomereba	mitomenakereba
		mitometa ra	mitomenakatta ra
	FORMAL	mitomemashita ra	mitomemasen deshita ra
PRESUMPTIVE:	PLAIN	mitomeru daroo	mitomenai daroo
	FORMAL	mitomeru deshoo	mitomenai deshoo
VOLITIONAL:	PLAIN	mitomeyoo	
	FORMAL	mitomemashoo	

	Affirmative		*Affirmative*
POTENTIAL	mitomerareru mitomereru	HONORIFIC	omitome ni naru omitome nasaru
PASSIVE	mitomerareru	HUMBLE	omitome suru omitome itasu
CAUSATIVE	mitomesaseru		
CAUS. PASSIVE	mitomesaserareru		

Examples:

1. *Chichi wa Nihon e no ryuugaku o mitomete kurenai.*
   My father wouldn't allow me to go to Japan to study.
2. *Yatto Nihon no daigaku no nyuugaku o mitomeraremashita.*
   At last, I was accepted into a Japanese university.
3. *Watashi no iu koto mo mitomete itadakemasen ka.*
   Won't you please accept what I'm saying too?
4. *Kare wa jibun no ayamari o mitomemashita.*
   He admitted that he was wrong.
5. *Kanojo wa shigoto no nooryoku o mitomerareta.*
   People recognized what a good worker she is.

見付かる to be found, discovered: (intrans.)

		Affirmative	*Negative*
PLAIN FORM:	PRESENT	mitsukaru	mitsukaranai
	PAST	mitsukatta	mitsukaranakatta
MASU FORM:	PRESENT	mitsukarimasu	mitsukarimasen
	PAST	mitsukarimashita	mitsukarimasen deshita
IMPERATIVE		(mitsukare)	(mitsukaru na)
TE FORM		mitsukatte	mitsukaranakute
CONDITIONAL:	PLAIN	mitsukareba	mitsukaranakereba
		mitsukatta ra	mitsukaranakatta ra
	FORMAL	mitsukarimashita ra	mitsukarimasen deshita ra
PRESUMPTIVE:	PLAIN	mitsukaru daroo	mitsukaranai daroo
	FORMAL	mitsukaru deshoo	mitsukaranai deshoo
VOLITIONAL:	PLAIN	(mitsukaroo)	
	FORMAL	(mitsukarimashoo)	

	Affirmative		*Affirmative*
POTENTIAL	(mitsukareru)	HONORIFIC	omitsukari ni naru
			omitsukari nasaru
PASSIVE	(mitsukarareru)	HUMBLE	(omitsukari suru)
			(omitsukari itasu)
CAUSATIVE	(mitsukaraseru)		
CAUS. PASSIVE	(mitsukaraserareru)		

Examples:

1. *Apaato ga mitsukatta?*
   Did you find an apartment?
   Un, ii no ga mitsukatta yo.
   Yes, I found a good one.
2. *Yatto hon ga mitsukarimashita.*
   At last, my book was found.
3. *Saifu ga mada mitsukaranai.*
   I have not found my wallet yet.
4. *Mitsukaru to hidoi me ni au zo.*
   If this is discovered, you'll be in terrible trouble.

見付ける to find, discover, look for: (trans.)

		Affirmative	*Negative*
PLAIN FORM:	PRESENT	mitsukeru	mitsukenai
	PAST	mitsuketa	mitsukenakatta
MASU FORM:	PRESENT	mitsukemasu	mitsukemasen
	PAST	mitsukemashita	mitsukemasen deshita
IMPERATIVE		mitsukero	mitsukeru na
TE FORM		mitsukete	mitsukenakute
CONDITIONAL:	PLAIN	mitsukereba	mitsukenakereba
		mitsuketa ra	mitsukenakatta ra
	FORMAL	mitsukemashita ra	mitsukemasen deshita ra
PRESUMPTIVE:	PLAIN	mitsukeru daroo	mitsukenai daroo
	FORMAL	mitsukeru deshoo	mitsukenai deshoo
VOLITIONAL:	PLAIN	mitsukeyoo	
	FORMAL	mitsukemashoo	

	Affirmative		*Affirmative*
POTENTIAL	mitsukerareru	HONORIFIC	(omitsuke ni naru)
	mitsukereru		(omitsuke nasaru)
PASSIVE	mitsukerareru	HUMBLE	(omitsuke suru)
			(omitsuke itasu)
CAUSATIVE	mitsukesaseru		
CAUS. PASSIVE	mitsukesaserareru		

Examples:

1. *Moo apaato o mitsukemashita ka.*
   Have you found an apartment yet?
   Hai, mitsukemashita.
   Yes, I have.
2. *Omoshiroi hon o mitsuketa node shookai shimasu.*
   I'd like to tell you about an interesting book I found.
3. *Yatto sono jijitsu o mitsukemashita.*
   I finally discovered that fact.
4. *Nihon de shigoto o mitsuke-tai.*
   I'd like to find a job in Japan.

もうかる to make a profit, be lucky: (intrans.)

		Affirmative	*Negative*
PLAIN FORM:	PRESENT	mookaru	mookaranai
	PAST	mookatta	mookaranakatta
MASU FORM:	PRESENT	mookarimasu	mookarimasen
	PAST	mookarimashita	mookarimasen deshita
IMPERATIVE		(mookare)	(mookaru na)
TE FORM		mookatte	mookaranakute
CONDITIONAL:	PLAIN	mookareba	mookaranakereba
		mookatta ra	mookaranakatta ra
	FORMAL	mookarimashita ra	mookarimasen deshita ra
PRESUMPTIVE:	PLAIN	mookaru daroo	mookaranai daroo
	FORMAL	mookaru deshoo	mookaranai deshoo
VOLITIONAL:	PLAIN	(mookaroo)	
	FORMAL	(mookarimashoo)	

	Affirmative		*Affirmative*
POTENTIAL	(mookareru)	HONORIFIC	(omookari ni naru)
			(omookari nasaru)
PASSIVE	(mookarareru)	HUMBLE	(omookari suru)
			(omookari itasu)
CAUSATIVE	(mookaraseru)		
CAUS. PASSIVE	(mookaraserareru)		

Examples:

1. *Kabu wa mookarimasu ka.*
   Do you make a profit on your stocks?
   Iie, amari mookarimasen.
   No, not very much.
2. *Pachinko de ikura mookarimashita ka.*
   How much did you win at pachinko?
   Go-hyaku en de ichi-man en mookarimashita.
   With five hundred yen, I won ten thousand yen.
3. *Kare ga kaisha made kuruma ni nosete kureta node mookatta.*
   I was lucky because my friend gave me a lift to the company.

もうける to make a profit, to have a child; 設ける to set up: (both trans.)

		Affirmative	*Negative*
PLAIN FORM:	PRESENT	mookeru	mookenai
	PAST	mooketa	mookenakatta
MASU FORM:	PRESENT	mookemasu	mookemasen
	PAST	mookemashita	mookemasen deshita
IMPERATIVE		mookero	mookeru na
TE FORM		mookete	mookenakute
CONDITIONAL:	PLAIN	mookereba	mookenakereba
		mooketa ra	mookenakatta ra
	FORMAL	mookemashita ra	mookemasen deshita ra
PRESUMPTIVE:	PLAIN	mookeru daroo	mookenai daroo
	FORMAL	mookeru deshoo	mookenai deshoo
VOLITIONAL:	PLAIN	mookeyoo	
	FORMAL	mookemashoo	

	Affirmative		*Affirmative*
POTENTIAL	mookerareru	HONORIFIC	omooke ni naru
	mookereru		omooke nasaru
PASSIVE	mookerareru	HUMBLE	omooke suru
			omooke itasu
CAUSATIVE	mookesaseru		
CAUS. PASSIVE	mookesaserareru		

Examples:

1. *Kare wa okane o mookemashita.*
   He made a profit.
2. *Keiba de ikura mookemashita ka.*
   How much did you make on horse racing?
   San-man en gurai mookemashita.
   I made about thirty thousand yen.
3. *Kanojo wa kodomo o hitori mookemashita.*
   She gave birth to a child.
4. *Kikai o mookete futari o awaseyoo.*
   I'll provide an opportunity for them to meet each other.

漏らす to let leak out, escape: (trans.)

		Affirmative	*Negative*
PLAIN FORM:	PRESENT	morasu	morasanai
	PAST	morashita	morasanakatta
MASU FORM:	PRESENT	morashimasu	morashimasen
	PAST	morashimashita	morashimasen deshita
IMPERATIVE		morase	morasu na
TE FORM		morashite	morasanakute
CONDITIONAL:	PLAIN	moraseba	morasanakereba
		morashita ra	morasanakatta ra
	FORMAL	morashimashita ra	morashimasen deshita ra
PRESUMPTIVE:	PLAIN	morasu daroo	morasanai daroo
	FORMAL	morasu deshoo	morasanai deshoo
VOLITIONAL:	PLAIN	morasoo	
	FORMAL	morashimashoo	

	Affirmative		*Affirmative*
POTENTIAL	moraseru	HONORIFIC	omorashi ni naru
			omorashi nasaru
PASSIVE	morasareru	HUMBLE	(omorashi suru)
			(omorashi itasu)
CAUSATIVE	morasaseru		
CAUS. PASSIVE	morasaserareru		

Examples:

1. *Himitsu o morasanaide kudasai.*
   Please don't reveal our secret.
2. *Kono kaaten wa hikari o soto ni morasanai.*
   This curtain does not let the light out.
3. *Kare no setsumei o kiki-morashite shimatta.*
   I did not catch his explanation.
4. *Kanojo wa honne o morashita.*
   She revealed her true intentions.
5. *Okashikute, warai o morashita.*
   It was so funny that I let out a laugh.

貰う to get, receive, to marry: (trans.)

		Affirmative	*Negative*
PLAIN FORM:	PRESENT	morau	morawanai
	PAST	moratta	morawanakatta
MASU FORM:	PRESENT	moraimasu	moraimasen
	PAST	moraimashita	moraimasen deshita
IMPERATIVE		morae	morau na
TE FORM		moratte	morawanakute
CONDITIONAL:	PLAIN	moraeba	morawanakereba
		moratta ra	morawanakatta ra
	FORMAL	moraimashita ra	moraimasen deshita ra
PRESUMPTIVE:	PLAIN	morau daroo	morawanai daroo
	FORMAL	morau deshoo	morawanai deshoo
VOLITIONAL:	PLAIN	moraoo	
	FORMAL	moraimashoo	

	Affirmative		*Affirmative*
POTENTIAL	moraeru	HONORIFIC	omorai ni naru
			omorai nasaru
PASSIVE	morawareru	HUMBLE	itadaku
CAUSATIVE	morawaseru		
CAUS. PASSIVE	morawaserareru		
	morawasareru		

Examples:

1. *Tomodachi ni/kara tegami o moraimashita.*
   I received a letter from a friend.
2. *Kore wa sensei ni/kara itadaita jisho desu.*
   This is a dictionary that I got from my teacher.
3. *Nihon-go o oshiete itadakemasen ka.*
   Would you mind teaching Japanese?
4. *Heya-dai wa kichin to haratte moraimasu yo.*
   You are required to pay the rent on time.
5. *Kare wa bijin no okusan o moratta.*
   He married a beautiful woman.

漏れる to leak out, escape: (intrans.)

		Affirmative	*Negative*
PLAIN FORM:	PRESENT	moreru	morenai
	PAST	moreta	morenakatta
MASU FORM:	PRESENT	moremasu	moremasen
	PAST	moremashita	moremasen deshita
IMPERATIVE		(morero)	(moreru na)
TE FORM		morete	morenakute
CONDITIONAL:	PLAIN	morereba	morenakereba
		moreta ra	morenakatta ra
	FORMAL	moremashita ra	moremasen deshita ra
PRESUMPTIVE:	PLAIN	moreru daroo	morenai daroo
	FORMAL	moreru deshoo	morenai deshoo
VOLITIONAL:	PLAIN	(moreyoo)	
	FORMAL	(moremashoo)	

	Affirmative		*Affirmative*
POTENTIAL	(morerareru)	HONORIFIC	(omore ni naru)
			(omore nasaru)
PASSIVE	(morerareru)	HUMBLE	(omore suru)
			(omore itasu)
CAUSATIVE	(moresaseru)		
CAUS. PASSIVE	(moresaserareru)		

Examples:

1. *Mizu ga morete iru.*
   Water is trickling out.
2. *Dooshite himitsu ga moreta'n desu ka.*
   How has our secret leaked out?
   Kare no kuchi kara moreta no kamo-shirenai.
   Perhaps he disclosed it.
3. *Kuruma kara gasorin ga morete imasu yo.*
   Your car is leaking gasoline.
4. *Kaaten no sukima kara akari ga morete imasu.*
   Light is shining through the opening between the curtains.

motomeru

求める to demand, ask, seek, buy: (trans.)

		Affirmative	*Negative*
PLAIN FORM:	PRESENT	motomeru	motomenai
	PAST	motometa	motomenakatta
MASU FORM:	PRESENT	motomemasu	motomemasen
	PAST	motomemashita	motomemasen deshita
IMPERATIVE		motomero	motomeru na
TE FORM		motomete	motomenakute
CONDITIONAL:	PLAIN	motomereba	motomenakereba
		motometa ra	motomenakatta ra
	FORMAL	motomemashita ra	motomemasen deshita ra
PRESUMPTIVE:	PLAIN	motomeru daroo	motomenai daroo
	FORMAL	motomeru deshoo	motomenai deshoo
VOLITIONAL:	PLAIN	motomeyoo	
	FORMAL	motomemashoo	

	Affirmative		*Affirmative*
POTENTIAL	motomerareru motomereru	HONORIFIC	omotome ni naru omotome nasaru
PASSIVE	motomerareru	HUMBLE	omotome suru omotome itasu
CAUSATIVE	motomesaseru		
CAUS. PASSIVE	motomesaserareru		

Examples:

1. *Shachoo ni menkai o motomemashita.*
   They requested an interview with the president.
2. *Eigyoobu-in motomu.*
   Wanted: Salesman.
3. *Koe o agete, tasuke o motometa.*
   He shouted for help.
4. *Ano hon o moo omotome ni narimashita ka.*
   Have you bought that book yet?
   Kore kara sugu motomeru tsumori desu.
   I plan to buy it right away.

持つ to have, hold, pay for, own: (trans.)

		Affirmative	*Negative*
PLAIN FORM:	PRESENT	motsu	motanai
	PAST	motta	motanakatta
MASU FORM:	PRESENT	mochimasu	mochimasen
	PAST	mochimashita	mochimasen deshita
IMPERATIVE		mote	motsu na
TE FORM		motte	motanakute
CONDITIONAL:	PLAIN	moteba	motanakereba
		motta ra	motanakatta ra
	FORMAL	mochimashita ra	mochimasen deshita ra
PRESUMPTIVE:	PLAIN	motsu daroo	motanai daroo
	FORMAL	motsu deshoo	motanai deshoo
VOLITIONAL:	PLAIN	motoo	
	FORMAL	mochimashoo	

	Affirmative		*Affirmative*
POTENTIAL	moteru	HONORIFIC	omochi ni naru
			omochi nasaru
PASSIVE	motareru	HUMBLE	omochi suru
			omochi itasu
CAUSATIVE	motaseru		
CAUS. PASSIVE	motaserareru		
	motasareru		

Examples:

1. *Sumimasen ga, nimotsu o motte kudasai.*
   Excuse me, but could you please hold the baggage?
2. *Watashi wa ima okane o motte imasen.*
   I don't have any money now.
3. *Nihon bunka ni kyoomi o omochi desu ka.*
   Are you interested in Japanese culture?
4. *Ryuugaku hiyoo o seifu ga motte kuremashita.*
   The government paid the expenses for my studying abroad.
5. *Chichi wa ooki na mise o motte imasu.*
   My father runs a big shop.

向ける to turn toward, point at: (trans.)

		Affirmative	*Negative*
PLAIN FORM:	PRESENT	mukeru	mukenai
	PAST	muketa	mukenakatta
MASU FORM:	PRESENT	mukemasu	mukemasen
	PAST	mukemashita	mukemasen deshita
IMPERATIVE		mukero	mukeru na
TE FORM		mukete	mukenakute
CONDITIONAL:	PLAIN	mukereba	mukenakereba
		muketa ra	mukenakatta ra
	FORMAL	mukemashita ra	mukemasen deshita ra
PRESUMPTIVE:	PLAIN	mukeru daroo	mukenai daroo
	FORMAL	mukeru deshoo	mukenai deshoo
VOLITIONAL:	PLAIN	mukeyoo	
	FORMAL	mukemashoo	

	Affirmative		*Affirmative*
POTENTIAL	mukerareru	HONORIFIC	omuke ni naru
	mukereru		omuke nasaru
PASSIVE	mukerareru	HUMBLE	omuke suru
			omuke itasu
CAUSATIVE	mukesaseru		
CAUS. PASSIVE	mukesaserareru		

Examples:

1. *Kare wa kyuu ni kao o kochira ni muketa.*
   He suddenly turned his face toward us.
2. *Kanojo wa pisutoru o otoko ni muketa.*
   She pointed her pistol at the man.
3. *Kare wa Nihon ni mukete, shuppatsu shita.*
   He set off for Japan.
4. *Sono hiniku wa watashi ni mukerareta.*
   That sarcasm was directed at me.
5. *Mondai kaiketsu ni mukete, doryoku shita.*
   They worked toward solving the problem.

向く to look toward, to suit: (intrans.);* むく to peel, strip off: (trans.)

		Affirmative	*Negative*
PLAIN FORM:	PRESENT	muku	mukanai
	PAST	muita	mukanakatta
MASU FORM:	PRESENT	mukimasu	mukimasen
	PAST	mukimashita	mukimasen deshita
IMPERATIVE		muke	muku na
TE FORM		muite	mukanakute
CONDITIONAL:	PLAIN	mukeba	mukanakereba
		muita ra	mukanakatta ra
	FORMAL	mukimashita ra	mukimasen deshita ra
PRESUMPTIVE:	PLAIN	muku daroo	mukanai daroo
	FORMAL	muku deshoo	mukanai deshoo
VOLITIONAL:	PLAIN	mukoo	
	FORMAL	mukimashoo	

	Affirmative		*Affirmative*
POTENTIAL	mukeru	HONORIFIC	omuki ni naru
			omuki nasaru
PASSIVE	mukareru	HUMBLE	omuki suru
			omuki itasu
CAUSATIVE	mukaseru		
CAUS. PASSIVE	mukaserareru		
	mukasareru		

Examples:

1. *Shashin o torimasu kara kochira o muite kudasai.*
   Please look this way. I'm going to take a photo.
2. *Kanojo wa shita o muita mama kotaemasen deshita.*
   She kept on looking downward and did not answer.
3. *Anata wa donna shigoto ni muite iru to omoimasu ka.*
   What kind of job do you think you are suitable for?
4. *Kono fuku wa wakai hito ni mukimasen.*
   These clothes are not suitable for young people.
5. *Jagaimo no kawa o muite kudasai.*
   Please peel the potato.

* The *muku* 向く meaning "to look toward, to suit" generally does not use either potential or passive forms.

musubu

結ぶ to tie, contract, connect, link: (trans.)

		Affirmative	*Negative*
PLAIN FORM:	PRESENT	musubu	musubanai
	PAST	musunda	musubanakatta
MASU FORM:	PRESENT	musubimasu	musubimasen
	PAST	musubimashita	musubimasen deshita
IMPERATIVE		musube	musubu na
TE FORM		musunde	musubanakute
CONDITIONAL:	PLAIN	musubeba	musubanakereba
		musunda ra	musubanakatta ra
	FORMAL	musubimashita ra	musubimasen deshita ra
PRESUMPTIVE:	PLAIN	musubu daroo	musubanai daroo
	FORMAL	musubu deshoo	musubanai deshoo
VOLITIONAL:	PLAIN	musuboo	
	FORMAL	musubimashoo	

	Affirmative		*Affirmative*
POTENTIAL	musuberu	HONORIFIC	omusubi ni naru
			omusubi nasaru
PASSIVE	musubareru	HUMBLE	omusubi suru
			omusubi itasu
CAUSATIVE	musubaseru		
CAUS. PASSIVE	musubaserareru		
	musubasareru		

Examples:

1. *Kanojo wa obi o musunda.*
   She tied her obi.
2. *Kono basu wa futatsu no toshi o musunde iru.*
   This bus connects two cities.
3. *Nihon no kaisha to keiyaku o musubemashita ka.*
   Were you able to get a contract with a Japanese company?
   Hai, musubemashita.
   Yes, we were able to.
4. *Futari wa juu nen-kan koosai shite, yatto musubaremashita.*
   The two finally married after seeing each other for ten years.

投げる to throw, pitch: (trans.)

		Affirmative	*Negative*
PLAIN FORM:	PRESENT	nageru	nagenai
	PAST	nageta	nagenakatta
MASU FORM:	PRESENT	nagemasu	nagemasen
	PAST	nagemashita	nagemasen deshita
IMPERATIVE		nagero	nageru na
TE FORM		nagete	nagenakute
CONDITIONAL:	PLAIN	nagereba	nagenakereba
		nageta ra	nagenakatta ra
	FORMAL	nagemashita ra	nagemasen deshita ra
PRESUMPTIVE:	PLAIN	nageru daroo	nagenai daroo
	FORMAL	nageru deshoo	nagenai deshoo
VOLITIONAL:	PLAIN	nageyoo	
	FORMAL	nagemashoo	

	Affirmative		*Affirmative*
POTENTIAL	nagerareru	HONORIFIC	onage ni naru
			onage nasaru
PASSIVE	nagerareru	HUMBLE	onage suru
			onage itasu
CAUSATIVE	nagesaseru		
CAUS. PASSIVE	nagesaserareru		

Examples:

1. *Kodomo ga booru o nagete imasu.*
   The children are playing catch-ball.
2. *Kare wa jinsei o nagete iru yoo da ne.*
   He seems to be throwing away his life.
3. *Waarudo Shiriizu de nagesasete kure.*
   Let me pitch in the World Series.
   Dame da. Omae no kata wa shin'yoo dekinai kara nagesase-takunai.
   Forget it! I don't want you to throw because I can't rely on your arm.
4. *Sai wa nagerareta.*
   The die is cast. (*lit.*, the dice have been thrown)

鳴く to cry (for birds, insects), to bark, roar, mew, etc.; 泣く to cry (for persons): (both intrans.)

		Affirmative	*Negative*
PLAIN FORM:	PRESENT	naku	nakanai
	PAST	naita	nakanakatta
MASU FORM:	PRESENT	nakimasu	nakimasen
	PAST	nakimashita	nakimasen deshita
IMPERATIVE		nake	naku na
TE FORM		naite	nakanakute
CONDITIONAL:	PLAIN	nakeba	nakanakereba
		naita ra	nakanakatta ra
	FORMAL	nakimashita ra	nakimasen deshita ra
PRESUMPTIVE:	PLAIN	naku daroo	nakanai daroo
	FORMAL	naku deshoo	nakanai deshoo
VOLITIONAL:	PLAIN	nakoo	
	FORMAL	nakimashoo	

	Affirmative		*Affirmative*
POTENTIAL	nakeru	HONORIFIC	onaki ni naru
			onaki nasaru
PASSIVE	nakareru	HUMBLE	onaki suru
			onaki itasu
CAUSATIVE	nakaseru		
CAUS. PASSIVE	nakaserareru		
	nakasareru		

Examples:

1. *Kanojo o nakasete shimatta.*
   I made my girlfriend cry.
2. *Tori ga naite imasu.*
   The bird is singing.
3. *Neko ga naite imasu.*
   The cat is meowing.
4. *Shiken ni ukari, ureshikute naita.*
   I cried for joy because I passed the examination.
5. *Naite mo waratte mo ato ichinichi de kotoshi wa owari desu.*
   Like it or not, there's only one day left in the old year. (*lit.,* cry or laugh)

無くなる to be missing, to run out; 亡くなる to die, pass away: (both intrans.)

		Affirmative	*Negative*
PLAIN FORM:	PRESENT	nakunaru	nakunaranai
	PAST	nakunatta	nakunaranakatta
MASU FORM:	PRESENT	nakunarimasu	nakunarimasen
	PAST	nakunarimashita	nakunarimasen deshita
IMPERATIVE		(nakunare)	(nakunaru na)
TE FORM		nakunatte	nakunaranakute
CONDITIONAL:	PLAIN	nakunareba	nakunaranakereba
		nakunatta ra	nakunaranakatta ra
	FORMAL	nakunarimashita ra	nakunarimasen deshita ra
PRESUMPTIVE:	PLAIN	nakunaru daroo	nakunaranai daroo
	FORMAL	nakunaru deshoo	nakunaranai deshoo
VOLITIONAL:	PLAIN	(nakunaroo)	
	FORMAL	(nakunarimashoo)	

	Affirmative		*Affirmative*
POTENTIAL	(nakunareru)	HONORIFIC	onakunari ni naru
			onakunari nasaru
PASSIVE	(nakunarareru)	HUMBLE	(onakunari suru)
			(onakunari itasu)
CAUSATIVE	nakunaraseru		
CAUS. PASSIVE	nakunaraserareru		
	nakunarasareru		

Examples:

1. *Hon ga nakunatta.*
   The book is lost.
2. *Kabu ni wa kyoomi ga nakunarimashita.*
   I have lost interest in stocks.
3. *Nakunaranai uchi ni tabete kudasai.*
   Please eat it before it is all gone.
4. *Juu-ji o sugiru to basu ga nakunarimasu kara kaerimasu.*
   Since there are no buses after ten o'clock, I must return home.
5. *Yamada-san wa kyonen onakunari ni narimashita.*
   Mr. Yamada died last year.

nakusu   Group 1

無くす to lose (things); 亡くす to lose (person):* (both trans.)

		Affirmative	*Negative*
PLAIN FORM:	PRESENT	nakusu	nakusanai
	PAST	nakushita	nakusanakatta
MASU FORM:	PRESENT	nakushimasu	nakushimasen
	PAST	nakushimashita	nakushimasen deshita
IMPERATIVE		nakuse	nakusu na
TE FORM		nakushite	nakusanakute
CONDITIONAL:	PLAIN	nakuseba	nakusanakereba
		nakushita ra	nakusanakatta ra
	FORMAL	nakushimashita ra	nakushimasen deshita ra
PRESUMPTIVE:	PLAIN	nakusu daroo	nakusanai daroo
	FORMAL	nakusu deshoo	nakusanai deshoo
VOLITIONAL:	PLAIN	nakusoo	
	FORMAL	nakushimashoo	

	Affirmative		*Affirmative*
POTENTIAL	nakuseru	HONORIFIC	onakushi ni naru
			onakushi nasaru
PASSIVE	nakusareru	HUMBLE	(onakushi suru)
			(onakushi itasu)
CAUSATIVE	nakusaseru		
CAUS. PASSIVE	nakusaserareru		

Examples:

1. *Saifu o nakushita.*
   I lost my wallet.
2. *Doko de tokei o nakushita'n desu ka.*
   Where did you lose your watch?
   Doko de nakushita ka zenzen wakaranai'n desu yo.
   I have no idea where I lost it.
3. *Benkyoo o tsuzukeru ki o nakushita.*
   I no longer have the heart to continue studying.
4. *Ryooshin o nakushite, san-nen ni narimasu.*
   It has been three years since my parents died.

* *Nakusu* 亡くす meaning "to lose (person)" generally does not use the imperative or volitional forms.

直る to be corrected, repaired;* 治る to recover, get well: (both intrans.)

		Affirmative	*Negative*
PLAIN FORM:	PRESENT	naoru	naoranai
	PAST	naotta	naoranakatta
MASU FORM:	PRESENT	naorimasu	naorimasen
	PAST	naorimashita	naoimasen deshita
IMPERATIVE		(naore)	(naoru na)
TE FORM		naotte	naoranakute
CONDITIONAL:	PLAIN	naoreba	naoranakereba
		naotta ra	naoranakatta ra
	FORMAL	naorimashita ra	naorimasen deshita ra
PRESUMPTIVE:	PLAIN	naoru daroo	naoranai daroo
	FORMAL	naoru deshoo	naoranai deshoo
VOLITIONAL:	PLAIN	(naoroo)	
	FORMAL	(naorimashoo)	

	Affirmative		*Affirmative*
POTENTIAL	(naoreru)	HONORIFIC	onaori ni naru
			onaori nasaru
PASSIVE	(naorareru)	HUMBLE	(onaori suru)
			(onaori itasu)
CAUSATIVE	naoraseru		
CAUS. PASSIVE	naoraserareru		

Examples:

1. *Nihon-go no hatsuon ga naotta.*
   My Japanese pronunciation was corrected.
2. *Tokei ga naorimashita.*
   The watch was fixed.
3. *Moo kaze wa naorimashita ka.*
   Have you gotten rid of your cold?
   Ee, sukkari yoku narimashita.
   Yes, I have completely recovered.
4. *Kare wa isshoo sono kuse ga naoranakatta.*
   He was never able to overcome that habit.

* Besides those forms listed above, the intransitive *naoru* 直る meaning "to be corrected, repaired" generally does not use any honorific, causative, or causative passive forms.

直す to correct, fix, change, 治す to cure: (both trans.)

		Affirmative	*Negative*
PLAIN FORM:	PRESENT	naosu	naosanai
	PAST	naoshita	naosanakatta
MASU FORM:	PRESENT	naoshimasu	naoshimasen
	PAST	naoshimashita	naoshimasen deshita
IMPERATIVE		naose	naosu na
TE FORM		naoshite	naosanakute
CONDITIONAL:	PLAIN	naoseba	naosanakereba
		naoshita ra	naosanakatta ra
	FORMAL	naoshimashita ra	naoshimasen deshita ra
PRESUMPTIVE:	PLAIN	naosu daroo	naosanai daroo
	FORMAL	naosu deshoo	naosanai deshoo
VOLITIONAL:	PLAIN	naosoo	
	FORMAL	naoshimashoo	

	Affirmative		*Affirmative*
POTENTIAL	naoseru	HONORIFIC	onaoshi ni naru
			onaoshi nasaru
PASSIVE	naosareru	HUMBLE	onaoshi suru
			onaoshi itasu
CAUSATIVE	naosaseru		
CAUS. PASSIVE	naosaserareru		

Examples:

1. *Nihon-go no hatsuon o naoshite kudasai.*
   Please correct my Japanese pronunciation.
2. *Kuruma o naoshite moraimashita.*
   I had my car fixed.
3. *Warui shuukan o naoshita hoo ga ii desu yo.*
   You should change your bad habits.
4. *Go-man en o doru ni naosu to ikura desu ka.*
   How much is fifty thousand yen in dollars?
5. *Byooki o naoshite moratta.*
   I had my illness treated.

並べる to line up, arrange, display: (trans.)

		Affirmative	*Negative*
PLAIN FORM:	PRESENT	naraberu	narabenai
	PAST	narabeta	narabenakatta
MASU FORM:	PRESENT	narabemasu	narabemasen
	PAST	narabemashita	narabemasen deshita
IMPERATIVE		narabero	naraberu na
TE FORM		narabete	narabenakute
CONDITIONAL:	PLAIN	narabereba	narabenakereba
		narabeta ra	narabenakatta ra
	FORMAL	narabemashita ra	narabemasen deshita ra
PRESUMPTIVE:	PLAIN	naraberu daroo	narabenai daroo
	FORMAL	naraberu deshoo	narabenai deshoo
VOLITIONAL:	PLAIN	narabeyoo	
	FORMAL	narabemashoo	

	Affirmative		*Affirmative*
POTENTIAL	naraberareru	HONORIFIC	onarabe ni naru
	narabereru		onarabe nasaru
PASSIVE	naraberareru	HUMBLE	onarabe suru
			onarabe itasu
CAUSATIVE	narabesaseru		
CAUS. PASSIVE	narabesaserareru		

Examples:

1. *Futari wa kyooshitsu de tsukue o narabete imasu.*
   Their desks were side by side in class.
2. *Isu o ni-retsu ni narabete kudasai.*
   Please line up the chairs in two rows.
3. *Ryoori o naraberu dake narabeta.*
   I lined up as many dishes as possible.
4. *Shinamono wa shookeesu ni narabete arimasu.*
   The goods are on display in the showcase.
5. *Watashi wa keisatsu ni shooko o naraberareta.*
   The police brought out all the evidence before me.

並ぶ to stand in a line, to equal: (intrans.)

		Affirmative	*Negative*
PLAIN FORM:	PRESENT	narabu	narabanai
	PAST	naranda	narabanakatta
MASU FORM:	PRESENT	narabimasu	narabimasen
	PAST	narabimashita	narabimasen deshita
IMPERATIVE		narabe	narabu na
TE FORM		narande	narabanakute
CONDITIONAL:	PLAIN	narabeba	narabanakereba
		naranda ra	narabanakatta ra
	FORMAL	narabimashita ra	narabimasen deshita ra
PRESUMPTIVE:	PLAIN	narabu daroo	narabanai daroo
	FORMAL	narabu deshoo	narabanai deshoo
VOLITIONAL:	PLAIN	naraboo	
	FORMAL	narabimashoo	

	Affirmative		*Affirmative*
POTENTIAL	naraberu	HONORIFIC	onarabi ni naru
			onarabi nasaru
PASSIVE	narabareru	HUMBLE	onarabi suru
			onarabi itasu
CAUSATIVE	narabaseru		
CAUS. PASSIVE	narabaserareru		
	narabasareru		

Examples:

1. *Ichi-retsu ni narande kudasai.*
   Please stand in a line.
2. *Eigakan no mae ni takusan no hito ga narande imasu.*
   Many people are lined up in front of the movie theater.
3. *Kono kuruma no nedan wa zero ga mutsu narande iru.*
   The price of this car has six zeros in it.
4. *Seiseki de yatto kare ni naranda.*
   I finally equaled him in grades.
5. *Nihon-go no kaiwa de wa kare ni narabu mono wa inai.*
   No one equals him in speaking Japanese.

習う to learn: (trans.)

		Affirmative	*Negative*
PLAIN FORM:	PRESENT	narau	narawanai
	PAST	naratta	narawanakatta
MASU FORM:	PRESENT	naraimasu	naraimasen
	PAST	naraimashita	naraimasen deshita
IMPERATIVE		narae	narau na
TE FORM		naratte	narawanakute
CONDITIONAL:	PLAIN	naraeba	narawanakereba
		naratta ra	narawanakatta ra
	FORMAL	naraimashita ra	naraimasen deshita ra
PRESUMPTIVE:	PLAIN	narau daroo	narawanai daroo
	FORMAL	narau deshoo	narawanai deshoo
VOLITIONAL:	PLAIN	naraoo	
	FORMAL	naraimashoo	

	Affirmative		*Affirmative*
POTENTIAL	naraeru	HONORIFIC	onarai ni naru
			onarai nasaru
PASSIVE	narawareru	HUMBLE	onarai suru
			onarai itasu
CAUSATIVE	narawaseru		
CAUS. PASSIVE	narawaserareru		
	narawasareru		

Examples:

1. *Dare ni/kara Nihon-go o naratta'n desu ka.*
   From whom did you learn Japanese?
   Nihon-jin no tomodachi ni/kara naratta'n desu.
   I learned from my Japanese friend.
2. *Yamada-san wa gitaa o naraita-gatte iru.*
   Mr. Yamada wants to learn how to play the guitar.
3. *Minna mo kare ni mi-naraoo.*
   Let's copy the way he does it.
4. *Narau yori narero.*
   Practice makes perfect.

慣れる to get used to, become skilled at: (intrans.)

		Affirmative	*Negative*
PLAIN FORM:	PRESENT	nareru	narenai
	PAST	nareta	narenakatta
MASU FORM:	PRESENT	naremasu	naremasen
	PAST	naremashita	naremasen deshita
IMPERATIVE		narero	nareru na
TE FORM		narete	narenakute
CONDITIONAL:	PLAIN	narereba	narenakereba
		nareta ra	narenakatta ra
	FORMAL	naremashita ra	naremasen deshita ra
PRESUMPTIVE:	PLAIN	nareru daroo	narenai daroo
	FORMAL	nareru deshoo	narenai deshoo
VOLITIONAL:	PLAIN	nareyoo	
	FORMAL	naremashoo	

	Affirmative		*Affirmative*
POTENTIAL	(narerareru)	HONORIFIC	onare ni naru
			onare nasaru
PASSIVE	(narerareru)	HUMBLE	(onare suru)
			(onare itasu)
CAUSATIVE	naresaseru		
CAUS. PASSIVE	naresaserareru		

Examples:

1. *Nihon no seikatsu ni naremashita ka.*
   Have you gotten used to living in Japan?
   Ee, sukkari naremashita.
   Yes, I've gotten completely used to it.
2. *Gaikoku-go ni narete inai.*
   I am not comfortable with foreign languages.
3. *Kanojo wa nareta tetsuki de fude o tsukatta.*
   She used her brush with a practiced hand.
4. *Atarashii kutsu ga yatto ashi ni narete kimashita.*
   These shoes are broken in at last.

なる *or* 成る to become; 鳴る to ring, sound:* (both intrans.)

		Affirmative	*Negative*
PLAIN FORM:	PRESENT	naru	naranai
	PAST	natta	naranakatta
MASU FORM:	PRESENT	narimasu	narimasen
	PAST	narimashita	narimasen deshita
IMPERATIVE		nare	naru na
TE FORM		natte	naranakute
CONDITIONAL:	PLAIN	nareba	naranakereba
		natta ra	naranakatta ra
	FORMAL	narimashita ra	narimasen deshita
PRESUMPTIVE:	PLAIN	naru daroo	naranai daroo
	FORMAL	naru deshoo	naranai deshoo
VOLITIONAL:	PLAIN	naroo	
	FORMAL	narimashoo	

	Affirmative		*Affirmative*
POTENTIAL	nareru	HONORIFIC	onari ni naru
			onari nasaru
PASSIVE	narareru	HUMBLE	(onari suru)
			(onari itasu)
CAUSATIVE	naraseru		
CAUS. PASSIVE	naraserareru		
	narasareru		

Examples:

1. *Kanji ga wakaru yoo ni narimashita.*
   I have come to understand Japanese characters.
2. *Itsu kara tabako o suwanaku natta no desu ka.*
   When did you give up smoking?
3. *Nihon de wa Shigatsu ni naru to gakkoo ga hajimarimasu.*
   In Japan, school begins in April.
4. *Saifu o nakushite, aoku natta.*
   Having lost my wallet, I turned pale.
5. *Denwa ga natte imasu.*
   The telephone is ringing.

* The verb *naru* 鳴る meaning "to ring, sound" generally does not use the imperative, volitional, potential, honorific, humble, or passive forms.

なさる to do:* (trans.)

		Affirmative	*Negative*
PLAIN FORM:	PRESENT	nasaru	nasaranai
	PAST	nasatta	nasaranakatta
MASU FORM:	PRESENT	nasaimasu**	nasaimasen
	PAST	nasaimashita	nasaimasen deshita
IMPERATIVE		nasare	nasaru na
TE FORM		nasatte	nasaranakute
CONDITIONAL:	PLAIN	nasareba	nasaranakereba
		nasatta ra	nasaranakatta ra
	FORMAL	nasaimashita ra	nasaimasen deshita ra
PRESUMPTIVE:	PLAIN	nasaru daroo	nasaranai daroo
	FORMAL	nasaru deshoo	nasaranai deshoo
VOLITIONAL:	PLAIN	nasaroo	
	FORMAL	nasaimashoo	

	Affirmative		*Affirmative*
POTENTIAL	nasareru	HONORIFIC	——
PASSIVE	nasarareru	HUMBLE	——
CAUSATIVE	nasaraseru		
CAUS. PASSIVE	nasaraserareru		

Examples:

1. *Ichinichi ni nan-jikan Nihon-go o benkyoo nasaimasu ka.*
   How many hours a day do you study Japanese?
   Yo jikan gurai itashimasu.
   I study about four hours.
2. *Suzuki Kyooju wa tenisu o nasaru to omoimasu ka.*
   Do you think Professor Suzuki plays tennis?
3. *Ima nani o nasatte iru'n desu ka.*
   What are you doing now?
   Yuujin ni tegami o kaite iru'n desu.
   I am writing a letter to a friend.

* *Nasaru* is the honorific equivalent of *suru.*
** For euphonic reasons, *nasaimasu* is used rather than *nasarimasu.*

眠る to sleep, fall asleep: (intrans.)

		Affirmative	*Negative*
PLAIN FORM:	PRESENT	nemuru	nemuranai
	PAST	nemutta	nemuranakatta
MASU FORM:	PRESENT	nemurimasu	nemurimasen
	PAST	nemurimashita	nemurimasen deshita
IMPERATIVE		nemure	nemuru na
TE FORM		nemutte	nemuranakute
CONDITIONAL:	PLAIN	nemureba	nemuranakereba
		nemutta ra	nemuranakatta ra
	FORMAL	nemurimashita ra	nemurimasen deshita ra
PRESUMPTIVE:	PLAIN	nemuru daroo	nemuranai daroo
	FORMAL	nemuru deshoo	nemuranai deshoo
VOLITIONAL:	PLAIN	nemuroo	
	FORMAL	nemurimashoo	

	Affirmative		*Affirmative*
POTENTIAL	nemureru	HONORIFIC	onemuri ni naru
			onemuri nasaru
PASSIVE	nemurareru	HUMBLE	(onemuri suru)
			(onemuri itasu)
CAUSATIVE	nemuraseru		
CAUS. PASSIVE	nemuraserareru		
	nemurasareru		

Examples:

1. *Yuube wa yoku nemuremashita ka.*
   Were you able to sleep well last night?
   Watashi wa gussuri nemuremashita.
   I slept soundly.
2. *Saikin yoku nemurenai'n desu.*
   I have not been able to sleep well recently.
3. *Koohii no sei de nemurenakatta.*
   The coffee prevented me from sleeping.
4. *Yasuraka ni nemutte kudasai.*
   Rest in peace.

寝る to go to bed, lie down: (intrans.)

		Affirmative	*Negative*
PLAIN FORM:	PRESENT	neru	nenai
	PAST	neta	nenakatta
MASU FORM:	PRESENT	nemasu	nemasen
	PAST	nemashita	nemasen deshita
IMPERATIVE		nero	neru na
TE FORM		nete	nenakute
CONDITIONAL:	PLAIN	nereba	nenakereba
		neta ra	nenakatta ra
	FORMAL	nemashita ra	nemasen deshita ra
PRESUMPTIVE:	PLAIN	neru daroo	nenai daroo
	FORMAL	neru deshoo	nenai deshoo
VOLITIONAL:	PLAIN	neyoo	
	FORMAL	nemashoo	

	Affirmative		*Affirmative*
POTENTIAL	nerareru	HONORIFIC	oyasumi ni naru
			oyasumi nasaru
PASSIVE	nerareru	HUMBLE	(oyasumi suru)
			(oyasumi itasu)
CAUSATIVE	nesaseru		
CAUS. PASSIVE	nesaserareru		

Examples:

1. *Itsumo nan-ji goro nemasu ka.*
   What time do you usually go to bed?
2. *Kare wa ne-nagara, hon o yonde iru.*
   He is reading a book while lying down.
3. *Neru mae ni ha o migakimasu ka.*
   Do you brush your teeth before going to bed?
4. *Hayaku nete, hayaku okiru.*
   Early to bed and early to rise.
5. *Nete mo samete mo, kare no koto o omotta.*
   He was constantly on my mind. (*lit.*, whether asleep or awake)

逃げる to run away, escape: (intrans.)

		Affirmative	*Negative*
PLAIN FORM:	PRESENT	nigeru	nigenai
	PAST	nigeta	nigenakatta
MASU FORM:	PRESENT	nigemasu	nigemasen
	PAST	nigemashita	nigemasen deshita
IMPERATIVE		nigero	nigeru na
TE FORM		nigete	nigenakute
CONDITIONAL:	PLAIN	nigereba	nigenakereba
		nigeta ra	nigenakatta ra
	FORMAL	nigemashita ra	nigemasen deshita ra
PRESUMPTIVE:	PLAIN	nigeru daroo	nigenai daroo
	FORMAL	nigeru deshoo	nigenai deshoo
VOLITIONAL:	PLAIN	nigeyoo	
	FORMAL	nigemashoo	

	Affirmative		*Affirmative*
POTENTIAL	nigerareru	HONORIFIC	onige ni naru
			onige nasaru
PASSIVE	nigerareru	HUMBLE	(onige suru)
			(onige itasu)
CAUSATIVE	nigesaseru		
CAUS. PASSIVE	nigesaserareru		

Examples:

1. *Hannin ni nigerareta.*
   The criminal got away from us.
2. *Tori ga kago kara nigeta.*
   The bird escaped from its cage.
3. *Doroboo wa kuruma de nigeta rashii.*
   It seems that the thief escaped by car.
4. *Nigeru ga kachi.*
   Discretion is wiser. (*lit.,* victory is attained by fleeing)
5. *Kare wa shitsumon kara umaku nigeta.*
   He deftly evaded the question.

煮る to boil: (trans.); 似る to look like, resemble: (intrans.)

		Affirmative	*Negative*
PLAIN FORM:	PRESENT	niru	ninai
	PAST	nita	ninakatta
MASU FORM:	PRESENT	nimasu	nimasen
	PAST	nimashita	nimasen deshita
IMPERATIVE		niro	niru na
TE FORM		nite	ninakute
CONDITIONAL:	PLAIN	nireba	ninakereba
		nita ra	ninakatta ra
	FORMAL	nimashita ra	nimasen deshita ra
PRESUMPTIVE:	PLAIN	niru daroo	ninai daroo
	FORMAL	niru deshoo	ninai deshoo
VOLITIONAL:	PLAIN	niyoo	
	FORMAL	nimashoo	

	Affirmative		*Affirmative*
POTENTIAL	nirareru	HONORIFIC	(oni ni naru)
			(oni nasaru)
PASSIVE	nirareru	HUMBLE	(oni suru)
			(oni itasu)
CAUSATIVE	nisaseru		
CAUS. PASSIVE	nisaserareru		
	nisasareru		

Examples:

1. *Jagaimo o niru to oishii desu.*
   Potatoes are delicious when boiled.
2. *Nita yasai wa suki desu ka.*
   Do you like boiled vegetables?
3. *Kare wa nite mo yaite mo kuenai hito da.*
   He is difficult to please. (*lit.,* Boiled or fried, he won't eat.)
4. *Anata wa otoosan ni nite imasu ne.*
   You look like your father, don't you?
5. *Kono akachan wa dare ni nite iru no daroo?*
   Who does this baby take after?

伸ばす to lengthen, stretch, spread out; 延ばす to postpone, extend: (both trans.)

		Affirmative	*Negative*
PLAIN FORM:	PRESENT	nobasu	nobasanai
	PAST	nobashita	nobasanakatta
MASU FORM:	PRESENT	nobashimasu	nobashimasen
	PAST	nobashimashita	nobashimasen deshita
IMPERATIVE		nobase	nobasu na
TE FORM		nobashite	nobasanakute
CONDITIONAL:	PLAIN	nobaseba	nobasanakereba
		nobashita ra	nobasanakatta ra
	FORMAL	nobashimashita ra	nobashimasen deshita ra
PRESUMPTIVE:	PLAIN	nobasu daroo	nobasanai daroo
	FORMAL	nobasu deshoo	nobasanai deshoo
VOLITIONAL:	PLAIN	nobasoo	
	FORMAL	nobashimashoo	

	Affirmative		*Affirmative*
POTENTIAL	nobaseru	HONORIFIC	onobashi ni naru
			onobashi nasaru
PASSIVE	nobasareru	HUMBLE	onobashi suru
			onobashi itasu
CAUSATIVE	nobasaseru		
CAUS. PASSIVE	nobasaserareru		

Examples:

1. *Kanojo wa kami o nagaku nobashite imasu.*
   She is letting her hair grow long.
2. *Te o nobashite, tabako o totta.*
   I reached out and took a cigarette.
3. *Seiseki o nobashite kureta sensei ni kansha shite imasu.*
   I am grateful to my teacher for helping me improve my grades.
4. *Nihon taizai o isshuukan nobashite kudasai.*
   Please extend my stay in Japan for one more week.
5. *Tsuma ga byooki de taoreta node, kikoku o nobasu tsumori desu.*
   As my wife has become sick, I'm going to postpone going back to my country.

nobiru　　　　　　　　　　　　　　　　　　　　**Group 2**

伸びる to grow, improve; 延びる to be extended, postpone: (both intrans.)

		Affirmative	*Negative*
PLAIN FORM:	PRESENT	nobiru	nobinai
	PAST	nobita	nobinakatta
MASU FORM:	PRESENT	nobimasu	nobimasen
	PAST	nobimashita	nobimasen deshita
IMPERATIVE		(nobiro)	(nobiru na)
TE FORM		nobite	nobinakute
CONDITIONAL:	PLAIN	nobireba	nobinakereba
		nobita ra	nobinakatta ra
	FORMAL	nobimashita ra	nobimasen deshita ra
PRESUMPTIVE:	PLAIN	nobiru daroo	nobinai daroo
	FORMAL	nobiru deshoo	nobinai deshoo
VOLITIONAL:	PLAIN	(nobiyoo)	
	FORMAL	(nobimashoo)	

	Affirmative		*Affirmative*
POTENTIAL	(nobirareru)	HONORIFIC	onobi ni naru
			onobi nasaru
PASSIVE	(nobirareru)	HUMBLE	(onobi suru)
			(onobi itasu)
CAUSATIVE	(nobisaseru)		
CAUS. PASSIVE	(nobisaserareru)		

Examples:

1. *Hantoshi de se ga juu-ichi senchi mo nobimashita.*
   I grew eleven centimeters in the last six months.
2. *Nihon-go no seiseki ga nobinai.*
   My grades in Japanese don't improve.
3. *Shiken ga nobita okage de benkyoo dekimasu.*
   Thanks to the postponing of the exam, I can study.
4. *Konogoro hi ga nobite kimashita ne.*
   The days are getting longer, aren't they?
5. *Taifuu no tame ni shuppatsu ga mikka nobita.*
   My departure has been postponed for three days because of a typhoon.

上る to go up; 登る to climb (steps, mountains): (both trans.);
昇る to rise: (intrans.)*

		Affirmative	Negative
PLAIN FORM:	PRESENT	noboru	noboranai
	PAST	nobotta	noboranakatta
MASU FORM:	PRESENT	noborimasu	noborimasen
	PAST	noborimashita	noborimasen deshita
IMPERATIVE		nobore	noboru na
TE FORM		nobotte	noboranakute
CONDITIONAL:	PLAIN	noboreba	noboranakereba
		nobotta ra	noboranakatta ra
	FORMAL	noborimashita ra	noborimasen deshita ra
PRESUMPTIVE:	PLAIN	noboru daroo	noboranai daroo
	FORMAL	noboru deshoo	noboranai deshoo
VOLITIONAL:	PLAIN	noboroo	
	FORMAL	noborimashoo	

	Affirmative		Affirmative
POTENTIAL	noboreru	HONORIFIC	onobori ni naru
			onobori nasaru
PASSIVE	noborareru	HUMBLE	onobori suru
			onobori itasu
CAUSATIVE	noboraseru		
CAUS. PASSIVE	noboraserareru		
	noborasareru		

Examples:

1. *Kaji kara kemuri ga noborimashita.*
   Smoke rose up from the fire.
2. *Sono hanashi de atama ni chi ga nobotta.*
   That story really upset me.
3. *Fuji-san ni nobotta koto ga arimasu ka.*
   Have you ever climbed Mount Fuji?
4. *Ishidan o nobotta tokoro ni, sakura no ki ga arimashita.*
   There was a cherry tree at the top of the stone steps.
5. *Hi ga noboru mae ni, jinja e inori ni dekaketa.*
   Before the sun rose, I went to the Shinto shrine to pray.

* The intransitive *noboru* 昇る meaning "to rise" generally does not use the potential, passive, honorific, humble, causative, or causative passive forms.

残る to remain: (intrans.)

		Affirmative	*Negative*
PLAIN FORM:	PRESENT	nokoru	nokoranai
	PAST	nokotta	nokoranakatta
MASU FORM:	PRESENT	nokorimasu	nokorimasen
	PAST	nokorimashita	nokorimasen deshita
IMPERATIVE		nokore	nokoru na
TE FORM		nokotte	nokoranakute
CONDITIONAL:	PLAIN	nokoreba	nokoranakereba
		nokotta ra	nokoranakatta ra
	FORMAL	nokorimashita ra	nokorimasen deshita ra
PRESUMPTIVE:	PLAIN	nokoru daroo	nokoranai daroo
	FORMAL	nokoru deshoo	nokoranai deshoo
VOLITIONAL:	PLAIN	nokoroo	
	FORMAL	nokorimashoo	

	Affirmative		*Affirmative*
POTENTIAL	(nokoreru)	HONORIFIC	onokori ni naru
			onokori nasaru
PASSIVE	(nokorareru)	HUMBLE	(onokori suru)
			(onokori itasu)
CAUSATIVE	(nokoraseru)		
CAUS. PASSIVE	(nokoraserareru)		

Examples:

1. *Hookago nokotte, benkyoo shita.*
   I stayed after school to study.
2. *Mikan ga takusan nokotte imasu.*
   There are many tangerines left over.
3. *Iya na nioi ga heya ni nokotte imasu.*
   A bad smell lingers in the room.
4. *Kare wa mada kenkyuushitsu ni nokotte imasu.*
   He is still in the study room.
5. *Zenzen okane ga nokotte inai.*
   There is no money remaining at all.

残す to save, leave behind (trans.)

		Affirmative	*Negative*
PLAIN FORM:	PRESENT	nokosu	nokosanai
	PAST	nokoshita	nokosanakatta
MASU FORM:	PRESENT	nokoshimasu	nokoshimasen
	PAST	nokoshimashita	nokoshimasen deshita
IMPERATIVE		nokose	nokosu na
TE FORM		nokoshite	nokosanakute
CONDITIONAL:	PLAIN	nokoseba	nokosanakereba
		nokoshita ra	nokosanakatta ra
	FORMAL	nokoshimashita ra	nokoshimasen deshita ra
PRESUMPTIVE:	PLAIN	nokosu daroo	nokosanai daroo
	FORMAL	nokosu deshoo	nokosanai deshoo
VOLITIONAL:	PLAIN	nokosoo	
	FORMAL	nokoshimashoo	

	Affirmative		*Affirmative*
POTENTIAL	nokoseru	HONORIFIC	onokoshi ni naru
			onokoshi nasaru
PASSIVE	nokosareru	HUMBLE	onokoshi suru
			onokoshi itasu
CAUSATIVE	nokosaseru		
CAUS. PASSIVE	nokosaserareru		

Examples:

1. *Nokosanaide zenbu tabete kudasai.*
   Please eat everything up.
2. *Shukudai o wasureta node sensei ni nokosaremashita.*
   The teacher made me stay because I forgot my homework.
3. *Kare wa roogo no tame ni okane o nokoshimashita.*
   He saved up money to use in his old age.
4. *Nokoshite oite, ashita tabeyoo.*
   Let's save it so we can eat it tomorrow.
5. *Kanojo wa yari-nokoshita koto o omoidashita.*
   She remembered that she had some things left to do.

飲む to drink, hold one's breath: (trans.)

		Affirmative	*Negative*
PLAIN FORM:	PRESENT	nomu	nomanai
	PAST	nonda	nomanakatta
MASU FORM:	PRESENT	nomimasu	nomimasen
	PAST	nomimashita	nomimasen deshita
IMPERATIVE		nome	nomu na
TE FORM		nonde	nomanakute
CONDITIONAL:	PLAIN	nomeba	nomanakereba
		nonda ra	nomanakatta ra
	FORMAL	nomimashita ra	nomimasen deshita ra
PRESUMPTIVE:	PLAIN	nomu daroo	nomanai daroo
	FORMAL	nomu deshoo	nomanai deshoo
VOLITIONAL:	PLAIN	nomoo	
	FORMAL	nomimashoo	

	Affirmative		*Affirmative*
POTENTIAL	nomeru	HONORIFIC	onomi ni naru
			onomi nasaru
PASSIVE	nomareru	HUMBLE	itadaku
CAUSATIVE	nomaseru		
CAUS. PASSIVE	nomaserareru		
	nomasareru		

Examples:

1. *Koohii o nomimashoo.*
   Let's drink some coffee.
2. *Ocha o nomi-nagara hanashi-atta.*
   They talked while drinking tea.
3. *Yamada-san wa ikka-getsu no kyuuryoo o hitoban de nonde shimatta.*
   Mr. Yamada spent a whole month's salary in one night's drinking.
4. *Kanojo o mite, isshun iki o nonda.*
   When I saw her, for a moment I froze. (*lit.,* swallowed my breath)
5. *Nonda ra noru na. Noru nara nomu na.*
   If you drink, don't drive. If you drive, don't drink.

乗る to ride, to participate, be fooled; 載る to be printed, be reported: (both intrans.)

		Affirmative	*Negative*
PLAIN FORM:	PRESENT	noru	noranai
	PAST	notta	noranakatta
MASU FORM:	PRESENT	norimasu	norimasen
	PAST	norimashita	norimasen deshita
IMPERATIVE		nore	noru na
TE FORM		notte	noranakute
CONDITIONAL:	PLAIN	noreba	noranakereba
		notta ra	noranakatta ra
	FORMAL	norimashita ra	norimasen deshita ra
PRESUMPTIVE:	PLAIN	noru daroo	noranai daroo
	FORMAL	noru deshoo	noranai deshoo
VOLITIONAL:	PLAIN	noroo	
	FORMAL	norimashoo	

	Affirmative		*Affirmative*
POTENTIAL	noreru	HONORIFIC	onori ni naru
			onori nasaru
PASSIVE	norareru	HUMBLE	onori suru
			onori itasu
CAUSATIVE	noraseru		
CAUS. PASSIVE	noraserareru		
	norasareru		

Examples:

1. *Jitensha ni notte, toshokan e/ni itta.*
   He rode a bicycle to the library.
2. *Mina-san, kono fune ni onori kudasai.*
   Everyone, please board this ship.
3. *Soodan ni notte kurenai ka.*
   May I discuss something with you?
4. *Sono te ni wa noranai yo.*
   I won't fall into such a trap.
5. *Jiken ga shinbun ni notta.*
   The affair was written up in the papers.

除く to leave out, omit; 覗く to look in; peep in: (both trans.)

		Affirmative	*Negative*
PLAIN FORM:	PRESENT	nozoku	nozokanai
	PAST	nozoita	nozokanakatta
MASU FORM:	PRESENT	nozokimasu	nozokimasen
	PAST	nozokimashita	nozokimasen deshita
IMPERATIVE		nozoke	nozoku na
TE FORM		nozoite	nozokanakute
CONDITIONAL:	PLAIN	nozokeba	nozokanakereba
		nozoita ra	nozokanakatta ra
	FORMAL	nozokimashita ra	nozokimasen deshita ra
PRESUMPTIVE:	PLAIN	nozoku daroo	nozokanai daroo
	FORMAL	nozoku deshoo	nozokanai deshoo
VOLITIONAL:	PLAIN	nozokoo	
	FORMAL	nozokimashoo	

	Affirmative		*Affirmative*
POTENTIAL	nozokeru	HONORIFIC	onozoki ni naru
			onozoki nasaru
PASSIVE	nozokareru	HUMBLE	(onozoki suru)
			(onozoki itasu)
CAUSATIVE	nozokaseru		
CAUS. PASSIVE	nozokaserareru		
	nozokasareru		

Examples:

1. *Kare no kotae wa ichidai o nozoite, dekite ita.*
   His answers were correct except for one.
2. *Saisho no go-peeji wa nozoite mo ii desu.*
   You may omit the first five pages.
3. *Watashi o nozoite, paatii ni ikita-gatte imasu.*
   Everybody wants to go to the party except me.
4. *Ano mise o nozoite miyoo yo.*
   Let's take a look in the shop.
5. *Poketto kara satsutaba ga nozoite ita.*
   A wad of bills was sticking out of his pocket. (*lit.,* peeping out)

脱ぐ to take off clothes: (trans.)

		Affirmative	*Negative*
PLAIN FORM:	PRESENT	nugu	nuganai
	PAST	nuida	nuganakatta
MASU FORM:	PRESENT	nugimasu	nugimasen
	PAST	nugimashita	nugimasen deshita
IMPERATIVE		nuge	nugu na
TE FORM		nuide	nuganakute
CONDITIONAL:	PLAIN	nugeba	nuganakereba
		nuida ra	nuganakatta ra
	FORMAL	nugimashita ra	nugimasen deshita ra
PRESUMPTIVE:	PLAIN	nugu daroo	nuganai daroo
	FORMAL	nugu deshoo	nuganai deshoo
VOLITIONAL:	PLAIN	nugoo	
	FORMAL	nugimashoo	

	Affirmative		*Affirmative*
POTENTIAL	nugeru	HONORIFIC	onugi ni naru
			onugi nasaru
PASSIVE	nugareru	HUMBLE	onugi suru
			onugi itasu
CAUSATIVE	nugaseru		
CAUS. PASSIVE	nugaserareru		
	nugasareru		

Examples:

1. *Fuku o nugaserareta.*
   I was forced to take off my clothes.
2. *Yoofuku o nuide, yukata o kita.*
   I undressed and put on a cotton kimono.
3. *Nihon de wa kutsu o nuide, heya ni agarimasu.*
   In Japan, you take off your shoes before entering a room.
4. *Koko de kooto o nuide mo ii desu ka.*
   May I take off my coat here?
   Hai, kekkoo desu. (Doozo, nuide kudasai.)
   Yes, please do.

濡れる to get wet, be moist: (intrans.)

		Affirmative	*Negative*
PLAIN FORM:	PRESENT	nureru	nurenai
	PAST	nureta	nurenakatta
MASU FORM:	PRESENT	nuremasu	nuremasen
	PAST	nuremashita	nuremasen deshita
IMPERATIVE		(nurero)	(nureru na)
TE FORM		nurete	nurenakute
CONDITIONAL:	PLAIN	nurereba	nurenakereba
		nureta ra	nurenakatta ra
	FORMAL	nuremashita ra	nuremasen deshita ra
PRESUMPTIVE:	PLAIN	nureru daroo	nurenai daroo
	FORMAL	nureru deshoo	nurenai deshoo
VOLITIONAL:	PLAIN	(nureyoo)	
	FORMAL	(nuremashoo)	

	Affirmative		*Affirmative*
POTENTIAL	(nurerareru)	HONORIFIC	onure ni naru
			onure nasaru
PASSIVE	(nurerareru)	HUMBLE	(onure suru)
			(onure itasu)
CAUSATIVE	(nuresaseru)		
CAUS. PASSIVE	(nuresaserareru)		

Examples:

1. *Ame de fuku ga nureta.*
   My clothes got wet in the rain.
2. *Kami ga nurete shimatta.*
   My hair got wet.
3. *Kanojo no me wa namida de nurete ita.*
   Her eyes were moist with tears.
4. *Nureta taoru o kashite kudasai.*
   Please lend me a wet towel.
5. *Sono yoofuku wa mada nurete imasu.*
   Those clothes are still wet.

塗る to paint, spread, put on (make-up): (trans.)

		Affirmative	*Negative*
PLAIN FORM:	PRESENT	nuru	nuranai
	PAST	nutta	nuranakatta
MASU FORM:	PRESENT	nurimasu	nurimasen
	PAST	nurimashita	nurimasen deshita
IMPERATIVE		nure	nuru na
TE FORM		nutte	nuranakute
CONDITIONAL:	PLAIN	nureba	nuranakereba
		nutta ra	nuranakatta ra
	FORMAL	nurimashita ra	nurimasen deshita ra
PRESUMPTIVE:	PLAIN	nuru daroo	nuranai daroo
	FORMAL	nuru deshoo	nuranai deshoo
VOLITIONAL:	PLAIN	nuroo	
	FORMAL	nurimashoo	

	Affirmative		*Affirmative*
POTENTIAL	nureru	HONORIFIC	onuri ni naru
			onuri nasaru
PASSIVE	nurareru	HUMBLE	onuri suru
			onuri itasu
CAUSATIVE	nuraseru		
CAUS. PASSIVE	nuraserareru		
	nurasareru		

Examples:

1. *Ie ni penki o nutte moratta.*
   I had my house painted.
2. *Pan ni bataa o nutte kudasai.*
   Please spread butter on the bread.
3. *Kabe o shiroku nuru tsumori desu.*
   I plan to paint the wall white.
4. *Boku no kao ni doro o nuranaide kudasai.*
   Please don't disgrace me. (*lit.*, don't spread mud on my face)
5. *Kanojo wa makka na kuchibeni o nutte iru.*
   She is putting on bright red lipstick.

盗む　to steal, do stealthily: (trans.)

		Affirmative	*Negative*
PLAIN FORM:	PRESENT	nusumu	nusumanai
	PAST	nusunda	nusumanakatta
MASU FORM:	PRESENT	nusumimasu	nusumimasen
	PAST	nusumimashita	nusumimasen deshita
IMPERATIVE		nusume	nusumu na
TE FORM		nusunde	nusumanakute
CONDITIONAL:	PLAIN	nusumeba	nusumanakereba
		nusunda ra	nusumanakatta ra
	FORMAL	nusumimashita ra	nusumimasen deshita ra
PRESUMPTIVE:	PLAIN	nusumu daroo	nusumanai daroo
	FORMAL	nusumu deshoo	nusumanai deshoo
VOLITIONAL:	PLAIN	nusumoo	
	FORMAL	nusumimashoo	

	Affirmative		*Affirmative*
POTENTIAL	nusumeru	HONORIFIC	onusumi ni naru
			onusumi nasaru
PASSIVE	nusumareru	HUMBLE	(onusumi suru)
			(onusumi itasu)
CAUSATIVE	nusumaseru		
CAUS. PASSIVE	nusumaserareru		
	nusumasareru		

Examples:

1. *Eigakan de saifu o nusumareta.*
   My wallet was stolen in the movie theater.
2. *Ginkoo ni doroboo ga nusumi ni hairimashita.*
   A thief broke into the bank.
3. *Kare wa kodomo ni okane o nusumaseta.*
   He made his child steal the money.
4. *Sensei no me o nusunde sake o nonda.*
   I drank saké behind the teacher's back.
5. *Karera wa hitome o nusunde atta.*
   They met secretly.

覚える to remember, memorize, learn: (trans.)

		Affirmative	*Negative*
PLAIN FORM:	PRESENT	oboeru	oboenai
	PAST	oboeta	oboenakatta
MASU FORM:	PRESENT	oboemasu	oboemasen
	PAST	oboemashita	oboemasen deshita
IMPERATIVE		oboero	oboeru na
TE FORM		oboete	oboenakute
CONDITIONAL:	PLAIN	oboereba	oboenakereba
		oboeta ra	oboenakatta ra
	FORMAL	oboemashita ra	oboemasen deshita ra
PRESUMPTIVE:	PLAIN	oboeru daroo	oboenai daroo
	FORMAL	oboeru deshoo	oboenai deshoo
VOLITIONAL:	PLAIN	oboeyoo	
	FORMAL	oboemashoo	

	Affirmative		*Affirmative*
POTENTIAL	oboerareru	HONORIFIC	ooboe ni naru
	oboereru		ooboe nasaru
PASSIVE	oboerareru	HUMBLE	(ooboe suru)
			(ooboe itasu)
CAUSATIVE	oboesaseru		
CAUS. PASSIVE	oboesaserareru		

Examples:

1. *Kanji ga nakanaka oboeraremasen.*
   I can't memorize Japanese characters easily.
2. *Nihon-go o oboeru no wa muzukashii ga, wasureru no wa yasashii desu.*
   It's difficult to learn Japanese, but easy to forget it.
3. *Watashi no koto o oboete imasu ka.*
   Do you remember me?
4. *Kore dake wa oboete oite kudasai.*
   Please just remember only this.
5. *Setsumei-sho o yomeba, tsukai-kata wa sugu oboeraremasu.*
   Read the explanation, and you'll understand at once how to use it.

落ちる to fall, come off: (intrans.)

		Affirmative	*Negative*
PLAIN FORM:	PRESENT	ochiru	ochinai
	PAST	ochita	ochinakatta
MASU FORM:	PRESENT	ochimasu	ochimasen
	PAST	ochimashita	ochimasen deshita
IMPERATIVE		ochiro	ochiru na
TE FORM		ochite	ochinakute
CONDITIONAL:	PLAIN	ochireba	ochinakereba
		ochita ra	ochinakatta ra
	FORMAL	ochimashita ra	ochimasen deshita ra
PRESUMPTIVE:	PLAIN	ochiru daroo	ochinai daroo
	FORMAL	ochiru deshoo	ochinai deshoo
VOLITIONAL:	PLAIN	ochiyoo	
	FORMAL	ochimashoo	

	Affirmative		*Affirmative*
POTENTIAL	(ochirareru)	HONORIFIC	oochi ni naru
			oochi nasaru
PASSIVE	(ochirareru)	HUMBLE	(oochi suru)
			(oochi itasu)
CAUSATIVE	ochisaseru		
CAUS. PASSIVE	ochisaserareru		

Examples:

1. *Shiken ni ochite gakkari shita.*
   I'm disappointed because I failed the examination.
2. *Hyaku-en dama ga yuka ni ochite ita.*
   A hundred yen coin has fallen on the floor.
3. *Shimi ga nakanaka ochinai.*
   The stain won't come out very easily.
4. *Yamada-san wa koi ni ochite, yoru mo nemurenai.*
   Since Mr. Yamada has fallen in love, he can't sleep very well at night.
5. *Kare no shuunyuu wa kyonen yori ochite iru.*
   His income has dropped since last year.

驚く to be surprised, amazed, shocked: (intrans.)

		Affirmative	*Negative*
PLAIN FORM:	PRESENT	odoroku	odorokanai
	PAST	odoroita	odorokanakatta
MASU FORM:	PRESENT	odorokimasu	odorokimasen
	PAST	odorokimashita	odorokimasen deshita
IMPERATIVE		odoroke	odoroku na
TE FORM		odoroite	odorokanakute
CONDITIONAL:	PLAIN	odorokeba	odorokanakereba
		odoroita ra	odorokanakatta ra
	FORMAL	odorokimashita ra	odorokimasen deshita ra
PRESUMPTIVE:	PLAIN	odoroku daroo	odorokanai daroo
	FORMAL	odoroku deshoo	odorokanai deshoo
VOLITIONAL:	PLAIN	odorokoo	
	FORMAL	odorokimashoo	

	Affirmative		*Affirmative*
POTENTIAL	(odorokeru)	HONORIFIC	oodoroki ni naru
			oodoroki nasaru
PASSIVE	(odorokareru)	HUMBLE	(oodoroki suru)
			(oodoroki itasu)
CAUSATIVE	odorokaseru		
CAUS. PASSIVE	odorokaserareru		
	odorokasareru		

Examples:

1. *Kare ga shinda to kiite, odorokimashita.*
   I was surprised to hear that he had died.
2. *Uta ga joozu na node odorokimashita.*
   We were surprised at how good the singing was.
3. *Odoroite, kare no kao o mita.*
   I stared back at him in surprise.
4. *Aa, odoroita!*
   What a surprise!
5. *Odoroita koto ni, ano kaisha wa toosan shita.*
   To my surprise, that company went bankrupt.

踊る to dance; 躍る to jump up, be excited: (both intrans.)

		Affirmative	*Negative*
PLAIN FORM:	PRESENT	odoru	odoranai
	PAST	odotta	odoranakatta
MASU FORM:	PRESENT	odorimasu	odorimasen
	PAST	odorimashita	odorimasen deshita
IMPERATIVE		odore	odoru na
TE FORM		odotte	odoranakute
CONDITIONAL:	PLAIN	odoreba	odoranakereba
		odotta ra	odoranakatta ra
	FORMAL	odorimashita ra	odorimasen deshita ra
PRESUMPTIVE:	PLAIN	odoru daroo	odoranai daroo
	FORMAL	odoru deshoo	odoranai deshoo
VOLITIONAL:	PLAIN	odoroo	
	FORMAL	odorimashoo	

	Affirmative		*Affirmative*
POTENTIAL	odoreru	HONORIFIC	oodori ni naru
			oodori nasaru
PASSIVE	odorareru	HUMBLE	oodori suru
			oodori itasu
CAUSATIVE	odoraseru		
CAUS. PASSIVE	odoraserareru		
	odorasareru		

Examples:

1. *Watashi to odotte kudasaimasen ka.*
   Could I please have this dance?
2. *Odori ni ikimashoo.*
   Let's go dancing.
3. *Odotte mo odoranakute mo sore wa jiyuu desu.*
   It does not matter whether you dance or not.
4. *Yorokobi de mune ga odorimashita.*
   My heart leaped with joy.
5. *Koi ga odotta.*
   A carp jumped out of the water (broke the surface).

起きる to wake up, get up, to occur:* (intrans.)

		Affirmative	*Negative*
PLAIN FORM:	PRESENT	okiru	okinai
	PAST	okita	okinakatta
MASU FORM:	PRESENT	okimasu	okimasen
	PAST	okimashita	okimasen deshita
IMPERATIVE		okiro	okiru na
TE FORM		okite	okinakute
CONDITIONAL:	PLAIN	okireba	okinakereba
		okita ra	okinakatta ra
	FORMAL	okimashita ra	okimasen deshita ra
PRESUMPTIVE:	PLAIN	okiru daroo	okinai daroo
	FORMAL	okiru deshoo	okinai deshoo
VOLITIONAL:	PLAIN	okiyoo	
	FORMAL	okimashoo	

	Affirmative		*Affirmative*
POTENTIAL	okirareru okireru	HONORIFIC	ooki ni naru ooki nasaru
PASSIVE	okirareru	HUMBLE	(ooki suru) (ooki itasu)
CAUSATIVE	okisaseru		
CAUS. PASSIVE	okisaserareru		

Examples:

1. *Kinoo nan-ji ni okimashita ka.*
   What time did you get up yesterday?
   Asa roku-ji ni okimashita.
   I got up at six o'clock in the morning.
2. *Yamada-san wa asa hayaku okirarenai.*
   Mr. Yamada can't get up early in the morning.
3. *Akachan ga okiru kara shizuka ni shite kudasai.*
   Please be quiet, or you'll wake up the baby.
4. *Saikin hen na jiken ga okite iru.*
   Recently strange things have been occurring.

* The verb *okiru* meaning "to occur" generally does not use the imperative, volitional, or honorific forms.

怒る to get angry; 起こる to occur: (both intrans.)

		Affirmative	Negative
PLAIN FORM:	PRESENT	okoru	okoranai
	PAST	okotta	okoranakatta
MASU FORM:	PRESENT	okorimasu	okorimasen
	PAST	okorimashita	okorimasen deshita
IMPERATIVE		okore	okoru na
TE FORM		okotte	okoranakute
CONDITIONAL:	PLAIN	okoreba	okoranakereba
		okotta ra	okoranakatta ra
	FORMAL	okorimashita ra	okorimasen deshita ra
PRESUMPTIVE:	PLAIN	okoru daroo	okoranai daroo
	FORMAL	okoru deshoo	okoranai deshoo
VOLITIONAL:	PLAIN	okoroo	
	FORMAL	okorimashoo	

	Affirmative		Affirmative
POTENTIAL	okoreru	HONORIFIC	ookori ni naru
			ookori nasaru
PASSIVE	okorareru	HUMBLE	(ookori suru)
			(ookori itasu)
CAUSATIVE	okoraseru		
CAUS. PASSIVE	okoraserareru		
	okorasareru		

Examples:

1. *Kanojo wa kankan ni okotte iru.*
   She is furious.
2. *Ano ko wa itsumo sensei ni okorarete iru.*
   That boy is always being scolded by the teacher.
3. *Kare o okoraseru to kowai yo.*
   If you make him angry, he becomes frightening.
4. *Osoroshii jiken ga okotta.*
   A terrible thing has occurred.
5. *Kono machi ni ooki na henka ga okotte iru.*
   A great change has taken place in this city.

起こす to wake up, make happen, pick (a person) up: (trans.)

		Affirmative	*Negative*
PLAIN FORM:	PRESENT	okosu	okosanai
	PAST	okoshita	okosanakatta
MASU FORM:	PRESENT	okoshimasu	okoshimasen
	PAST	okoshimashita	okoshimasen deshita
IMPERATIVE		okose	okosu na
TE FORM		okoshite	okosanakute
CONDITIONAL:	PLAIN	okoseba	okosanakereba
		okoshita ra	okosanakatta ra
	FORMAL	okoshimashita ra	okoshimasen deshita ra
PRESUMPTIVE:	PLAIN	okosu daroo	okosanai daroo
	FORMAL	okosu deshoo	okosanai deshoo
VOLITIONAL:	PLAIN	okosoo	
	FORMAL	okoshimashoo	

	Affirmative		*Affirmative*
POTENTIAL	okoseru	HONORIFIC	ookoshi ni naru
			ookoshi nasaru
PASSIVE	okosareru	HUMBLE	ookoshi suru
			ookoshi itasu
CAUSATIVE	okosaseru		
CAUS. PASSIVE	okosaserareru		

Examples:

1. *Asu no asa shichi-ji ni okoshite kudasai.*
   Please wake me at seven o'clock tomorrow morning.
2. *Haha ni go-ji ni okosareta.*
   My mother woke me at five o'clock.
3. *Kare wa mata kimagure o okoshite iru.*
   He is being whimsical again.
4. *Kare wa jigyoo o okoshita.*
   He initiated a project.
5. *Koronda kodomo o okoshite ageta.*
   I helped a child who had fallen get back on his feet.

置く to put, keep, leave: (trans.)

		Affirmative	*Negative*
PLAIN FORM:	PRESENT	oku	okanai
	PAST	oita	okanakatta
MASU FORM:	PRESENT	okimasu	okimasen
	PAST	okimashita	okimasen deshita
IMPERATIVE		oke	oku na
TE FORM		oite	okanakute
CONDITIONAL:	PLAIN	okeba	okanakereba
		oita ra	okanakatta ra
	FORMAL	okimashita ra	okimasen deshita ra
PRESUMPTIVE:	PLAIN	oku daroo	okanai daroo
	FORMAL	oku deshoo	okanai deshoo
VOLITIONAL:	PLAIN	okoo	
	FORMAL	okimashoo	

	Affirmative		*Affirmative*
POTENTIAL	okeru	HONORIFIC	ooki ni naru
			ooki nasaru
PASSIVE	okareru	HUMBLE	ooki suru
			ooki itasu
CAUSATIVE	okaseru		
CAUS. PASSIVE	okaserareru		
	okasareru		

Examples:

1. *Tana ni hon ga okarete iru.*
   There are books placed on the shelf.
2. *Nimotsu o oku basho ga nai.*
   There is no place to put my luggage.
3. *Ano mise wa donna mono o oite imasu ka.*
   What kinds of goods does that store have?
   Yunyuu-hin o oite imasu.
   It has imported goods.
4. *Kare wa kurushii tachiba ni okarete iru.*
   He has been put in a difficult situation.

遅れる to be late for, be delayed, be far behind: (intrans.)

		Affirmative	*Negative*
PLAIN FORM:	PRESENT	okureru	okurenai
	PAST	okureta	okurenakatta
MASU FORM:	PRESENT	okuremasu	okuremasen
	PAST	okuremashita	okuremasen deshita
IMPERATIVE		okurero	okureru na
TE FORM		okurete	okurenakute
CONDITIONAL:	PLAIN	okurereba	okurenakereba
		okureta ra	okurenakatta ra
	FORMAL	okuremashita ra	okuremasen deshita ra
PRESUMPTIVE:	PLAIN	okureru daroo	okurenai daroo
	FORMAL	okureru deshoo	okurenai deshoo
VOLITIONAL:	PLAIN	okureyoo	
	FORMAL	okuremashoo	

	Affirmative		*Affirmative*
POTENTIAL	okurerareru	HONORIFIC	ookure ni naru
	okurereru		ookure nasaru
PASSIVE	okurerareru	HUMBLE	(ookure suru)
			(ookure itasu)
CAUSATIVE	okuresaseru		
CAUS. PASSIVE	okuresaserareru		

Examples:

1. *Kiri no tame hikooki wa ni-jikan okureta.*
   The plane was delayed two hours because of fog.
2. *Kaisha ni okureta.*
   I was late for work.
3. *Gakkoo ni okurenai yoo ni isoida.*
   I hurried so as not to be late for school.
4. *Kono kurasu no shindo wa doo desu ka.*
   How is this class progressing along?
   Chotto okurete imasu.
   They are a little behind (the other classes).

送る to send, see off: (trans.)

		Affirmative	*Negative*
PLAIN FORM:	PRESENT	okuru	okuranai
	PAST	okutta	okuranakatta
MASU FORM:	PRESENT	okurimasu	okurimasen
	PAST	okurimashita	okurimasen deshita
IMPERATIVE		okure	okuru na
TE FORM		okutte	okuranakute
CONDITIONAL:	PLAIN	okureba	okuranakereba
		okutta ra	okuranakatta ra
	FORMAL	okurimashita ra	okurimasen deshita ra
PRESUMPTIVE:	PLAIN	okuru daroo	okuranai daroo
	FORMAL	okuru deshoo	okuranai deshoo
VOLITIONAL:	PLAIN	okuroo	
	FORMAL	okurimashoo	

	Affirmative		*Affirmative*
POTENTIAL	okureru	HONORIFIC	ookuri ni naru
			ookuri nasaru
PASSIVE	okurareru	HUMBLE	ookuri suru
			ookuri itasu
CAUSATIVE	okuraseru		
CAUS. PASSIVE	okuraserareru		
	okurasareru		

Examples:

1. *Okane o okutte kudasai.*
   Please send some money.
2. *Eki made ookuri itashimashoo.*
   I'll go to the station to see you off.
3. *Shinbun-sha ni toosho ga okurarete kita.*
   The newspaper has received letters to the editor.
4. *Okutte kurete arigatoo.*
   Thank you for seeing me (to my house).
5. *Narita Kuukoo made kanojo o okuri ni ikimashita.*
   I went to Narita Airport to see her off.

思う to think: (trans.)

		Affirmative	*Negative*
PLAIN FORM:	PRESENT	omou	omowanai
	PAST	omotta	omowanakatta
MASU FORM:	PRESENT	omoimasu	omoimasen
	PAST	omoimashita	omoimasen deshita
IMPERATIVE		omoe	omou na
TE FORM		omotte	omowanakute
CONDITIONAL:	PLAIN	omoeba	omowanakereba
		omotta ra	omowanakatta ra
	FORMAL	omoimashita ra	omoimasen deshita ra
PRESUMPTIVE:	PLAIN	omou daroo	omowanai daroo
	FORMAL	omou deshoo	omowanai deshoo
VOLITIONAL:	PLAIN	omooo	
	FORMAL	omoimashoo	

	Affirmative		*Affirmative*
POTENTIAL	omoeru	HONORIFIC	oomoi ni naru
			oomoi nasaru
PASSIVE	omowareru	HUMBLE	zonji ageru
			oomoi suru
CAUSATIVE	omowaseru		oomoi itasu
CAUS. PASSIVE	omowaserareru		
	omowasareru		

Examples:

1. *Anata no iu toori da to omoimasu.*
   I think that what you say is correct.
2. *Nihon o doo omoimasu ka.*
   What do you think of Japan?
   Omoshiroi kuni da to omoimasu.
   I think Japan is an interesting country.
3. *Kare wa isha da to wa omoenai.*
   I would not have thought that he is a doctor.
4. *Kare wa shoorai shachoo ni naru to omowarete iru.*
   He is regarded as being the future president of the company.

折れる to be broken, to give in, to turn, be folded: (intrans.)*

		Affirmative	*Negative*
PLAIN FORM:	PRESENT	oreru	orenai
	PAST	oreta	orenakatta
MASU FORM:	PRESENT	oremasu	oremasen
	PAST	oremashita	oremasen deshita
IMPERATIVE		(orero)	(oreru na)
TE FORM		orete	orenakute
CONDITIONAL:	PLAIN	orereba	orenakereba
		oreta ra	orenakatta ra
	FORMAL	oremashita ra	oremasen deshita ra
PRESUMPTIVE:	PLAIN	oreru daroo	orenai daroo
	FORMAL	oreru deshoo	orenai deshoo
VOLITIONAL:	PLAIN	(oreyoo)	
	FORMAL	(oremashoo)	

	Affirmative		*Affirmative*
POTENTIAL	(orerareru)	HONORIFIC	oore ni naru
			oore nasaru
PASSIVE	(orerareru)	HUMBLE	(oore suru)
			(oore itasu)
CAUSATIVE	(oresaseru)		
CAUS. PASSIVE	(oresaserareru)		

Examples:

1. *Zasshi no hyooshi ga orete iru.*
   The magazine cover is folded.
2. *Eda ga orete imasu ne.*
   The branch has broken off, hasn't it?
3. *Sono kado o migi ni oreru to yuubinkyoku ga arimasu.*
   If you turn right at that corner, there is a post office.
4. *Kono shigoto wa hone ga oremasu ne.*
   This work is difficult. (*lit.*, breaks the bones)
5. *Kami wa mittsu ni orete imasu.*
   The paper is folded in three.

* As with other verbs indicating movement, *oreru,* when meaning "to turn," may take a direct object, thus giving an idea of "going through a defined area." (*See* example 3.)

降りる to get off, fall; 下りる to come down, to be issued: (both trans.)

		Affirmative	*Negative*
PLAIN FORM:	PRESENT	oriru	orinai
	PAST	orita	orinakatta
MASU FORM:	PRESENT	orimasu	orimasen
	PAST	orimashita	orimasen deshita
IMPERATIVE		oriro	oriru na
TE FORM		orite	orinakute
CONDITIONAL:	PLAIN	orireba	orinakereba
		orita ra	orinakatta ra
	FORMAL	orimashita ra	orimasen deshita ra
PRESUMPTIVE:	PLAIN	oriru daroo	orinai daroo
	FORMAL	oriru deshoo	orinai deshoo
VOLITIONAL:	PLAIN	oriyoo	
	FORMAL	orimashoo	

	Affirmative		*Affirmative*
POTENTIAL	orirareru	HONORIFIC	oori ni naru
			oori nasaru
PASSIVE	orirareru	HUMBLE	oori suru
			oori itasu
CAUSATIVE	orisaseru		
CAUS. PASSIVE	orisaserareru		

Examples:

1. *Kaidan o orita.*
   I came down the stairs.
2. *Kare wa mado kara tobi-orita.*
   He jumped out the window.
3. *Oriru kata ga sumu made omachi kudasai.*
   Please wait until those passengers getting off have finished (getting off).
4. *Roku-juu-go sai de nenkin ga orita.*
   I was entitled to a pension at age sixty-five.
5. *Yatto biza ga orita.*
   My visa has been issued at last.

折る to fold, break, bend: (trans.)

		Affirmative	*Negative*
PLAIN FORM:	PRESENT	oru	oranai
	PAST	otta	oranakatta
MASU FORM:	PRESENT	orimasu	orimasen
	PAST	orimashita	orimasen deshita
IMPERATIVE		ore	oru na
TE FORM		otte	oranakute
CONDITIONAL:	PLAIN	oreba	oranakereba
		otta ra	oranakatta ra
	FORMAL	orimashita ra	orimasen deshita ra
PRESUMPTIVE:	PLAIN	oru daroo	oranai daroo
	FORMAL	oru deshoo	oranai deshoo
VOLITIONAL:	PLAIN	oroo	
	FORMAL	orimashoo	

	Affirmative		*Affirmative*
POTENTIAL	oreru	HONORIFIC	oori ni naru
			oori nasaru
PASSIVE	orareru	HUMBLE	oori suru
			oori itasu
CAUSATIVE	oraseru		
CAUS. PASSIVE	oraserareru		
	orasareru		

Examples:

1. *Sakura no eda o oranaide kudasai.*
   Don't break the branches of the cherry tree.
2. *Yubi o otte, ichi kara juu made kazoete kudasai.*
   Please count from one to ten on your fingers.
3. *Kanojo no tame ni orizuru o orimashoo.*
   Let's fold paper cranes for her.
4. *Ashi no hone o otte shimatta.*
   I broke a bone in my leg.
5. *Hanashi no koshi o oranaide kudasai.*
   Please don't interrupt us while we're talking.

押える to hold, catch; 抑える to suppress, control: (both trans.)

		Affirmative	*Negative*
PLAIN FORM:	PRESENT	osaeru	osaenai
	PAST	osaeta	osaenakatta
MASU FORM:	PRESENT	osaemasu	osaemasen
	PAST	osaemashita	osaemasen deshita
IMPERATIVE		osaero	osaeru na
TE FORM		osaete	osaenakute
CONDITIONAL:	PLAIN	osaereba	osaenakereba
		osaeta ra	osaenakatta ra
	FORMAL	osaemashita ra	osaemasen deshita ra
PRESUMPTIVE:	PLAIN	osaeru daroo	osaenai daroo
	FORMAL	osaeru deshoo	osaenai deshoo
VOLITIONAL:	PLAIN	osaeyoo	
	FORMAL	osaemashoo	

	Affirmative		*Affirmative*
POTENTIAL	osaerareru	HONORIFIC	oosae ni naru
	osaereru		oosae nasaru
PASSIVE	osaerareru	HUMBLE	oosae suru
			oosae itasu
CAUSATIVE	osaesaseru		
CAUS. PASSIVE	osaesaserareru		

Examples:

1. *Kare no datsuzei no shooko o osaeta.*
   They got hold of proof of his tax evasion.
2. *Ugokenai yoo ni kare no te-ashi o osaeta.*
   We held his arms and legs down so that he couldn't move.
3. *Kanojo wa jibun no kanjoo o osaerarenai.*
   She can't restrain her emotions.
4. *Nihon wa yushutsu o osaenakereba narimasen.*
   Japan has to restrict its exports.
5. *Kare wa koe o osaete hanashita.*
   He spoke in a low voice.

教える to teach, tell, show: (trans.)

		Affirmative	*Negative*
PLAIN FORM:	PRESENT	oshieru	oshienai
	PAST	oshieta	oshienakatta
MASU FORM:	PRESENT	oshiemasu	oshiemasen
	PAST	oshiemashita	oshiemasen deshita
IMPERATIVE		oshiero	oshieru na
TE FORM		oshiete	oshienakute
CONDITIONAL:	PLAIN	oshiereba	oshienakereba
		oshieta ra	oshienakatta ra
	FORMAL	oshiemashita ra	oshiemasen deshita ra
PRESUMPTIVE:	PLAIN	oshieru daroo	oshienai daroo
	FORMAL	oshieru deshoo	oshienai deshoo
VOLITIONAL:	PLAIN	oshieyoo	
	FORMAL	oshiemashoo	

	Affirmative		*Affirmative*
POTENTIAL	oshierareru oshiereru	HONORIFIC	ooshie ni naru ooshie nasaru
PASSIVE	oshierareru	HUMBLE	ooshie suru ooshie itasu
CAUSATIVE	oshiesaseru		
CAUS. PASSIVE	oshiesaserareru		

Examples:

1. *Kanojo ni Nihon-go o oshiete imasu.*
   I am teaching her Japanese.
2. *Kanojo wa kare ni Nihon-go o oshiete ageta.*
   She taught him Japanese.
3. *Keeki no tsukuri-kata o oshiete kudasai.*
   Please show me how to bake a cake.
4. *Kodomo ni michi o oshierareta.*
   I was given directions by a child.
5. *Namae o oshiete kudasaimasen ka.*
   May I have your name, please?

押す to push, press, stamp: (trans.)

		Affirmative	*Negative*
PLAIN FORM:	PRESENT	osu	osanai
	PAST	oshita	osanakatta
MASU FORM:	PRESENT	oshimasu	oshimasen
	PAST	oshimashita	oshimasen deshita
IMPERATIVE		ose	osu na
TE FORM		oshite	osanakute
CONDITIONAL:	PLAIN	oseba	osanakereba
		oshita ra	osanakatta ra
	FORMAL	oshimashita ra	oshimasen deshita ra
PRESUMPTIVE:	PLAIN	osu daroo	osanai daroo
	FORMAL	osu deshoo	osanai deshoo
VOLITIONAL:	PLAIN	osoo	
	FORMAL	oshimashoo	

	Affirmative		*Affirmative*
POTENTIAL	oseru	HONORIFIC	ooshi ni naru
			ooshi nasaru
PASSIVE	osareru	HUMBLE	ooshi suru
			ooshi itasu
CAUSATIVE	osaseru		
CAUS. PASSIVE	osaserareru		
	osasareru		

Examples:

1. *Ushiro kara osanaide.*
   Don't push from behind.
2. *Hiza o osu to, itamu'n desu yo.*
   My knee hurts when I press on it.
3. *Koko ni hanko o oshite kudasai.*
   Please stamp your seal here.
4. *Kare no taido ni osarete nani mo ienakatta.*
   I was so overcome with his attitude that I couldn't say anything.
5. *Tenisu no shiai de watashi wa kanojo ni osareppanashi datta.*
   In the tennis match, I was constantly being pressured by her.

落とす to drop, remove, lose: (trans.)

		Affirmative	*Negative*
PLAIN FORM:	PRESENT	otosu	otosanai
	PAST	otoshita	otosanakatta
MASU FORM:	PRESENT	otoshimasu	otoshimasen
	PAST	otoshimashita	otoshimasen deshita
IMPERATIVE		otose	otosu na
TE FORM		otoshite	otosanakute
CONDITIONAL:	PLAIN	otoseba	otosanakereba
		otoshita ra	otosanakatta ra
	FORMAL	otoshimashita ra	otoshimasen deshita ra
PRESUMPTIVE:	PLAIN	otosu daroo	otosanai daroo
	FORMAL	otosu deshoo	otosanai deshoo
VOLITIONAL:	PLAIN	otosoo	
	FORMAL	otoshimashoo	

	Affirmative		*Affirmative*
POTENTIAL	otoseru	HONORIFIC	ootoshi ni naru
			ootoshi nasaru
PASSIVE	otosareru	HUMBLE	ootoshi suru
			ootoshi itasu
CAUSATIVE	otosaseru		
CAUS. PASSIVE	otosaserareru		

Examples:

1. *Mado kara gomi o otosanaide kudasai.*
   Please don't drop the rubbish from the window.
2. *Motto supiido o otoshite kudasai.*
   Please slow down more.
3. *Seetaa no yogore o arai-otoshita.*
   I washed away the stain on the sweater.
4. *Anata ni ii-otoshita koto ga aru.*
   There is something I forgot to say to you.
5. *Sensei wa gojutten miman wa otosu to itta.*
   The teacher said that those who get scores under fifty won't pass.

追う to run after, drive out; 負う to bear: (both trans.)

		Affirmative	*Negative*
PLAIN FORM:	PRESENT	ou	owanai
	PAST	otta	owanakatta
MASU FORM:	PRESENT	oimasu	oimasen
	PAST	oimashita	oimasen deshita
IMPERATIVE		oe	ou na
TE FORM		otte	owanakute
CONDITIONAL:	PLAIN	oeba	owanakereba
		otta ra	owanakatta ra
	FORMAL	oimashita ra	oimasen deshita ra
PRESUMPTIVE:	PLAIN	ou daroo	owanai daroo
	FORMAL	ou deshoo	owanai deshoo
VOLITIONAL:	PLAIN	ooo	
	FORMAL	oimashoo	

	Affirmative		*Affirmative*
POTENTIAL	oeru	HONORIFIC	ooi ni naru
			ooi nasaru
PASSIVE	owareru	HUMBLE	ooi suru
			ooi itasu
CAUSATIVE	owaseru		
CAUS. PASSIVE	owaserareru		
	owasareru		

Examples:

1. *Kare wa keisatsu ni owarete iru.*
   He is being pursued by the police.
2. *Mainichi shigoto ni owarete iru.*
   I am bombarded with work everyday.
3. *Kanojo wa itsumo yume o otte iru.*
   She is always pursuing big dreams.
4. *Watashi no kodomo wa hontoo ni te ni oenai.*
   My child is quite beyond my control.
5. *Sono koto ni wa sekinin o oi-kaneru.*
   I cannot bear responsibility for that.

終わる to be finished, be over: (intrans.)

		Affirmative	*Negative*
PLAIN FORM:	PRESENT	owaru	owaranai
	PAST	owatta	owaranakatta
MASU FORM:	PRESENT	owarimasu	owarimasen
	PAST	owarimashita	owarimasen deshita
IMPERATIVE		oware	owaru na
TE FORM		owatte	owaranakute
CONDITIONAL:	PLAIN	owareba	owaranakereba
		owatta ra	owaranakatta ra
	FORMAL	owarimashita ra	owarimasen deshita ra
PRESUMPTIVE:	PLAIN	owaru daroo	owaranai daroo
	FORMAL	owaru deshoo	owaranai deshoo
VOLITIONAL:	PLAIN	owaroo	
	FORMAL	owarimashoo	

	Affirmative		*Affirmative*
POTENTIAL	owareru	HONORIFIC	oowari ni naru
			oowari nasaru
PASSIVE	owarareru	HUMBLE	(oowari suru)
			(oowari itasu)
CAUSATIVE	owaraseru		
CAUS. PASSIVE	owaraserareru		
	owarasareru		

Examples:

1. *Jugyoo ga ato jup-pun de owaru.*
   Classes will end in ten minutes.
2. *Go-ji ni shigoto ga owarimasu ka.*
   Do you finish work at five o'clock?
3. *Sensoo ga hayaku owatte hoshii.*
   I'd like the war to come to an end soon.
4. *Sono hon o yomi-owatta ra, watashi ni kashite kudasai.*
   After finishing that book, please lend it to me.
5. *Kotae o kaki-owatta ra, dashite kudasai.*
   Please hand in your answers after you've finished writing.

泳ぐ to swim: (intrans.)

		Affirmative	*Negative*
PLAIN FORM:	PRESENT	oyogu	oyoganai
	PAST	oyoida	oyoganakatta
MASU FORM:	PRESENT	oyogimasu	oyogimasen
	PAST	oyogimashita	oyogimasen deshita
IMPERATIVE		oyoge	oyogu na
TE FORM		oyoide	oyoganakute
CONDITIONAL:	PLAIN	oyogeba	oyoganakereba
		oyoida ra	oyoganakatta ra
	FORMAL	oyogimashita ra	oyogimasen deshita ra
PRESUMPTIVE:	PLAIN	oyogu daroo	oyoganai daroo
	FORMAL	oyogu deshoo	oyoganai deshoo
VOLITIONAL:	PLAIN	oyogoo	
	FORMAL	oyogimashoo	

	Affirmative		*Affirmative*
POTENTIAL	oyogeru	HONORIFIC	ooyogi ni naru
			ooyogi nasaru
PASSIVE	oyogareru	HUMBLE	(ooyogi suru)
			(ooyogi itasu)
CAUSATIVE	oyogaseru		
CAUS. PASSIVE	oyogaserareru		
	oyogasareru		

Examples:

1. *Dore gurai oyogemasu ka.*
   How far can you swim?
   Zenzen oyogenai'n desu.
   I cannot swim at all.
2. *Kawa o oyoide watatta.*
   I swam across the river.
3. *Mizuumi de oyoida koto ga arimasu ka.*
   Have you swum in a lake?
   Iie, arimasen. Itsumo puuru de oyogimasu.
   No, I haven't. I always swim in a pool.

下がる to fall, drop, hang: (intrans.)

		Affirmative	*Negative*
PLAIN FORM:	PRESENT	sagaru	sagaranai
	PAST	sagatta	sagaranakatta
MASU FORM:	PRESENT	sagarimasu	sagarimasen
	PAST	sagarimashita	sagarimasen deshita
IMPERATIVE		sagare	sagaru na
TE FORM		sagatte	sagaranakute
CONDITIONAL:	PLAIN	sagareba	sagaranakereba
		sagatta ra	sagaranakatta ra
	FORMAL	sagarimashita ra	sagarimasen deshita ra
PRESUMPTIVE:	PLAIN	sagaru daroo	sagaranai daroo
	FORMAL	sagaru deshoo	sagaranai deshoo
VOLITIONAL:	PLAIN	sagaroo	
	FORMAL	sagarimashoo	

	Affirmative		*Affirmative*
POTENTIAL	(sagareru)	HONORIFIC	osagari ni naru
			osagari nasaru
PASSIVE	(sagarareru)	HUMBLE	(osagari suru)
			(osagari itasu)
CAUSATIVE	(sagaraseru)		
CAUS. PASSIVE	(sagaraserareru)		

Examples:

1. *Zubon ga sagatte imasu yo.*
   Your trousers are falling down.
2. *Mado ni kaaten ga sagatte iru.*
   A curtain is hanging in the window.
3. *En ga agari, doru ga sagatte iru.*
   The yen is rising and the dollar is dropping.
4. *Asu wa kion ga sagaru daroo.*
   The temperature probably will fall tomorrow.
5. *Nihon-go no seiseki ga mata sagatte shimatta.*
   My grades for Japanese fell again.

探す *or* 捜す to look for, investigate: (trans.)

		Affirmative	*Negative*
PLAIN FORM:	PRESENT	sagasu	sagasanai
	PAST	sagashita	sagasanakatta
MASU FORM:	PRESENT	sagashimasu	sagashimasen
	PAST	sagashimashita	sagashimasen deshita
IMPERATIVE		sagase	sagasu na
TE FORM		sagashite	sagasanakute
CONDITIONAL:	PLAIN	sagaseba	sagasanakereba
		sagashita ra	sagasanakatta ra
	FORMAL	sagashimashita ra	sagashimasen deshita ra
PRESUMPTIVE:	PLAIN	sagasu daroo	sagasanai daroo
	FORMAL	sagasu deshoo	sagasanai deshoo
VOLITIONAL:	PLAIN	sagasoo	
	FORMAL	sagashimashoo	

	Affirmative		*Affirmative*
POTENTIAL	sagaseru	HONORIFIC	osagashi ni naru
			osagashi nasaru
PASSIVE	sagasareru	HUMBLE	osagashi suru
			osagashi itasu
CAUSATIVE	sagasaseru		
CAUS. PASSIVE	sagasaserareru		

Examples:

1. *Nani o sagashite iru no?*
   What are you looking for?
2. *Apaato o sagasu no ni kuroo shimashita.*
   I had trouble finding the apartment.
3. *Jisho de tango o sagashite kudasai.*
   Please look up the word in a dictionary.
4. *Takaramono wa tsui ni sagasenakatta.*
   In the end, they weren't able to find the treasure.
5. *Eigo no sensei o sagashite iru tokoro desu.*
   We now are looking for an English teacher.

下げる to lower, hang, pull back: (trans.)

		Affirmative	*Negative*
PLAIN FORM:	PRESENT	sageru	sagenai
	PAST	sageta	sagenakatta
MASU FORM:	PRESENT	sagemasu	sagemasen
	PAST	sagemashita	sagemasen deshita
IMPERATIVE		sagero	sageru na
TE FORM		sagete	sagenakute
CONDITIONAL:	PLAIN	sagereba	sagenakereba
		sageta ra	sagenakatta ra
	FORMAL	sagemashita ra	sagemasen deshita ra
PRESUMPTIVE:	PLAIN	sageru daroo	sagenai daroo
	FORMAL	sageru deshoo	sagenai deshoo
VOLITIONAL:	PLAIN	sageyoo	
	FORMAL	sagemashoo	

	Affirmative		*Affirmative*
POTENTIAL	sagerareru	HONORIFIC	osage ni naru
	sagereru		osage nasaru
PASSIVE	sagerareru	HUMBLE	osage suru
			osage itasu
CAUSATIVE	sagesaseru		
CAUS. PASSIVE	sagesaserareru		

Examples:

1. *Kanojo wa sensei ni atama o sageta.*
   She bowed to her teacher.
2. *Shigoto de misu o shite, kyuuryoo o sagerareta.*
   After making mistakes at work, my wages were lowered.
3. *Chokin o sagete, Nihon e/ni iku tsumori desu.*
   I plan to go to Japan after withdrawing my savings.
4. *Motto ondo o sagete kudasai.*
   Please lower the temperature even more.
5. *Kare wa otoko o sageta.*
   He lost face as a man.

裂ける to tear, split: (intrans.);* 避ける to avoid, keep away from: (trans.)

		Affirmative	*Negative*
PLAIN FORM:	PRESENT	sakeru	sakenai
	PAST	saketa	sakenakatta
MASU FORM:	PRESENT	sakemasu	sakemasen
	PAST	sakemashita	sakemasen deshita
IMPERATIVE		sakero	sakeru na
TE FORM		sakete	sakenakute
CONDITIONAL:	PLAIN	sakereba	sakenakereba
		saketa ra	sakenakatta ra
	FORMAL	sakemashita ra	sakemasen deshita ra
PRESUMPTIVE:	PLAIN	sakeru daroo	sakenai daroo
	FORMAL	sakeru deshoo	sakenai deshoo
VOLITIONAL:	PLAIN	sakeyoo	
	FORMAL	sakemashoo	

	Affirmative		*Affirmative*
POTENTIAL	sakerareru sakereru	HONORIFIC	osake ni naru osake nasaru
PASSIVE	sakerareru	HUMBLE	(osake suru) (osake itasu)
CAUSATIVE	sakesaseru		
CAUS. PASSIVE	sakesaserareru		

Examples:

1. *Tsume-komi-sugite, fukuro ga sakete shimatta.*
   I stuffed too much in the bag, and it tore.
2. *Sore wa kuchi ga sakete mo ienai.*
   Nothing will make me reveal it.
3. *Kore wa sakete toorenai mondai da.*
   This is a problem we have to face.
4. *Sutoraiki totsunyuu wa sakerarenai daroo.*
   We probably can't avoid a strike confrontation.
5. *Kare wa kurasu no nakama kara sakerarete iru.*
   He is ostracized by his classmates.

* The intransitive verb *sakeru* 裂ける meaning "to tear, split" generally does not use the potential, passive, honorific, humble, causative, or causative passive forms.

咲く to bloom: (intrans.);* 裂く to tear; 割く to make (time), to cut: (both trans.)

		Affirmative	*Negative*
PLAIN FORM:	PRESENT	saku	sakanai
	PAST	saita	sakanakatta
MASU FORM:	PRESENT	sakimasu	sakimasen
	PAST	sakimashita	sakimasen deshita
IMPERATIVE		sake	saku na
TE FORM		saite	sakanakute
CONDITIONAL:	PLAIN	sakeba	sakanakereba
		saita ra	sakanakatta ra
	FORMAL	sakimashita ra	sakimasen deshita ra
PRESUMPTIVE:	PLAIN	saku daroo	sakanai daroo
	FORMAL	saku deshoo	sakanai deshoo
VOLITIONAL:	PLAIN	sakoo	
	FORMAL	sakimashoo	

	Affirmative		*Affirmative*
POTENTIAL	sakeru	HONORIFIC	osaki ni naru
			osaki nasaru
PASSIVE	sakareru	HUMBLE	osaki suru
			osaki itasu
CAUSATIVE	sakaseru		
CAUS. PASSIVE	sakaserareru		
	sakasareru		

Examples:

1. *Sakura no hana ga saki-hajimeta.*
   The cherry blossoms have begun to blossom.
2. *Omoide-banashi ni hana ga saita.*
   They had a lively conversation about the good old days.
3. *Zutazuta ni fuku o sakareta.*
   My clothes were ripped to shreds.
4. *Futari no naka o sakanaide kudasai.*
   Please don't cause a rift between the two people.
5. *O-jikan o jup-pun hodo saite kudasaimasen ka.*
   Could you please spare ten minutes for me?

---

* The intransitive verb *saku* 咲く meaning "to bloom" does not generally use the volitional, potential, passive, honorific, humble, causative, or causative passive forms.

支える to support, keep: (trans.)

		Affirmative	*Negative*
PLAIN FORM:	PRESENT	sasaeru	sasaenai
	PAST	sasaeta	sasaenakatta
MASU FORM:	PRESENT	sasaemasu	sasaemasen
	PAST	sasaemashita	sasaemasen deshita
IMPERATIVE		sasaero	sasaeru na
TE FORM		sasaete	sasaenakute
CONDITIONAL:	PLAIN	sasaereba	sasaenakereba
		sasaeta ra	sasaenakatta ra
	FORMAL	sasaemashita ra	sasaemasen deshita ra
PRESUMPTIVE:	PLAIN	sasaeru daroo	sasaenai daroo
	FORMAL	sasaeru deshoo	sasaenai deshoo
VOLITIONAL:	PLAIN	sasaeyoo	
	FORMAL	sasaemashoo	

	Affirmative		*Affirmative*
POTENTIAL	sasaerareru sasaereru	HONORIFIC	osasae ni naru osasae nasaru
PASSIVE	sasaerareru	HUMBLE	osasae suru osasae itasu
CAUSATIVE	sasaesaseru		
CAUS. PASSIVE	sasaesaserareru		

Examples:

1. *Kare wa tsue de karada o sasaete iru.*
   He is supporting himself with a stick.
2. *Kare wa dai-kazoku o sasaete ikanakereba narimasen.*
   He has to support a large family.
3. *Ojisan wa watashi no kyooiku no hiyoo o sasaete kureta.*
   My uncle bore the cost of my education.
4. *Kanojo o sasaete ageta ra doo desu ka.*
   How about giving her support (with your affection?)
5. *Teki no koogeki kara jinchi o sasae-kirenai.*
   We can't maintain our position due to the enemy's assault.

誘う to invite, ask, tempt: (trans.)

		Affirmative	*Negative*
PLAIN FORM:	PRESENT	sasou	sasowanai
	PAST	sasotta	sasowanakatta
MASU FORM:	PRESENT	sasoimasu	sasoimasen
	PAST	sasoimashita	sasoimasen deshita
IMPERATIVE		sasoe	sasou na
TE FORM		sasotte	sasowanakute
CONDITIONAL:	PLAIN	sasoeba	sasowanakereba
		sasotta ra	sasowanakatta ra
	FORMAL	sasoimashita ra	sasoimasen deshita ra
PRESUMPTIVE:	PLAIN	sasou daroo	sasowanai daroo
	FORMAL	sasou deshoo	sasowanai deshoo
VOLITIONAL:	PLAIN	sasooo	
	FORMAL	sasoimashoo	

	Affirmative		*Affirmative*
POTENTIAL	sasoeru	HONORIFIC	osasoi ni naru
			osasoi nasaru
PASSIVE	sasowareru	HUMBLE	osasoi suru
			osasoi itasu
CAUSATIVE	sasowaseru		
CAUS. PASSIVE	sasowaserareru		
	sasowasareru		

Examples:

1. *Sensei o paatii ni osasoi shita.*
   I invited my teacher to the party.
2. *Kimi mo sasou kara koi yo.*
   You're invited too, so be sure to come.
3. *Kyooto ni ikoo to sasowaremashita.*
   I was invited to go to Kyoto.
4. *Tekido no undoo wa shokuyoku o sasou.*
   Moderate exercise will increase your appetite.
5. *Kare wa karera ni sasowarete, hanzai o okashita.*
   Deceived by their urging, he committed the crime.

指す to point to, call on; 刺す to pierce, sting; 差す to insert, put up: (all trans.)

		Affirmative	*Negative*
PLAIN FORM:	PRESENT	sasu	sasanai
	PAST	sashita	sasanakatta
MASU FORM:	PRESENT	sashimasu	sashimasen
	PAST	sashimashita	sashimasen deshita
IMPERATIVE		sase	sasu na
TE FORM		sashite	sasanakute
CONDITIONAL:	PLAIN	saseba	sasanakereba
		sashita ra	sasanakatta ra
	FORMAL	sashimashita ra	sasimasen deshita ra
PRESUMPTIVE:	PLAIN	sasu daroo	sasanai daroo
	FORMAL	sasu deshoo	sasanai deshoo
VOLITIONAL:	PLAIN	sasoo	
	FORMAL	sashimashoo	

	Affirmative		*Affirmative*
POTENTIAL	saseru	HONORIFIC	osashi ni naru
			osashi nasaru
PASSIVE	sasareru	HUMBLE	osashi suru
			osashi itasu
CAUSATIVE	sasaseru		
CAUS. PASSIVE	sasaserareru		
	sasasareru		

Examples:

1. *Nihon-go no jugyoo de sasareta.*
   I was called upon during Japanese class.
2. *Mushi ni ashi o sasareta.*
   I was bitten on the leg by an insect.
3. *Kanojo ga itta kotoba wa mune o sashita.*
   What she said pierced my heart.
4. *Tsukareta node megusuri o sashita.*
   Since I was tired, I used some eyedrops.
5. *Ame ga yanda noni, kanojo wa mada kasa o sashite iru.*
   She has her umbrella up even though it has stopped raining.

騒ぐ to be noisy: (intrans.)

		Affirmative	*Negative*
PLAIN FORM:	PRESENT	sawagu	sawaganai
	PAST	sawaida	sawaganakatta
MASU FORM:	PRESENT	sawagimasu	sawagimasen
	PAST	sawagimashita	sawagimasen deshita
IMPERATIVE		sawage	sawagu na
TE FORM		sawaide	sawaganakute
CONDITIONAL:	PLAIN	sawageba	sawaganakereba
		sawaida ra	sawaganakatta ra
	FORMAL	sawagimashita ra	sawagimasen deshita ra
PRESUMPTIVE:	PLAIN	sawagu daroo	sawaganai daroo
	FORMAL	sawagu deshoo	sawaganai deshoo
VOLITIONAL:	PLAIN	sawagoo	
	FORMAL	sawagimashoo	

	Affirmative		*Affirmative*
POTENTIAL	sawageru	HONORIFIC	osawagi ni naru
			osawagi nasaru
PASSIVE	sawagareru	HUMBLE	osawagi suru
			osawagi itasu
CAUSATIVE	sawagaseru		
CAUS. PASSIVE	sawagaserareru		
	sawagasareru		

Examples:

1. *Kyooshitsu de sawaganaide kudasai.*
   Don't make a ruckus in the classroom.
2. *O-sake o nonde, sawaide iru hito wa dare desu ka.*
   Who is that drunk making a nuisance of himself?
3. *Sakuya wa mune ga sawaide nemurenakatta.*
   Last night I felt restless and could not sleep.
4. *Watashi ga sawaida ra, doroboo wa nigete itta.*
   When I made lots of noise, the thief ran away.
5. *Sawagu na, ochitsuke yo.*
   Keep calm, and don't get excited.

縛る to tie, bind: (trans.)

		Affirmative	*Negative*
PLAIN FORM:	PRESENT	shibaru	shibaranai
	PAST	shibatta	shibaranakatta
MASU FORM:	PRESENT	shibarimasu	shibarimasen
	PAST	shibarimashita	shibarimasen deshita
IMPERATIVE		shibare	shibaru na
TE FORM		shibatte	shibaranakute
CONDITIONAL:	PLAIN	shibareba	shibaranakereba
		shibatta ra	shibaranakatta ra
	FORMAL	shibarimashita ra	shibarimasen deshita ra
PRESUMPTIVE:	PLAIN	shibaru daroo	shibaranai daroo
	FORMAL	shibaru deshoo	shibaranai deshoo
VOLITIONAL:	PLAIN	shibaroo	
	FORMAL	shibarimashoo	

	Affirmative		*Affirmative*
POTENTIAL	shibareru	HONORIFIC	oshibari ni naru
			oshibari nasaru
PASSIVE	shibarareru	HUMBLE	oshibari suru
			oshibari itasu
CAUSATIVE	shibaraseru		
CAUS. PASSIVE	shibaraserareru		
	shibarasareru		

Examples:

1. *Gootoo ni ryoote o shibarareta.*
   Both my hands were bound by the burglar.
2. *Inu o kui ni shibatte oita.*
   I tied the dog to a post.
3. *Kare wa ichinichi-juu shigoto ni shibararete ita.*
   He was tied up with work all day.
4. *Dooshite shuushoku shinai'n desu ka.*
   Why don't you find work?
   Jikan ni shibarareru no wa kirai desu.
   I hate to be bound by time.

shikaru

叱る to scold: (trans.)

		Affirmative	*Negative*
PLAIN FORM:	PRESENT	shikaru	shikaranai
	PAST	shikatta	shikaranakatta
MASU FORM:	PRESENT	shikarimasu	shikarimasen
	PAST	shikarimashita	shikarimasen deshita
IMPERATIVE		shikare	shikaru na
TE FORM		shikatte	shikaranakute
CONDITIONAL:	PLAIN	shikareba	shikaranakereba
		shikatta ra	shikaranakatta ra
	FORMAL	shikarimashita ra	shikarimasen deshita ra
PRESUMPTIVE:	PLAIN	shikaru daroo	shikaranai daroo
	FORMAL	shikaru deshoo	shikaranai deshoo
VOLITIONAL:	PLAIN	shikaroo	
	FORMAL	shikarimashoo	

	Affirmative		*Affirmative*
POTENTIAL	shikareru	HONORIFIC	oshikari ni naru
			oshikari nasaru
PASSIVE	shikarareru	HUMBLE	oshikari suru
			oshikari itasu
CAUSATIVE	shikaraseru		
CAUS. PASSIVE	shikaraserareru		
	shikarasareru		

Examples:

1. *Chikoku shite shikarareta.*
   I was scolded for being late.
2. *Anata wa kodomo o shikari-sugiru.*
   You scold the child too much.
3. *Shigoto de sake o nonde, jooshi ni shikarareta.*
   My boss scolded me for drinking on the job.
4. *Shikarareru zo.*
   You'll catch it.
5. *Otoosan wa kibishiku karera o shikarimashita.*
   Father severely scolded them.

敷く　to spread, lay, promulgate (a law): (trans.)

		Affirmative	*Negative*
PLAIN FORM:	PRESENT	shiku	shikanai
	PAST	shiita	shikanakatta
MASU FORM:	PRESENT	shikimasu	shikimasen
	PAST	shikimashita	shikimasen deshita
IMPERATIVE		shike	shiku na
TE FORM		shiite	shikanakute
CONDITIONAL:	PLAIN	shikeba	shikanakereba
		shiita ra	shikanakatta ra
	FORMAL	shikimashita ra	shikimasen deshita ra
PRESUMPTIVE:	PLAIN	shiku daroo	shikanai daroo
	FORMAL	shiku deshoo	shikanai deshoo
VOLITIONAL:	PLAIN	shikoo	
	FORMAL	shikimashoo	

	Affirmative		*Affirmative*
POTENTIAL	shikeru	HONORIFIC	oshiki ni naru
			oshiki nasaru
PASSIVE	shikareru	HUMBLE	oshiki suru
			oshiki itasu
CAUSATIVE	shikaseru		
CAUS. PASSIVE	shikaserareru		
	shikasareru		

Examples:

1. *Nihon-jin wa tatami ni futon o shiite nemasu.*
   Japanese lay out bedding on the tatami and go to sleep.
2. *Yuka ni akai juutan o shiki-tai.*
   I want to lay a red carpet on the floor.
3. *Kare wa nyooboo no shiri ni shikarete iru.*
   He is under his wife's thumb. (*lit.,* flattened by wife's derrière)
4. *Kono machi made tetsudoo o shiku keikaku wa nai.*
   There are no plans to extend the railroad to this town.
5. *Hanran hassei no toki, seifu wa kuni-juu ni kaigenrei o shiku daroo.*
   In case a revolt rises up, the government probably will place the whole country under martial law.

shimaru

閉まる be closed, shut; 締まる be tight, firm, be thrifty: (both intrans.)

		Affirmative	*Negative*
PLAIN FORM:	PRESENT	shimaru	shimaranai
	PAST	shimatta	shimaranakatta
MASU FORM:	PRESENT	shimarimasu	shimarimasen
	PAST	shimarimashita	shimarimasen deshita
IMPERATIVE		shimare	shimaru na
TE FORM		shimatte	shimaranakute
CONDITIONAL:	PLAIN	shimareba	shimaranakereba
		shimatta ra	shimaranakatta ra
	FORMAL	shimarimashita ra	shimarimasen deshita ra
PRESUMPTIVE:	PLAIN	shimaru daroo	shimaranai daroo
	FORMAL	shimaru deshoo	shimaranai deshoo
VOLITIONAL:	PLAIN	shimaroo	
	FORMAL	shimarimashoo	

	Affirmative		*Affirmative*
POTENTIAL	(shimareru)	HONORIFIC	oshimari ni naru
			oshimari nasaru
PASSIVE	(shimarareru)	HUMBLE	(oshimari suru)
			(oshimari itasu)
CAUSATIVE	shimaraseru		
CAUS. PASSIVE	shimaraserareru		

Examples:

1. *Doa wa jidooteki ni shimarimasu.*
   The door shuts automatically.
2. *Toshokan wa roku-ji ni shimaru.*
   The library closes at six o'clock.
3. *Kutsu-himo ga kataku shimatte ite, hodokenai.*
   The shoestring is tied so tightly that I can't undo it.
4. *Shimaranai hanashi da.*
   It is a pointless speech.
5. *Kanojo wa kekkon shite kara shimatte kita.*
   She has become thrifty since her marriage.

しまう to put away, put back, finish, end up doing: (intrans. and trans.)

		Affirmative	*Negative*
PLAIN FORM:	PRESENT	shimau	shimawanai
	PAST	shimatta	shimawanakatta
MASU FORM:	PRESENT	shimaimasu	shimaimasen
	PAST	shimaimashita	shimaimasen deshita
IMPERATIVE		shimae	shimau na
TE FORM		shimatte	shimawanakute
CONDITIONAL:	PLAIN	shimaeba	shimawanakereba
		shimatta ra	shimawanakatta ra
	FORMAL	shimaimashita ra	shimaimasen deshita ra
PRESUMPTIVE:	PLAIN	shimau daroo	shimawanai daroo
	FORMAL	shimau deshoo	shimawanai deshoo
VOLITIONAL:	PLAIN	shimaoo	
	FORMAL	shimaimashoo	

	Affirmative		*Affirmative*
POTENTIAL	shimaeru	HONORIFIC	oshimai ni naru
			oshimai nasaru
PASSIVE	shimawareru	HUMBLE	oshimai suru
			oshimai itasu
CAUSATIVE	shimawaseru		
CAUS. PASSIVE	shimawaserareru		
	shimawasareru		

Examples:

1. *Kore o tsukue no hikidashi ni shimatte kudasai.*
   Please put this away in the desk drawer.
2. *Jisho o tsukutta ra, honbako ni shimai-nasai.*
   Put the dictionary back in the bookcase after using it.
3. *Shukudai o yatte shimaimashita.*
   I have finished my homework.
4. *Kono shoosetsu o yonde shimatta.*
   I finished reading this novel.
5. *Kinoo katta keeki o zenbu tabete shimatta.*
   I've eaten up all the cake I bought yesterday.

閉める *or* 締める to shut, close, tie, fasten; 占める to take, hold, occupy: (both trans.)

		Affirmative	*Negative*
PLAIN FORM:	PRESENT	shimeru	shimenai
	PAST	shimeta	shimenakatta
MASU FORM:	PRESENT	shimemasu	shimemasen
	PAST	shimemashita	shimemasen deshita
IMPERATIVE		shimero	shimeru na
TE FORM		shimete	shimenakute
CONDITIONAL:	PLAIN	shimereba	shimenakereba
		shimeta ra	shimenakatta ra
	FORMAL	shimemashita ra	shimemasen deshita ra
PRESUMPTIVE:	PLAIN	shimeru daroo	shimenai daroo
	FORMAL	shimeru deshoo	shimenai deshoo
VOLITIONAL:	PLAIN	shimeyoo	
	FORMAL	shimemashoo	

	Affirmative		*Affirmative*
POTENTIAL	shimerareru shimereru	HONORIFIC	oshime ni naru oshime nasaru
PASSIVE	shimerareru	HUMBLE	oshime suru oshime itasu
CAUSATIVE	shimesaseru		
CAUS. PASSIVE	shimesaserareru		

Examples:

1. *Mado o shimete kudasai.*
   Please close the window.
2. *Kare wa akai nekutai o shimete imasu.*
   He is wearing a red tie.
3. *Suidoo no sen o shime-wasureta.*
   I forgot to turn off the water.
4. *Kare wa kaisha de juuyoo na chii o shimete iru.*
   He has an important position in the firm.
5. *Denki seihin wa yushutsu no roku-wari o shimete iru.*
   Electrical appliances hold a sixty-percent share of our exports.

示す to show, indicate, point out: (trans.)

		Affirmative	*Negative*
PLAIN FORM:	PRESENT	shimesu	shimesanai
	PAST	shimeshita	shimesanakatta
MASU FORM:	PRESENT	shimeshimasu	shimeshimasen
	PAST	shimeshimashita	shimeshimasen deshita
IMPERATIVE		shimese	shimesu na
TE FORM		shimeshite	shimesanakute
CONDITIONAL:	PLAIN	shimeseba	shimesanakereba
		shimeshita ra	shimesanakatta ra
	FORMAL	shimeshimashita ra	shimeshimasen deshita ra
PRESUMPTIVE:	PLAIN	shimesu daroo	shimesanai daroo
	FORMAL	shimesu deshoo	shimesanai deshoo
VOLITIONAL:	PLAIN	shimesoo	
	FORMAL	shimeshimashoo	

	Affirmative		*Affirmative*
POTENTIAL	shimeseru	HONORIFIC	oshimeshi ni naru
			oshimeshi nasaru
PASSIVE	shimesareru	HUMBLE	oshimeshi suru
			oshimeshi itasu
CAUSATIVE	shimesaseru		
CAUS. PASSIVE	shimesaserareru		

Examples:

1. *Ondokei wa reika juu-do o shimeshita.*
   The thermometer indicated ten degrees below zero.
2. *Shachoo wa watashi no keikaku ni nanshoku o oshimeshi ni narimashita.*
   The company president showed his disapproval of my plan.
3. *Kare wa watashi no itta koto ni kyoomi o shimesanakatta.*
   He showed no interest in what I said.
4. *Anata ni tehon o shimeshimashoo.*
   I will give you a good example.
5. *Sore ga chizu no doko ni aru ka shimeshite kudasai.*
   Please show me where it is on the map.

信じる to believe, be confident of: (trans.)

		Affirmative	*Negative*
PLAIN FORM:	PRESENT	shinjiru	shinjinai
	PAST	shinjita	shinjinakatta
MASU FORM:	PRESENT	shinjimasu	shinjimasen
	PAST	shinjimashita	shinjimasen deshita
IMPERATIVE		shinjiro	shinjiru na
TE FORM		shinjite	shinjinakute
CONDITIONAL:	PLAIN	shinjireba	shinjinakereba
		shinjita ra	shinjinakatta ra
	FORMAL	shinjimashita ra	shinjimasen deshita ra
PRESUMPTIVE:	PLAIN	shinjiru daroo	shinjinai daroo
	FORMAL	shinjiru deshoo	shinjinai deshoo
VOLITIONAL:	PLAIN	shinjiyoo	
	FORMAL	shinjimashoo	

	Affirmative		*Affirmative*
POTENTIAL	shinjirareru	HONORIFIC	oshinji ni naru
	shinjireru		oshinji nasaru
PASSIVE	shinjirareru	HUMBLE	oshinji suru
			oshinji itasu
CAUSATIVE	shinjisaseru		
CAUS. PASSIVE	shinjisaserareru		

Examples:

1. *Watashi wa kanojo no seikoo o shinjite imasu.*
   I am sure she will succeed.
2. *Kare no iu koto wa shinjiraremasen.*
   I can't believe what he says.
3. *Tooji chikyuu wa taira da to shinjirarete ita.*
   In those days, the earth was believed to be flat.
4. *Watashi wa otto o shinjite imasu.*
   I trust my husband.
5. *Kanojo wa hito no kotoba o sugu shinji-yasui.*
   She easily believes other people's stories.

死ぬ to die, pass away: (intrans.)

		Affirmative	*Negative*
PLAIN FORM:	PRESENT	shinu	shinanai
	PAST	shinda	shinanakatta
MASU FORM:	PRESENT	shinimasu	shinimasen
	PAST	shinimashita	shinimasen deshita
IMPERATIVE		shine	shinu na
TE FORM		shinde	shinanakute
CONDITIONAL:	PLAIN	shineba	shinanakereba
		shinda ra	shinanakatta ra
	FORMAL	shinimashita ra	shinimasen deshita ra
PRESUMPTIVE:	PLAIN	shinu daroo	shinanai daroo
	FORMAL	shinu deshoo	shinanai deshoo
VOLITIONAL:	PLAIN	shinoo	
	FORMAL	shinimashoo	

	Affirmative		*Affirmative*
POTENTIAL	shineru	HONORIFIC	onakunari ni naru
			onakunari nasaru
PASSIVE	shinareru	HUMBLE	(onakunari suru)
			(onakunari itasu)
CAUSATIVE	shinaseru		
CAUS. PASSIVE	shinaserareru		
	shinasareru		

Examples:

1. *Watashi ga jus-sai datta toki, kootsuu-jiko de haha wa shinda.*
   My mother died in a traffic accident when I was ten years old.
2. *Chichi ga shinde kara go-nen ni naru.*
   It has been five years since my father died.
3. *Sonna koto o suru yori shinda hoo ga ii.*
   I would rather die than do such a thing.
4. *Kono e wa shinde imasu.*
   There is no life in this picture.
5. *Okashikute shini-soo deshita.*
   I nearly died of laughter.

調べる to investigate, study, search, check up: (trans.)

		Affirmative	*Negative*
PLAIN FORM:	PRESENT	shiraberu	shirabenai
	PAST	shirabeta	shirabenakatta
MASU FORM:	PRESENT	shirabemasu	shirabemasen
	PAST	shirabemashita	shirabemasen deshita
IMPERATIVE		shirabero	shiraberu na
TE FORM		shirabete	shirabenakute
CONDITIONAL:	PLAIN	shirabereba	shirabenakereba
		shirabeta ra	shirabenakatta ra
	FORMAL	shirabemashita ra	shirabemasen deshita ra
PRESUMPTIVE:	PLAIN	shiraberu daroo	shirabenai daroo
	FORMAL	shiraberu deshoo	shirabenai deshoo
VOLITIONAL:	PLAIN	shirabeyoo	
	FORMAL	shirabemashoo	

	Affirmative		*Affirmative*
POTENTIAL	shiraberareru	HONORIFIC	oshirabe ni naru
	shirabereru		oshirabe nasaru
PASSIVE	shiraberareru	HUMBLE	oshirabe suru
			oshirabe itasu
CAUSATIVE	shirabesaseru		
CAUS. PASSIVE	shirabesaserareru		

Examples:

1. *Wakaranai kotoba wa jisho de shirabero.*
   Look up in the dictionary any words you don't know.
2. *Keisatsu ga hannin o shirabete iru.*
   The police are interrogating the suspect.
3. *Kare wa kekkan ga aru ka doo ka kikai o shirabeta.*
   He inspected the machines for defects.
4. *Watashi wa zeikan ni suutsukeesu o shiraberareta.*
   My suitcase was searched by the customs officer.
5. *Kare wa Nihon no shuukyoo ni tsuite shiraberu tame ni toshokan e itta.*
   He went to the library to study about Japanese religion.

知る to know, become aware of, become familiar with: (trans.)

		Affirmative	*Negative*
PLAIN FORM:	PRESENT	shiru	shiranai
	PAST	shitta	shiranakatta
MASU FORM:	PRESENT	shirimasu	shirimasen
	PAST	shirimashita	shirimasen deshita
IMPERATIVE		shire	shiru na
TE FORM		shitte	shiranakute
CONDITIONAL:	PLAIN	shireba	shiranakereba
		shitta ra	shiranakatta ra
	FORMAL	shirimashita ra	shirimasen deshita ra
PRESUMPTIVE:	PLAIN	shiru daroo	shiranai daroo
	FORMAL	shiru deshoo	shiranai deshoo
VOLITIONAL:	PLAIN	shiroo	
	FORMAL	shirimashoo	

	Affirmative		*Affirmative*
POTENTIAL	shireru	HONORIFIC	oshiri ni naru
			oshiri nasaru
			gozonji de irassharu
PASSIVE	shirareru	HUMBLE	zonjiru
			shoochi suru
			shoochi itasu
CAUSATIVE	shiraseru		
CAUS. PASSIVE	shiraserareru		
	shirasareru		

Examples:

1. *Anata wa Nihon-go o shitte imasu ka.*
   Do you know Japanese?
   Hai, shitte imasu.
   Yes, I do.
   Iie, shirimasen.
   No, I don't.
2. *Kare wa jibun no ketten o shiranai.*
   He is not aware of his own faults.
3. *Sore wa watashi no shitta koto ja nai.*
   That's none of my business.

従う to follow, obey, go along with: (intrans.)

		Affirmative	*Negative*
PLAIN FORM:	PRESENT	shitagau	shitagawanai
	PAST	shitagatta	shitagawanakatta
MASU FORM:	PRESENT	shitagaimasu	shitagaimasen
	PAST	shitagaimashita	shitagaimasen deshita
IMPERATIVE		shitagae	shitagau na
TE FORM		shitagatte	shitagawanakute
CONDITIONAL:	PLAIN	shitagaeba	shitagawanakereba
		shitagatta ra	shitagawanakatta ra
	FORMAL	shitagaimashita ra	shitagaimasen deshita ra
PRESUMPTIVE:	PLAIN	shitagau daroo	shitagawanai daroo
	FORMAL	shitagau deshoo	shitagawanai deshoo
VOLITIONAL:	PLAIN	shitagaoo	
	FORMAL	shitagaimashoo	

	Affirmative		*Affirmative*
POTENTIAL	shitagaeru	HONORIFIC	oshitagai ni naru
			oshitagai nasaru
PASSIVE	shitagawareru	HUMBLE	oshitagai suru
			oshitagai itasu
CAUSATIVE	shitagawaseru		
CAUS. PASSIVE	shitagawaserareru		
	shitagawasareru		

Examples:

1. *Kisoku ni wa shitagawanakereba narimasen.*
   One must abide by the rules.
2. *Watashi-tachi wa annai-nin ni shitagatte, Kyooto o ryokoo shita.*
   We toured Kyoto, following the guide.
3. *Ryuukoo ga kawaru to, kanojo wa itsumo sore ni shitagaimasu.*
   When fashion changes, she always goes along with it.
4. *Kimi no chuukoku ni shitagaimasu.*
   I will follow your advice.
5. *Ryooshin no iu koto ni shitagatta hoo ga ii yo.*
   You had better listen to what your parents say.

沈める to sink, submerge; 静める to quiet, calm, suppress: (both trans.)

		Affirmative	*Negative*
PLAIN FORM:	PRESENT	shizumeru	shizumenai
	PAST	shizumeta	shizumenakatta
MASU FORM:	PRESENT	shizumemasu	shizumemasen
	PAST	shizumemashita	shizumemasen deshita
IMPERATIVE		shizumero	shizumeru na
TE FORM		shizumete	shizumenakute
CONDITIONAL:	PLAIN	shizumereba	shizumenakereba
		shizumeta ra	shizumenakatta ra
	FORMAL	shizumemashita ra	shizumemasen deshita ra
PRESUMPTIVE:	PLAIN	shizumeru daroo	shizumenai daroo
	FORMAL	shizumeru deshoo	shizumenai deshoo
VOLITIONAL:	PLAIN	shizumeyoo	
	FORMAL	shizumemashoo	

	Affirmative		*Affirmative*
POTENTIAL	shizumerareru shizumereru	HONORIFIC	oshizume ni naru oshizume nasaru
PASSIVE	shizumerareru	HUMBLE	oshizume suru oshizume itasu
CAUSATIVE	shizumesaseru		
CAUS. PASSIVE	shizumesaserareru		

Examples:

1. *Sono sensuikan wa suu-seki no senpaku o shizumeta.*
   That submarine sank several ships.
2. *Kookuu-bokan wa sensuikan ni shizumerareta.*
   The aircraft carrier was sunk by the submarine.
3. *Gen-seifu de wa mohaya bukka o shizumeraremasen.*
   The present government cannot suppress prices any longer.
4. *Kare no koofun o shizumeru no wa muzukashi-soo desu.*
   It seems difficult to calm down his excitement.
5. *Keisatsu wa demotai o shizumerarenakatta.*
   The police could not pacify the demonstrators.

沈む to sink, feel depressed (intrans.)

		Affirmative	*Negative*
PLAIN FORM:	PRESENT	shizumu	shizumanai
	PAST	shizunda	shizumanakatta
MASU FORM:	PRESENT	shizumimasu	shizumimasen
	PAST	shizumimashita	shizumimasen deshita
IMPERATIVE		shizume	shizumu na
TE FORM		shizunde	shizumanakute
CONDITIONAL:	PLAIN	shizumeba	shizumanakereba
		shizunda ra	shizumanakatta ra
	FORMAL	shizumimashita ra	shizumimasen deshita ra
PRESUMPTIVE:	PLAIN	shizumu daroo	shizumanai daroo
	FORMAL	shizumu deshoo	shizumanai deshoo
VOLITIONAL:	PLAIN	shizumoo	
	FORMAL	shizumimashoo	

	Affirmative		*Affirmative*
POTENTIAL	(shizumeru)	HONORIFIC	oshizumi ni naru
			oshizumi nasaru
PASSIVE	(shizumareru)	HUMBLE	(oshizumi suru)
			(oshizumi itasu)
CAUSATIVE	shizumaseru		
CAUS. PASSIVE	shizumaserareru		
	shizumasareru		

Examples:

1. *Taiyoo wa higashi ni nobori, nishi ni shizumu.*
   The sun rises in the east and sets in the west.
2. *Taifuu de fune ga shizunda.*
   The ship sank in the typhoon.
3. *Kanojo wa kanashimi ni shizunde imasu.*
   She is deep in sorrow.
4. *Tochi ga nana-senchi shizunda.*
   The ground sank seven centimeters.
5. *Kodai no fune ga kaitei ni shizunde iru.*
   An ancient ship lays sunken on the bottom of the sea.

育てる to bring up, raise, rear: (trans.)

		Affirmative	*Negative*
PLAIN FORM:	PRESENT	sodateru	sodatenai
	PAST	sodateta	sodatenakatta
MASU FORM:	PRESENT	sodatemasu	sodatemasen
	PAST	sodatemashita	sodatemasen deshita
IMPERATIVE		sodatero	sodateru na
TE FORM		sodatete	sodatenakute
CONDITIONAL:	PLAIN	sodatereba	sodatenakereba
		sodateta ra	sodatenakatta ra
	FORMAL	sodatemashita ra	sodatemasen deshita ra
PRESUMPTIVE:	PLAIN	sodateru daroo	sodatenai daroo
	FORMAL	sodateru deshoo	sodatenai deshoo
VOLITIONAL:	PLAIN	sodateyoo	
	FORMAL	sodatemashoo	

	Affirmative		*Affirmative*
POTENTIAL	sodaterareru	HONORIFIC	osodate ni naru
	sodatereru		osodate nasaru
PASSIVE	sodaterareru	HUMBLE	osodate suru
			osodate itasu
CAUSATIVE	sodatesaseru		
CAUS. PASSIVE	sodatesaserareru		

Examples:

1. *Kanojo wa hitori de san-nin no kodomo o sodateta.*
   She brought up three children by herself.
2. *Kare wa ryooshin ni amayakasarete, sodaterareta.*
   He was brought up by parents who spoiled him.
3. *Karera wa nan-zen-too mo no ushi o sodatete iru.*
   They raise thousands of cattle.
4. *Chichi wa bara no hana o daiji ni sodatete imasu.*
   My father carefully tends to his roses.
5. *Otoosan ga kanojo no ongaku no sainoo o sodatemashita.*
   Her father fostered her musical talent.

育つ to grow up, be brought up, be raised: (intrans.)

		Affirmative	*Negative*
PLAIN FORM:	PRESENT	sodatsu	sodatanai
	PAST	sodatta	sodatanakatta
MASU FORM:	PRESENT	sodachimasu	sodachimasen
	PAST	sodachimashita	sodachimasen deshita
IMPERATIVE		sodate	sodatsu na
TE FORM		sodatte	sodatanakute
CONDITIONAL:	PLAIN	sodateba	sodatanakereba
		sodatta ra	sodatanakatta ra
	FORMAL	sodachimashita ra	sodachimasen deshita ra
PRESUMPTIVE:	PLAIN	sodatsu daroo	sodatanai daroo
	FORMAL	sodatsu deshoo	sodatanai deshoo
VOLITIONAL:	PLAIN	sodatoo	
	FORMAL	sodachimashoo	

	Affirmative		*Affirmative*
POTENTIAL	(sodateru)	HONORIFIC	osodachi ni naru
			osodachi nasaru
PASSIVE	(sodatareru)	HUMBLE	(osodachi suru)
			(osodachi itasu)
CAUSATIVE	sodataseru		
CAUS. PASSIVE	sodataserareru		

Examples:

1. *Watashi wa Tookyoo de umarete, Tookyoo de sodachimashita.*
   I was born and brought up in Tokyo.
2. *Tokai de sodatta kodomo wa hiyowa desu.*
   A city-bred child is delicate.
3. *Samui kikoo de wa painappuru wa sodachimasen.*
   Pineapples can't be grown in cold climates.
4. *Kanojo wa rippa na musume ni sodatta.*
   She has grown into a fine girl.
5. *Oya wa nakute mo, ko wa sodatsu.*
   Nature can be a good mother.

過ぎる to pass, exceed; (attached to a verb, adjective, or adverb) to be too ~: (intrans.)*

		Affirmative	*Negative*
PLAIN FORM:	PRESENT	sugiru	suginai
	PAST	sugita	suginakatta
MASU FORM:	PRESENT	sugimasu	sugimasen
	PAST	sugimashita	sugimasen deshita
IMPERATIVE		sugiro	sugiru na
TE FORM		sugite	suginakute
CONDITIONAL:	PLAIN	sugireba	suginakereba
		sugita ra	suginakatta ra
	FORMAL	sugimashita ra	sugimasen deshita ra
PRESUMPTIVE:	PLAIN	sugiru daroo	suginai daroo
	FORMAL	sugiru deshoo	suginai deshoo
VOLITIONAL:	PLAIN	sugiyoo	
	FORMAL	sugimashoo	

	Affirmative		*Affirmative*
POTENTIAL	(sugirareru)	HONORIFIC	osugi ni naru
			osugi nasaru
PASSIVE	(sugirareru)	HUMBLE	(osugi suru)
			(osugi itasu)
CAUSATIVE	sugisaseru		
CAUS. PASSIVE	sugisaserareru		

Examples:

1. *Natsu wa sugita.*
   Summer is over.
2. *Kono kenkyuu o hajimete kara, go-nen ga sugite shimaimashita.*
   Five years have passed since I started this research.
3. *Densha wa ichi-jikan mae ni Oosaka o sugimashita.*
   The train passed Osaka one hour ago.
4. *Kono hon wa watashi ni wa muzukashi-sugiru.*
   This book is too difficult for me.
5. *Kare wa yonjus-sai o sugite iru.*
   He is over forty years old.

* Classified as an intransitive verb, but also used as a transitive verb. (*See* examples 3, 5.)

過ごす to pass time, spend time, get through: (trans.)

		Affirmative	*Negative*
PLAIN FORM:	PRESENT	sugosu	sugosanai
	PAST	sugoshita	sugosanakatta
MASU FORM:	PRESENT	sugoshimasu	sugoshimasen
	PAST	sugoshimashita	sugoshimasen deshita
IMPERATIVE		sugose	sugosu na
TE FORM		sugoshite	sugosanakute
CONDITIONAL:	PLAIN	sugoseba	sugosanakereba
		sugoshita ra	sugosanakatta ra
	FORMAL	sugoshimashita ra	sugoshimasen deshita ra
PRESUMPTIVE:	PLAIN	sugosu daroo	sugosanai daroo
	FORMAL	sugosu deshoo	sugosanai deshoo
VOLITIONAL:	PLAIN	sugosoo	
	FORMAL	sugoshimashoo	

	Affirmative		*Affirmative*
POTENTIAL	sugoseru	HONORIFIC	osugoshi ni naru
			osugoshi nasaru
PASSIVE	sugosareru	HUMBLE	(osugoshi suru)
			(osugoshi itasu)
CAUSATIVE	sugosaseru		
CAUS. PASSIVE	sugosaserareru		

Examples:

1. *Tookyoo de ikka-getsu sugoshimashita.*
   I spent a month in Tokyo.
2. *Sakuban watashi-tachi wa kanojo no uchi de tanoshii toki o sugoshita.*
   We had a good time at her place last night.
3. *Jaa, fuyu-yasumi o tanoshiku sugoshite ne.*
   Well, be sure and have a pleasant winter vacation.
4. *Jikan o muda ni sugosu na.*
   Don't waste your time.
5. *Kore dake no shokuryoo ga areba, fuyu o sugoseru daroo.*
   With this much food, we'll be able to make it through the winter.

好く to like: (trans.); 空く to become empty;* 透く to have gaps, be transparent:* (both intrans.)

		Affirmative	*Negative*
PLAIN FORM:	PRESENT	suku	sukanai
	PAST	suita	sukanakatta
MASU FORM:	PRESENT	sukimasu	sukimasen
	PAST	sukimashita	sukimasen deshita
IMPERATIVE		suke	suku na
TE FORM		suite	sukanakute
CONDITIONAL:	PLAIN	sukeba	sukanakereba
		suita ra	sukanakatta ra
	FORMAL	sukimashita ra	sukimasen deshita ra
PRESUMPTIVE:	PLAIN	suku daroo	sukanai daroo
	FORMAL	suku deshoo	sukanai deshoo
VOLITIONAL:	PLAIN	sukoo	
	FORMAL	sukimashoo	

	Affirmative		*Affirmative*
POTENTIAL	sukeru	HONORIFIC	osuki ni naru
			osuki nasaru
PASSIVE	sukareru	HUMBLE	(osuki suru)
			(osuki itasu)
CAUSATIVE	sukaseru		
CAUS. PASSIVE	sukaserareru		

Examples:

1. *Kare wa minna ni sukarete iru.*
   He is liked by everybody.
2. *Minna ni sukareru hito ni nari-tai.*
   I want to become a person liked by all.
3. *Densha wa konde imashita ka, suite imashita ka.*
   Was the train crowded or was it empty?
4. *Onaka ga suita.*
   I am hungry.
5. *Kare wa ha ga suite iru.*
   He has gaps between his teeth.

* The intransitive verbs *suku* meaning "to become empty" 空く and "to have gaps, be transparent" 透く do not generally use volitional, potential, passive, honorific, humble, causative, or causative passive forms.

住む to live; 済む to end, be over;* 澄む to become clear:*
(all intrans.)

		Affirmative	*Negative*
PLAIN FORM:	PRESENT	sumu	sumanai
	PAST	sunda	sumanakatta
MASU FORM:	PRESENT	sumimasu	sumimasen
	PAST	sumimashita	sumimasen deshita
IMPERATIVE		sume	sumu na
TE FORM		sunde	sumanakute
CONDITIONAL:	PLAIN	sumeba	sumanakereba
		sunda ra	sumanakatta ra
	FORMAL	sumimashita ra	sumimasen deshita ra
PRESUMPTIVE:	PLAIN	sumu daroo	sumanai daroo
	FORMAL	sumu deshoo	sumanai deshoo
VOLITIONAL:	PLAIN	sumoo	
	FORMAL	sumimashoo	

	Affirmative		*Affirmative*
POTENTIAL	sumeru	HONORIFIC	osumi ni naru
			osumi nasaru
PASSIVE	sumareru	HUMBLE	(osumi suru)
			(osumi itasu)
CAUSATIVE	sumaseru		
CAUS. PASSIVE	sumaserareru		
	sumasareru		

Examples:

1. *Ane wa ryooshin to issho ni sunde imasu.*
   My elder sister is living with our parents.
2. *Kaigi wa san-ji ni sumimashita.*
   The meeting ended at three o'clock.
3. *Shigoto ga sunda ra, koohii demo nomi ni ikimashoo.*
   Let's go have some coffee after work.
4. *Kore wa okane de sumu mondai de wa nai.*
   This is not a matter that can be settled with money.
5. *Tsuki ga sunde iru.*
   The moon is shining clear.

* The verbs *sumu* meaning "to end, be over" 済む and "to become clear" 澄む generally do not use the imperative, volitional, potential, passive, humble, or honorific forms.

する to do, make, to have a value, price: (trans. and intrans.)

		Affirmative	*Negative*
PLAIN FORM:	PRESENT	suru	shinai
	PAST	shita	shinakatta
MASU FORM:	PRESENT	shimasu	shimasen
	PAST	shimashita	shimasen deshita
IMPERATIVE		shiro	suru na
TE FORM		shite	shinakute
CONDITIONAL:	PLAIN	sureba	shinakereba
		shita ra	shinakatta ra
	FORMAL	shimashita ra	shimasen deshita ra
PRESUMPTIVE:	PLAIN	suru daroo	shinai daroo
	FORMAL	suru deshoo	shinai deshoo
VOLITIONAL:	PLAIN	shiyoo	
	FORMAL	shimashoo	

	Affirmative		*Affirmative*
POTENTIAL	dekiru	HONORIFIC	nasaru
PASSIVE	sareru	HUMBLE	itasu
CAUSATIVE	saseru		
CAUS. PASSIVE	saserareru		

Examples:

1. *Nichiyoobi ni nani o shimasu ka.*
   What are you going to do on Sunday?
   Suru koto ga ippai arimasu.
   I have many things to do.
2. *Otoosan wa nani o shite imasu ka. (Sensei o shite imasu.)*
   What does your father do? (He is a teacher.)
3. *Watashi wa musuko o isha ni shi-tai.*
   I want my son to become a doctor.
4. *Sono tokei wa ikura shimashita ka.*
   How much did that watch cost?

進める to advance, promote; 勧める to recommend: (both trans.)

		Affirmative	*Negative*
PLAIN FORM:	PRESENT	susumeru	susumenai
	PAST	susumeta	susumenakatta
MASU FORM:	PRESENT	susumemasu	susumemasen
	PAST	susumemashita	susumemasen deshita
IMPERATIVE		susumero	susumeru na
TE FORM		susumete	susumenakute
CONDITIONAL:	PLAIN	susumereba	susumenakereba
		susumeta ra	susumenakatta ra
	FORMAL	susumemashita ra	susumemasen deshita ra
PRESUMPTIVE:	PLAIN	susumeru daroo	susumenai daroo
	FORMAL	susumeru deshoo	susumenai deshoo
VOLITIONAL:	PLAIN	susumeyoo	
	FORMAL	susumemashoo	

	Affirmative		*Affirmative*
POTENTIAL	susumerareru	HONORIFIC	osusume ni naru
	susumereru		osusume nasaru
PASSIVE	susumerareru	HUMBLE	osusume suru
			osusume itasu
CAUSATIVE	susumesaseru		
CAUS. PASSIVE	susumesaserareru		

Examples:

1. *Kono keikaku o susumete kudasai.*
   Please go ahead with this plan.
2. *Kono choomiryoo wa shokuyoku o susumemasu.*
   This seasoning helps improve the flavor. (*lit.*, promotes the appetite)
3. *Tokei o ichi-jikan susumete oita.*
   I set the clock ahead by an hour.
4. *Sensei ga kono jisho o susumete kureta.*
   The teacher recommended this dictionary.
5. *Chichi wa watashi ni gaikoku ryuugaku o susumeta.*
   My father encouraged me to study abroad.

進む to advance, progress, go forward: (intrans.)*

		Affirmative	*Negative*
PLAIN FORM:	PRESENT	susumu	susumanai
	PAST	susunda	susumanakatta
MASU FORM:	PRESENT	susumimasu	susumimasen
	PAST	susumimashita	susumimasen deshita
IMPERATIVE		susume	susumu na
TE FORM		susunde	susumanakute
CONDITIONAL:	PLAIN	susumeba	susumanakereba
		susunda ra	susumanakatta ra
	FORMAL	susumimashita ra	susumimasen deshita ra
PRESUMPTIVE:	PLAIN	susumu daroo	susumanai daroo
	FORMAL	susumu deshoo	susumanai deshoo
VOLITIONAL:	PLAIN	susumoo	
	FORMAL	susumimashoo	

	Affirmative		*Affirmative*
POTENTIAL	susumeru	HONORIFIC	osusumi ni naru
			osusumi nasaru
PASSIVE	susumareru	HUMBLE	(osusumi suru)
			(osusumi itasu)
CAUSATIVE	susumaseru		
CAUS. PASSIVE	susumaserareru		
	susumasareru		

Examples:

1. *Wareware wa hayashi no naka o go-kiro susunda.*
   We advanced five kilometers through the woods.
2. *Kono kuni no kagaku gijutsu wa taihen susunde imasu.*
   Scientific technology is very advanced in this country.
3. *Kooji wa kyuusoku ni susunde iru.*
   The construction work is moving ahead rapidly.
4. *Chikagoro doomo shoku ga susumanai.*
   For some reason, I don't seem to have much of an appetite recently.
5. *Watashi no tokei wa ichinichi ni go-fun susumimasu.*
   My watch gains five minutes a day.

* As with other verbs indicating movement, *susumu* may take a direct object, thus giving an idea of "going through a defined area." (*See* example 1.)

捨てる to throw away, abandon, desert: (trans.)

		Affirmative	*Negative*
PLAIN FORM:	PRESENT	suteru	sutenai
	PAST	suteta	sutenakatta
MASU FORM:	PRESENT	sutemasu	sutemasen
	PAST	sutemashita	sutemasen deshita
IMPERATIVE		sutero	suteru na
TE FORM		sutete	sutenakute
CONDITIONAL:	PLAIN	sutereba	sutenakereba
		suteta ra	sutenakatta ra
	FORMAL	sutemashita ra	sutemasen deshita ra
PRESUMPTIVE:	PLAIN	suteru daroo	sutenai daroo
	FORMAL	suteru deshoo	sutenai deshoo
VOLITIONAL:	PLAIN	suteyoo	
	FORMAL	sutemashoo	

	Affirmative		*Affirmative*
POTENTIAL	suterareru sutereru	HONORIFIC	osute ni naru osute nasaru
PASSIVE	suterareru	HUMBLE	osute suru osute itasu
CAUSATIVE	sutesaseru		
CAUS. PASSIVE	sutesaserareru		

Examples:

1. *Dooro ni gomi o sutenaide kudasai.*
   Please don't litter in the street.
2. *Kono koinu wa dare ga suteta no daroo ka.*
   I wonder who abandoned this puppy?
3. *Mada tsukaeru mono o sutete wa ikemasen.*
   Don't throw away things you can still use.
4. *Kare wa chii o suteta.*
   He threw away his social standing.
5. *Kanojo wa otto ni suterareta.*
   She was deserted by her husband.

吸う to take a breath, inhale, suck, absorb: (trans.)

		Affirmative	*Negative*
PLAIN FORM:	PRESENT	suu	suwanai
	PAST	sutta	suwanakatta
MASU FORM:	PRESENT	suimasu	suimasen
	PAST	suimashita	suimasen deshita
IMPERATIVE		sue	suu na
TE FORM		sutte	suwanakute
CONDITIONAL:	PLAIN	sueba	suwanakereba
		sutta ra	suwanakatta ra
	FORMAL	suimashita ra	suimasen deshita ra
PRESUMPTIVE:	PLAIN	suu daroo	suwanai daroo
	FORMAL	suu deshoo	suwanai deshoo
VOLITIONAL:	PLAIN	suoo	
	FORMAL	suimashoo	

	Affirmative		*Affirmative*
POTENTIAL	sueru	HONORIFIC	osui ni naru
			osui nasaru
PASSIVE	suwareru	HUMBLE	(osui suru)
			(osui itasu)
CAUSATIVE	suwaseru		
CAUS. PASSIVE	suwaserareru		
	suwasareru		

Examples:

1. *Koko de tabako o sutte mo ii desu ka.*
   May I smoke here?
2. *Fukaku iki o sutte, soshite yukkuri haite kudasai.*
   Please breathe in deeply and then exhale slowly.
3. *Akachan ga okaasan no oppai o suu.*
   A baby suckles at her mother's breast.
4. *Kono suitori-gami wa inku o yoku suimasu.*
   This blotting paper absorbs ink well.
5. *Onna wa kane o sui-torareta.*
   The woman had her money swindled out of her.

座る to sit down, take a seat: (intrans.)

		Affirmative	*Negative*
PLAIN FORM:	PRESENT	suwaru	suwaranai
	PAST	suwatta	suwaranakatta
MASU FORM:	PRESENT	suwarimasu	suwarimasen
	PAST	suwarimashita	suwarimasen deshita
IMPERATIVE		suware	suwaru na
TE FORM		suwatte	suwaranakute
CONDITIONAL:	PLAIN	suwareba	suwaranakereba
		suwatta ra	suwaranakatta ra
	FORMAL	suwarimashita ra	suwarimasen deshita ra
PRESUMPTIVE:	PLAIN	suwaru daroo	suwaranai daroo
	FORMAL	suwaru deshoo	suwaranai deshoo
VOLITIONAL:	PLAIN	suwaroo	
	FORMAL	suwarimashoo	

	Affirmative		*Affirmative*
POTENTIAL	suwareru	HONORIFIC	osuwari ni naru
			osuwari nasaru
PASSIVE	suwarareru	HUMBLE	(osuwari suru)
			(osuwari itasu)
CAUSATIVE	suwaraseru		
CAUS. PASSIVE	suwaraserareru		
	suwarasareru		

Examples:

1. *Doozo koko ni suwatte kudasai.*
   Please sit down here.
2. *Doozo osuwari kudasai.*
   Please have a seat.
3. *Roojin wa yuka ni suwatte ita.*
   The old man was sitting on the floor.
4. *Kodomo wa piano ni mukatte suwatta.*
   The child sat down at the piano.
5. *Kono sofaa ni san-nin wa suwarenai.*
   Three people can't sit on this sofa.

食べる　to eat, to live on: (trans.)

		Affirmative	*Negative*
PLAIN FORM:	PRESENT	taberu	tabenai
	PAST	tabeta	tabenakatta
MASU FORM:	PRESENT	tabemasu	tabemasen
	PAST	tabemashita	tabemasen deshita
IMPERATIVE		tabero	taberu na
TE FORM		tabete	tabenakute
CONDITIONAL:	PLAIN	tabereba	tabenakereba
		tabeta ra	tabenakatta ra
	FORMAL	tabemashita ra	tabemasen deshita ra
PRESUMPTIVE:	PLAIN	taberu daroo	tabenai daroo
	FORMAL	taberu deshoo	tabenai deshoo
VOLITIONAL:	PLAIN	tabeyoo	
	FORMAL	tabemashoo	

	Affirmative		*Affirmative*
POTENTIAL	taberareru	HONORIFIC	otabe ni naru
	tabereru		otabe nasaru
			meshiagaru
PASSIVE	taberareru	HUMBLE	itadaku
CAUSATIVE	tabesaseru		
CAUS. PASSIVE	tabesaserareru		

Examples:

1. *Nihon-jin wa shushoku to shite, kome o taberu.*
   For Japanese, rice is a staple food.
2. *Kono kinoko wa taberarenai.*
   This mushroom is not edible.
3. *Asa-gohan o tabemashita ka.*
   Have you had your breakfast?
4. *Hito-tsuki go-man en de wa tabete ikenai.*
   We cannot live on fifty thousand yen a month.
5. *Nante kawaii akachan deshoo. Tabete shimai-tai wa.*
   What a cute baby! He's so adorable! (*lit.*, like to eat up)

たまる to be saved, accumulated, piled up: (intrans.)

		Affirmative	Negative
PLAIN FORM:	PRESENT	tamaru	tamaranai
	PAST	tamatta	tamaranakatta
MASU FORM:	PRESENT	tamarimasu	tamarimasen
	PAST	tamarimashita	tamarimasen deshita
IMPERATIVE		(tamare)	(tamaru na)
TE FORM		tamatte	tamaranakute
CONDITIONAL:	PLAIN	tamareba	tamaranakereba
		tamatta ra	tamaranakatta ra
	FORMAL	tamarimashita ra	tamarimasen deshita ra
PRESUMPTIVE:	PLAIN	tamaru daroo	tamaranai daroo
	FORMAL	tamaru deshoo	tamaranai deshoo
VOLITIONAL:	PLAIN	(tamaroo)	
	FORMAL	(tamarimashoo)	

	Affirmative		Affirmative
POTENTIAL	(tamareru)	HONORIFIC	otamari ni naru
			otamari nasaru
PASSIVE	(tamarareru)	HUMBLE	(otamari suru)
			(otamari itasu)
CAUSATIVE	tamaraseru		
CAUS. PASSIVE	tamaraserareru		

Examples:

1. *Ichi-man en tamatta.*
   I have saved ten thousand yen.
2. *Tsukue no ue ni hokori ga tamatte iru.*
   Dust has accumulated on the desk.
3. *Yachin ga nika-getsu bun tamatte iru.*
   I am two months behind with my rent.
4. *Shakkin ga juu-man en tamatta.*
   The debt has grown to one hundred thousand yen.
5. *Kare wa shigoto ga tamatte ita node paatii ni ikanakatta.*
   He had so much work left to do that he didn't go to the party.

ためる   to save, store up, accumulate: (trans.)

		Affirmative	*Negative*
PLAIN FORM:	PRESENT	tameru	tamenai
	PAST	tameta	tamenakatta
MASU FORM:	PRESENT	tamemasu	tamemasen
	PAST	tamemashita	tamemasen deshita
IMPERATIVE		tamero	tameru na
TE FORM		tamete	tamenakute
CONDITIONAL:	PLAIN	tamereba	tamenakereba
		tameta ra	tamenakatta ra
	FORMAL	tamemashita ra	tamemasen deshita ra
PRESUMPTIVE:	PLAIN	tameru daroo	tamenai daroo
	FORMAL	tameru deshoo	tamenai deshoo
VOLITIONAL:	PLAIN	tameyoo	
	FORMAL	tamemashoo	

	Affirmative		*Affirmative*
POTENTIAL	tamerareru	HONORIFIC	otame ni naru
	tamereru		otame nasaru
PASSIVE	tamerareru	HUMBLE	(otame suru)
			(otame itasu)
CAUSATIVE	tamesaseru		
CAUS. PASSIVE	tamesaserareru		

Examples:

1. *Okane o tamete, terebi o kau tsumori desu.*
   I intend to save my money to buy a TV set.
2. *Kono chihoo de wa amamizu o tamete, sore o inryoo-sui ni tsukau.*
   In this area they save rainwater and use it for drinking water.
3. *Kare wa shigoto o tame-sugita.*
   He has let too much work pile up.
4. *Wakai uchi ni chishiki o tamete oke.*
   Accumulate knowledge while you are young.
5. *Risu wa konomi o tameru.*
   A squirrel stores away nuts.

試す to test, try: (trans.)

		Affirmative	*Negative*
PLAIN FORM:	PRESENT	tamesu	tamesanai
	PAST	tameshita	tamesanakatta
MASU FORM:	PRESENT	tameshimasu	tameshimasen
	PAST	tameshimashita	tameshimasen deshita
IMPERATIVE		tamese	tamesu na
TE FORM		tameshite	tamesanakute
CONDITIONAL:	PLAIN	tameseba	tamesanakereba
		tameshita ra	tamesanakatta ra
	FORMAL	tameshimashita ra	tameshimasen deshita ra
PRESUMPTIVE:	PLAIN	tamesu daroo	tamesanai daroo
	FORMAL	tamesu deshoo	tamesanai deshoo
VOLITIONAL:	PLAIN	tamesoo	
	FORMAL	tameshimashoo	

	Affirmative		*Affirmative*
POTENTIAL	tameseru	HONORIFIC	otameshi ni naru
			otameshi nasaru
PASSIVE	tamesareru	HUMBLE	otameshi suru
			otameshi itasu
CAUSATIVE	tamesaseru		
CAUS. PASSIVE	tamesaserareru		

Examples:

1. *Watashi wa hito o tamesu no wa kirai desu.*
   I don't like to test people.
2. *Shuppatsu suru mae ni bureeki o tameshita hoo ga ii.*
   You had better check the brakes before you start out.
3. *Kare wa sono kikai ga ugoku ka doo ka moo ichido tameshita.*
   He tested that machine once more to see if it would work.
4. *Nando mo tameshite mita ga, seikoo shinakatta.*
   I tried and tried, but could not succeed.
5. *Saisho umaku ikanakatta ra, moo ichido tameshite goran.*
   If at first you don't succeed, try again.

頼む to ask a person to do, reserve (tickets), to rely on: (trans.)

		Affirmative	*Negative*
PLAIN FORM:	PRESENT	tanomu	tanomanai
	PAST	tanonda	tanomanakatta
MASU FORM:	PRESENT	tanomimasu	tanomimasen
	PAST	tanomimashita	tanomimasen deshita
IMPERATIVE		tanome	tanomu na
TE FORM		tanonde	tanomanakute
CONDITIONAL:	PLAIN	tanomeba	tanomanakereba
		tanonda ra	tanomanakatta ra
	FORMAL	tanomimashita ra	tanomimasen deshita ra
PRESUMPTIVE:	PLAIN	tanomu daroo	tanomanai daroo
	FORMAL	tanomu deshoo	tanomanai deshoo
VOLITIONAL:	PLAIN	tanomoo	
	FORMAL	tanomimashoo	

	Affirmative		*Affirmative*
POTENTIAL	tanomeru	HONORIFIC	otanomi ni naru
			otanomi nasaru
PASSIVE	tanomareru	HUMBLE	otanomi suru
			otanomi itasu
CAUSATIVE	tanomaseru		
CAUS. PASSIVE	tanomaserareru		
	tanomasareru		

Examples:

1. *Kare ni tanomareru to, iya to ienai.*
   I can't say no if he asks me.
2. *Kare ni hon o kashite kure to tanonda ga, kotowarareta.*
   I asked him to lend me his book, but he refused.
3. *Tanomu kara watashi ni kamawanaide kudasai.*
   I'm asking you to please leave me alone.
4. *Ongaku-kai no kippu o tanomimashita ka.*
   Have you reserved tickets for the concert?
5. *Karera wa kazu o tanonde, suki-katte o shita.*
   Relying on the strength of numbers, they did whatever they liked.

楽しむ to enjoy oneself, take pleasure in, have a good time: (trans.)

		Affirmative	*Negative*
PLAIN FORM:	PRESENT	tanoshimu	tanoshimanai
	PAST	tanoshinda	tanoshimanakatta
MASU FORM:	PRESENT	tanoshimimasu	tanoshimimasen
	PAST	tanoshimimashita	tanoshimimasen deshita
IMPERATIVE		tanoshime	tanoshimu na
TE FORM		tanoshinde	tanoshimanakute
CONDITIONAL:	PLAIN	tanoshimeba	tanoshimanakereba
		tanoshinda ra	tanoshimanakatta ra
	FORMAL	tanoshimimashita ra	tanoshimimasen deshita ra
PRESUMPTIVE:	PLAIN	tanoshimu daroo	tanoshimanai daroo
	FORMAL	tanoshimu deshoo	tanoshimanai deshoo
VOLITIONAL:	PLAIN	tanoshimoo	
	FORMAL	tanoshimimashoo	

	Affirmative		*Affirmative*
POTENTIAL	tanoshimeru	HONORIFIC	otanoshimi ni naru
			otanoshimi nasaru
PASSIVE	tanoshimareru	HUMBLE	(otanoshimi suru)
			(otanoshimi itasu)
CAUSATIVE	tanoshimaseru		
CAUS. PASSIVE	tanoshimaserareru		

Examples:

1. *Watashi wa tokidoki manga o yonde tanoshimimasu.*
   I sometimes amuse myself by reading comics.
2. *Nichiyoobi ni doraibu o tanoshimoo to omotte iru.*
   I've been thinking about going for a drive on Sunday.
3. *Kare wa gaikoku-kitte o atsumete tanoshinde ita.*
   He took delight in collecting foreign stamps.
4. *Yamada-san wa hitori de terebi o mite tanoshinde imasu.*
   Mr. Yamada is having a good time watching television by himself.
5. *Paatii o tanoshimimashita ka. (Juubun tanoshimimashita.)*
   Did you enjoy the party? (I enjoyed it very much.)

倒れる to fall down, collapse: (intrans.)

		Affirmative	*Negative*
PLAIN FORM:	PRESENT	taoreru	taorenai
	PAST	taoreta	taorenakatta
MASU FORM:	PRESENT	taoremasu	taoremasen
	PAST	taoremashita	taoremasen deshita
IMPERATIVE		taorero	taoreru na
TE FORM		taorete	taorenakute
CONDITIONAL:	PLAIN	taorereba	taorenakereba
		taoreta ra	taorenakatta ra
	FORMAL	taoremashita ra	taoremasen deshita ra
PRESUMPTIVE:	PLAIN	taoreru daroo	taorenai daroo
	FORMAL	taoreru deshoo	taorenai deshoo
VOLITIONAL:	PLAIN	taoreyoo	
	FORMAL	taoremashoo	

	Affirmative		*Affirmative*
POTENTIAL	taorerareru	HONORIFIC	otaore ni naru
			otaore nasaru
PASSIVE	taorerareru	HUMBLE	(otaore suru)
			(otaore itasu)
CAUSATIVE	taoresaseru		
CAUS. PASSIVE	taoresaserareru		

Examples:

1. *Haha wa ki o ushinatte, yuka ni taoremashita.*
   My mother lost consciousness and fell to the floor.
2. *Kinoo no jishin de too ga taoreta.*
   The tower was toppled by the earthquake yesterday.
3. *Aomuke ni taoremashita.*
   I fell flat on my back.
4. *Chichi wa hiroo de taoreta.*
   My father collapsed from exhaustion.
5. *Gen-naikaku wa kantan ni wa taorenai daroo.*
   The present Cabinet probably will not collapse easily.

倒す to throw down, knock down, defeat, not repay: (trans.)

		Affirmative	*Negative*
PLAIN FORM:	PRESENT	taosu	taosanai
	PAST	taoshita	taosanakatta
MASU FORM:	PRESENT	taoshimasu	taoshimasen
	PAST	taoshimashita	taoshimasen deshita
IMPERATIVE		taose	taosu na
TE FORM		taoshite	taosanakute
CONDITIONAL:	PLAIN	taoseba	taosanakereba
		taoshita ra	taosanakatta ra
	FORMAL	taoshimashita ra	taoshimasen deshita ra
PRESUMPTIVE:	PLAIN	taosu daroo	taosanai daroo
	FORMAL	taosu deshoo	taosanai deshoo
VOLITIONAL:	PLAIN	taosoo	
	FORMAL	taoshimashoo	

	Affirmative		*Affirmative*
POTENTIAL	taoseru	HONORIFIC	otaoshi ni naru
			otaoshi nasaru
PASSIVE	taosareru	HUMBLE	(otaoshi suru)
			(otaoshi itasu)
CAUSATIVE	taosaseru		
CAUS. PASSIVE	taosaserareru		

Examples:

1. *Sakuya no arashi ga takusan no ki o taoshita.*
   Last night's storm blew down many trees.
2. *Sooji o shite ite, ukkari shite kabin o taoshita.*
   I carelessly knocked over the vase while cleaning.
3. *Kare wa tenisu no shiai de kyooteki o taoshita.*
   In the tennis match, he defeated a powerful opponent.
4. *Gen-naikaku o taosu beki da to kare wa shuchoo shita.*
   He insisted that the present Cabinet should be overthrown.
5. *Kare wa shakkin o taoshite kieta.*
   He evaded paying off his debts and vanished.

足りる to be enough, be sufficient, suffice: (intrans.)

		Affirmative	*Negative*
PLAIN FORM:	PRESENT	tariru	tarinai
	PAST	tarita	tarinakatta
MASU FORM:	PRESENT	tarimasu	tarimasen
	PAST	tarimashita	tarimasen deshita
IMPERATIVE		(tariro)	(tariru na)
TE FORM		tarite	tarinakute
CONDITIONAL:	PLAIN	tarireba	tarinakereba
		tarita ra	tarinakatta ra
	FORMAL	tarimashita ra	tarimasen deshita ra
PRESUMPTIVE:	PLAIN	tariru daroo	tarinai daroo
	FORMAL	tariru deshoo	tarinai deshoo
VOLITIONAL:	PLAIN	(tariyoo)	
	FORMAL	(tarimashoo)	

	Affirmative		*Affirmative*
POTENTIAL	(tarirareru)	HONORIFIC	otari ni naru
			otari nasaru
PASSIVE	(tarirareru)	HUMBLE	(otari suru)
			(otari itasu)
CAUSATIVE	tarisaseru		
CAUS. PASSIVE	tarisaserareru		

Examples:

1. *Ichi-man en areba tariru.*
   Ten thousand yen will suffice.
2. *Okane ga ichi-man en tarinai.*
   I am ten thousand yen short.
3. *Sen en ni go-juu en tarinai.*
   We're fifty yen short of a thousand yen.
4. *Moo shigoto ni kyoomi ga nakunatta to ieba tariyoo.*
   Suffice it to say that I am no longer interested in my job.
5. *Kare wa keiken ga tarimasen.*
   He is lacking in experience.

確かめる to make sure, check, verify: (trans.)

		Affirmative	*Negative*
PLAIN FORM:	PRESENT	tashikameru	tashikamenai
	PAST	tashikameta	tashikamenakatta
MASU FORM:	PRESENT	tashikamemasu	tashikamemasen
	PAST	tashikamemashita	tashikamemasen deshita
IMPERATIVE		tashikamero	tashikameru na
TE FORM		tashikamete	tashikamenakute
CONDITIONAL:	PLAIN	tashikamereba	tashikamenakereba
		tashikameta ra	tashikamenakatta ra
	FORMAL	tashikamemashita ra	tashikamemasen deshita ra
PRESUMPTIVE:	PLAIN	tashikameru daroo	tashikamenai daroo
	FORMAL	tashikameru deshoo	tashikamenai deshoo
VOLITIONAL:	PLAIN	tashikameyoo	
	FORMAL	tashikamemashoo	

	Affirmative		*Affirmative*
POTENTIAL	tashikamerareru	HONORIFIC	otashikame ni naru
	tashikamereru		otashikame nasaru
PASSIVE	tashikamerareru	HUMBLE	(otashikame suru)
			(otashikame itasu)
CAUSATIVE	tashikamesaseru		
CAUS. PASSIVE	tashikamesaserareru		

Examples:

1. *O-kyaku ga tsuita ka doo ka tashikameru tame ni jimusho ni denwa shita.*
   I telephoned my office to make sure that the customer had arrived.
2. *Hikooki no toochaku jikan o denwa de tashikamemashita.*
   I telephoned and verified the arrival time of the plane.
3. *Kore ga tadashii ka doo ka tashikamete kudasai.*
   Please check to see whether this is correct or not.
4. *Sore wa shinjitsu de aru koto ga tashikamerareta.*
   The truth of it was confirmed.
5. *Kanojo no ikoo o tashikame-tai.*
   I'd like to verify her intentions.

助かる to be saved, rescued, spared: (intrans.)

		Affirmative	*Negative*
PLAIN FORM:	PRESENT	tasukaru	tasukaranai
	PAST	tasukatta	tasukaranakatta
MASU FORM:	PRESENT	tasukarimasu	tasukarimasen
	PAST	tasukarimashita	tasukarimasen deshita
IMPERATIVE		(tasukare)	(tasukaru na)
TE FORM		tasukatte	tasukaranakute
CONDITIONAL:	PLAIN	tasukareba	tasukaranakereba
		tasukatta ra	tasukaranakatta ra
	FORMAL	tasukarimashita ra	tasukarimasen deshita ra
PRESUMPTIVE:	PLAIN	tasukaru daroo	tasukaranai daroo
	FORMAL	tasukaru deshoo	tasukaranai deshoo
VOLITIONAL:	PLAIN	tasukaroo	
	FORMAL	tasukarimashoo	

	Affirmative			*Affirmative*
POTENTIAL	(tasukareru)	HONORIFIC		otasukari ni naru
				otasukari nasaru
PASSIVE	(tasukarareru)	HUMBLE		(otasukari suru)
				(otasukari itasu)
CAUSATIVE	tasukaraseru			
CAUS. PASSIVE	tasukaraserareru			

Examples:

1. *Shoonen wa kawa ni ochita ga, tasukatta.*
   The boy fell into the river but he was rescued.
2. *Hiyoo ga tasukatta.*
   I was spared the expenses.
3. *Sono kanja wa tasukaru mikomi wa arimasen.*
   It does not look like that patient can be helped.
4. *Kono kikai de watashi wa ooini tasukatte iru.*
   This machine helps me out a great deal.
5. *Kono kuni wa bukka ga yasui node tasukarimasu.*
   I am thankful that prices are low in this country.

tasukeru

助ける to help, save, rescue: (trans.)

		Affirmative	*Negative*
PLAIN FORM:	PRESENT	tasukeru	tasukenai
	PAST	tasuketa	tasukenakatta
MASU FORM:	PRESENT	tasukemasu	tasukemasen
	PAST	tasukemashita	tasukemasen deshita
IMPERATIVE		tasukero	tasukeru na
TE FORM		tasukete	tasukenakute
CONDITIONAL:	PLAIN	tasukereba	tasukenakereba
		tasuketa ra	tasukenakatta ra
	FORMAL	tasukemashita ra	tasukemasen deshita ra
PRESUMPTIVE:	PLAIN	tasukeru daroo	tasukenai daroo
	FORMAL	tasukeru deshoo	tasukenai deshoo
VOLITIONAL:	PLAIN	tasukeyoo	
	FORMAL	tasukemashoo	

	Affirmative		*Affirmative*
POTENTIAL	tasukerareru	HONORIFIC	otasuke ni naru
	tasukereru		otasuke nasaru
PASSIVE	tasukerareru	HUMBLE	otasuke suru
			otasuke itasu
CAUSATIVE	tasukesaseru		
CAUS. PASSIVE	tasukesaserareru		

Examples:

1. *Kare wa kawa ni ochita shoonen o tasukemashita.*
   He rescued a boy who had fallen in the river.
2. *Haha ga watashi no shukudai o tasukete kuremashita.*
   My mother helped me with my homework.
3. *Watashi wa shintai-shoogaisha o tasukeru tame ni hataraki-tai.*
   I want to work to help the physically handicapped.
4. *Inochi dake wa tasukete kudasai.*
   Please just spare my life.
5. *Ten wa mizukara tasukeru mono o tasukeru.*
   God helps those who help themselves.

立てる to stand, to erect, raise, establish; 建てる to build (both trans.)

		Affirmative	*Negative*
PLAIN FORM:	PRESENT	tateru	tatenai
	PAST	tateta	tatenakatta
MASU FORM:	PRESENT	tatemasu	tatemasen
	PAST	tatemashita	tatemasen deshita
IMPERATIVE		tatero	tateru na
TE FORM		tatete	tatenakute
CONDITIONAL:	PLAIN	tatereba	tatenakereba
		tateta ra	tatenakatta ra
	FORMAL	tatemashita ra	tatemasen deshita ra
PRESUMPTIVE:	PLAIN	tateru daroo	tatenai daroo
	FORMAL	tateru deshoo	tatenai deshoo
VOLITIONAL:	PLAIN	tateyoo	
	FORMAL	tatemashoo	

	Affirmative		*Affirmative*
POTENTIAL	taterareru	HONORIFIC	otate ni naru
	tatereru		otate nasaru
PASSIVE	taterareru	HUMBLE	otate suru
			otate itasu
CAUSATIVE	tatesaseru		
CAUS. PASSIVE	tatesaserareru		

Examples:

1. *Anata wa tamago o tateraremasu ka.*
   Can you stand an egg on its end?
2. *Torakku wa suna-bokori o tateta.*
   The truck raised a cloud of dust.
3. *Kare no gyooseki o kinen shite, doozoo ga tateraremashita.*
   A bronze statue was erected in memory of his achievements.
4. *Kare wa hyaku-meetoru kyoosoo de shin-kiroku o tateta.*
   He established a new record in the 100-meter dash.
5. *Yoshida-san wa saikin ie o tatemashita.*
   Mr. Yoshida recently built a house.

立つ to stand, rise; 建つ to be built;* 経つ to pass, elapse:* (all intrans.)

		Affirmative	*Negative*
PLAIN FORM:	PRESENT	tatsu	tatanai
	PAST	tatta	tatanakatta
MASU FORM:	PRESENT	tachimasu	tachimasen
	PAST	tachimashita	tachimasen deshita
IMPERATIVE		tate	tatsu na
TE FORM		tatte	tatanakute
CONDITIONAL:	PLAIN	tateba	tatanakereba
		tatta ra	tatanakatta ra
	FORMAL	tachimashita ra	tachimasen deshita ra
PRESUMPTIVE:	PLAIN	tatsu daroo	tatanai daroo
	FORMAL	tatsu deshoo	tatanai deshoo
VOLITIONAL:	PLAIN	tatoo	
	FORMAL	tachimashoo	

	Affirmative		*Affirmative*
POTENTIAL	tateru	HONORIFIC	otachi ni naru
			otachi nasaru
PASSIVE	tatareru	HUMBLE	(otachi suru)
			(otachi itasu)
CAUSATIVE	tataseru		
CAUS. PASSIVE	tataserareru		
	tatasareru		

Examples:

1. *Keikan ga machi-kado ni tatte iru.*
   A policeman is standing at the street corner.
2. *Ashi ga shibirete tatemasen.*
   I can't stand up because my legs have gone to sleep.
3. *Kuruma ga tooru to suna-bokori ga tatta.*
   A cloud of dust rose when cars passed.
4. *Kooen ni kinenhi ga tatta.*
   The monument was erected in the park.
5. *Kare ga koko ni kite kara go-nen ga tachimashita.*
   Five years have passed since he came here.

* The verbs *tatsu* meaning "to be built" 建つ and "to pass, elapse" 経つ generally do not use the imperative, volitional, potential, honorific, humble, passive, causative, or causative passive forms.

頼る to depend on, rely on: (intrans.)*

		Affirmative	*Negative*
PLAIN FORM:	PRESENT	tayoru	tayoranai
	PAST	tayotta	tayoranakatta
MASU FORM:	PRESENT	tayorimasu	tayorimasen
	PAST	tayorimashita	tayorimasen deshita
IMPERATIVE		tayore	tayoru na
TE FORM		tayotte	tayoranakute
CONDITIONAL:	PLAIN	tayoreba	tayoranakereba
		tayotta ra	tayoranakatta ra
	FORMAL	tayorimashita ra	tayorimasen deshita ra
PRESUMPTIVE:	PLAIN	tayoru daroo	tayoranai daroo
	FORMAL	tayoru deshoo	tayoranai deshoo
VOLITIONAL:	PLAIN	tayoroo	
	FORMAL	tayorimashoo	

	Affirmative		*Affirmative*
POTENTIAL	tayoreru	HONORIFIC	otayori ni naru
			otayori nasaru
PASSIVE	tayorareru	HUMBLE	otayori suru
			otayori itasu
CAUSATIVE	tayoraseru		
CAUS. PASSIVE	tayoraserareru		

Examples:

1. *Karera wa shuunyuu-gen o yooton ni tayotte iru.*
   They depend on hog raising as a source of income.
2. *Kimi wa sonna ni tanin ni tayotte wa ikenai.*
   You must not depend so much on others.
3. *Kare wa kanemochi no oya ni tayoranaide shusse shita.*
   He advanced his career without relying on his rich parents.
4. *Komatta koto ga okite mo, watashi ni tasuke o motomete tayoru na.*
   Even if you get into trouble, don't look to me for help.
5. *Kanojo wa ani o tayotte, Tookyoo ni kimashita.*
   She came to Tokyo counting on her older brother's help.

* Also used like a transitive verb. (*See* example 5.)

tazuneru   Group 2

尋ねる to ask, look for, search; 訪ねる to visit: (both trans.)

		Affirmative	*Negative*
PLAIN FORM:	PRESENT	tazuneru	tazunenai
	PAST	tazuneta	tazunenakatta
MASU FORM:	PRESENT	tazunemasu	tazunemasen
	PAST	tazunemashita	tazunemasen deshita
IMPERATIVE		tazunero	tazuneru na
TE FORM		tazunete	tazunenakute
CONDITIONAL:	PLAIN	tazunereba	tazunenakereba
		tazuneta ra	tazunenakatta ra
	FORMAL	tazunemashita ra	tazunemasen deshita ra
PRESUMPTIVE:	PLAIN	tazuneru daroo	tazunenai daroo
	FORMAL	tazuneru deshoo	tazunenai deshoo
VOLITIONAL:	PLAIN	tazuneyoo	
	FORMAL	tazunemashoo	

	Affirmative		*Affirmative*
POTENTIAL	tazunerareru	HONORIFIC	otazune ni naru
			otazune nasaru
PASSIVE	tazunerareru	HUMBLE	otazune suru
			otazune itasu
CAUSATIVE	tazunesaseru		
CAUS. PASSIVE	tazunesaserareru		

Examples:

1. *Anata ni tazune-tai koto ga arimasu.*
   I have a question to ask you.
2. *Kare wa watashi ni sono jiken no koto o kiita ka to tazuneta.*
   He asked if I had heard of that incident.
3. *Kuwashii koto wa tantoosha ni otazune kudasai.*
   For further information, please ask the person in charge.
4. *Watashi wa Kyooto no o-tera ya jinja o tazunemashita.*
   I visited temples and shrines in Kyoto.
5. *Senjitsu kare o jimusho ni tazunemashita.*
   I called on him at his office the other day.

手伝う to help, assist: (trans.)

		Affirmative	*Negative*
PLAIN FORM:	PRESENT	tetsudau	tetsudawanai
	PAST	tetsudatta	tetsudawanakatta
MASU FORM:	PRESENT	tetsudaimasu	tetsudaimasen
	PAST	tetsudaimashita	tetsudaimasen deshita
IMPERATIVE		tetsudae	tetsudau na
TE FORM		tetsudatte	tetsudawanakute
CONDITIONAL:	PLAIN	tetsudaeba	tetsudawanakereba
		tetsudatta ra	tetsudawanakatta ra
	FORMAL	tetsudaimashita ra	tetsudaimasen deshita ra
PRESUMPTIVE:	PLAIN	tetsudau daroo	tetsudawanai daroo
	FORMAL	tetsudau deshoo	tetsudawanai deshoo
VOLITIONAL:	PLAIN	tetsudaoo	
	FORMAL	tetsudaimashoo	

	Affirmative		*Affirmative*
POTENTIAL	tetsudaeru	HONORIFIC	otetsudai ni naru
			otetsudai nasaru
PASSIVE	tetsudawareru	HUMBLE	otetsudai suru
			otetsudai itasu
CAUSATIVE	tetsudawaseru		
CAUS. PASSIVE	tetsudawaserareru		
	tetsudawasareru		

Examples:

1. *Sumimasen ga, kono shigoto o tetsudatte kudasai.*
   I'm sorry to trouble you, but could you help with this job?
   Yorokonde otetsudai shimasu.
   I would be glad to help you.
2. *Nani ka tetsudau koto ga arimasu ka?*
   Can I do anything to help you?
3. *Kare ga watashi no taipu o tetsudatte kuremashita.*
   He helped me with the typing.
4. *Obaasan ga basu kara oriru no o tetsudatta.*
   I helped the old lady get off the bus.

飛ばす to let fly, to skip (over), spread (a rumor): (trans.)

		Affirmative	*Negative*
PLAIN FORM:	PRESENT	tobasu	tobasanai
	PAST	tobashita	tobasanakatta
MASU FORM:	PRESENT	tobashimasu	tobashimasen
	PAST	tobashimashita	tobashimasen deshita
IMPERATIVE		tobase	tobasu na
TE FORM		tobashite	tobasanakute
CONDITIONAL:	PLAIN	tobaseba	tobasanakereba
		tobashita ra	tobasanakatta ra
	FORMAL	tobashimashita ra	tobashimasen deshita ra
PRESUMPTIVE:	PLAIN	tobasu daroo	tobasanai daroo
	FORMAL	tobasu deshoo	tobasanai deshoo
VOLITIONAL:	PLAIN	tobasoo	
	FORMAL	tobashimashoo	

	Affirmative		*Affirmative*
POTENTIAL	tobaseru	HONORIFIC	otobashi ni naru
			otobashi nasaru
PASSIVE	tobasareru	HUMBLE	(otobashi suru)
			(otobashi itasu)
CAUSATIVE	tobasaseru		
CAUS. PASSIVE	tobasaserareru		

Examples:

1. *Kaze ga booshi o tobashita.*
   The wind blew my hat off.
2. *Shoonen wa kami-hikooki o tobashita.*
   The boy let fly a paper airplane.
3. *Kare wa mizuumi made zen-sokuryoku de kuruma o tobashimashita.*
   He drove his car at top speed to the lake.
4. *Kono hon no muzukashii tokoro wa tobashite mo yoi.*
   You may skip the difficult parts of this book.
5. *Dema o tobasanai de kure.*
   Don't spread false rumors.

飛ぶ to fly, jump, take to the air (intrans.)*

		Affirmative	*Negative*
PLAIN FORM:	PRESENT	tobu	tobanai
	PAST	tonda	tobanakatta
MASU FORM:	PRESENT	tobimasu	tobimasen
	PAST	tobimashita	tobimasen deshita
IMPERATIVE		tobe	tobu na
TE FORM		tonde	tobanakute
CONDITIONAL:	PLAIN	tobeba	tobanakereba
		tonda ra	tobanakatta ra
	FORMAL	tobimashita ra	tobimasen deshita ra
PRESUMPTIVE:	PLAIN	tobu daroo	tobanai daroo
	FORMAL	tobu deshoo	tobanai deshoo
VOLITIONAL:	PLAIN	toboo	
	FORMAL	tobimashoo	

	Affirmative		*Affirmative*
POTENTIAL	toberu	HONORIFIC	otobi ni naru
			otobi nasaru
PASSIVE	tobareru	HUMBLE	(otobi suru)
			(otobi itasu)
CAUSATIVE	tobaseru		
CAUS. PASSIVE	tobaserareru		
	tobasareru		

Examples:

1. *Shiroi tori ga umi no ue o tonde imasu.*
   A white bird is flying over the ocean.
2. *Kare wa hashiri-takatobi de ni-meetoru tonda.*
   He jumped two meters in the high jump.
3. *Kare wa tadachi ni Pari e tonda.*
   He flew immediately to Paris.
4. *Hanashi wa inu no koto kara gorufu ni tonda.*
   The conversation jumped from dogs to golf.
5. *Kono hon wa tobu yoo ni urete iru.*
   This book is selling like hotcakes.

* As with other verbs indicating movement, *tobu* may take a direct object, thus giving an idea of "going through a defined area." (*See* example 1.)

届ける to report, notify, send, deliver: (trans.)

		Affirmative	*Negative*
PLAIN FORM:	PRESENT	todokeru	todokenai
	PAST	todoketa	todokenakatta
MASU FORM:	PRESENT	todokemasu	todokemasen
	PAST	todokemashita	todokemasen deshita
IMPERATIVE		todokero	todokeru na
TE FORM		todokete	todokenakute
CONDITIONAL:	PLAIN	todokereba	todokenakereba
		todoketa ra	todokenakatta ra
	FORMAL	todokemashita ra	todokemasen deshita ra
PRESUMPTIVE:	PLAIN	todokeru daroo	todokenai daroo
	FORMAL	todokeru deshoo	todokenai deshoo
VOLITIONAL:	PLAIN	todokeyoo	
	FORMAL	todokemashoo	

	Affirmative		*Affirmative*
POTENTIAL	todokerareru todokereru	HONORIFIC	otodoke ni naru otodoke nasaru
PASSIVE	todokerareru	HUMBLE	otodoke suru otodoke itasu
CAUSATIVE	todokesaseru		
CAUS. PASSIVE	todokesaserareru		

Examples:

1. *Maiasa shinbun o todokete kudasai.*
   Please deliver the newspaper every morning.
2. *Kare wa kanojo no tanjoobi ni hanataba o todoketa.*
   He sent her a bouquet of flowers on her birthday.
3. *Juusho no henkoo o shiyakusho ni todokemashita.*
   I notified the city office of my change of address.
4. *Chooki-kekkin no baai wa, sono riyuu o kaisha ni todokenakereba naranai.*
   In cases of long absences, you must inform the company of the reason.
5. *Dooshite kare wa higai o keisatsu ni todokenakatta no daroo.*
   I wonder why he didn't report the damage to the police?

届く to reach, arrive: (intrans.)

		Affirmative	*Negative*
PLAIN FORM:	PRESENT	todoku	todokanai
	PAST	todoita	todokanakatta
MASU FORM:	PRESENT	todokimasu	todokimasen
	PAST	todokimashita	todokimasen deshita
IMPERATIVE		(todoke)	(todoku na)
TE FORM		todoite	todokanakute
CONDITIONAL:	PLAIN	todokeba	todokanakereba
		todoita ra	todokanakatta ra
	FORMAL	todokimashita ra	todokimasen deshita ra
PRESUMPTIVE:	PLAIN	todoku daroo	todokanai daroo
	FORMAL	todoku deshoo	todokanai deshoo
VOLITIONAL:	PLAIN	(todokoo)	
	FORMAL	(todokimashoo)	

	Affirmative		*Affirmative*
POTENTIAL	(todokeru)	HONORIFIC	otodoki ni naru
			otodoki nasaru
PASSIVE	(todokareru)	HUMBLE	(otodoki suru)
			(otodoki itasu)
CAUSATIVE	todokaseru		
CAUS. PASSIVE	todokaserareru		
	todokasareru		

Examples:

1. *Anata no tegami ga kinoo todokimashita.*
   Your letter reached me yesterday.
2. *Kare ga dekaketa ato de dengon ga todoita.*
   The message arrived after he had left.
3. *Kanojo no koe wa kawa no mukoo-gawa made todokanai deshoo.*
   Her voice probably won't carry to the other side of the river.
4. *Kare wa roku-jus-sai ni te ga todoku.*
   He is close to sixty years old.
5. *Kono tana wa taka-sugite, watashi ni wa todokimasen.*
   This shelf is too high for me to reach.

解ける to become untied, be solved; 溶ける to dissolve, melt: (both intrans.)

		Affirmative	*Negative*
PLAIN FORM:	PRESENT	tokeru	tokenai
	PAST	toketa	tokenakatta
MASU FORM:	PRESENT	tokemasu	tokemasen
	PAST	tokemashita	tokemasen deshita
IMPERATIVE		(tokero)	(tokeru na)
TE FORM		tokete	tokenakute
CONDITIONAL:	PLAIN	tokereba	tokenakereba
		toketa ra	tokenakatta ra
	FORMAL	tokemashita ra	tokemasen deshita ra
PRESUMPTIVE:	PLAIN	tokeru daroo	tokenai daroo
	FORMAL	tokeru deshoo	tokenai deshoo
VOLITIONAL:	PLAIN	(tokeyoo)	
	FORMAL	(tokemashoo)	

	Affirmative		*Affirmative*
POTENTIAL	(tokerareru)	HONORIFIC	otoke ni naru
			otoke nasaru
PASSIVE	(tokerareru)	HUMBLE	(otoke suru)
			(otoke itasu)
CAUSATIVE	tokesaseru		
CAUS. PASSIVE	tokesaserareru		

Examples:

1. *Tootoo nazo ga tokenakatta.*
   In the end, the puzzle could not be solved.
2. *Kutsuhimo ga tokete iru.*
   The shoestring is coming untied.
3. *Kare no gokai wa nakanaka tokenakatta.*
   So far, he can't be convinced otherwise. (*lit.,* untie his misunderstanding)
4. *Shio wa mizu ni tokemasu.*
   Salt dissolves in water.
5. *Kono kinzoku wa netsu de tokemasu.*
   This metal melts with heat.

解く to untie, unfasten, solve, to relieve of a post: (trans.)

		Affirmative	*Negative*
PLAIN FORM:	PRESENT	toku	tokanai
	PAST	toita	tokanakatta
MASU FORM:	PRESENT	tokimasu	tokimasen
	PAST	tokimashita	tokimasen deshita
IMPERATIVE		toke	toku na
TE FORM		toite	tokanakute
CONDITIONAL:	PLAIN	tokeba	tokanakereba
		toita ra	tokanakatta ra
	FORMAL	tokimashita ra	tokimasen deshita ra
PRESUMPTIVE:	PLAIN	toku daroo	tokanai daroo
	FORMAL	toku deshoo	tokanai deshoo
VOLITIONAL:	PLAIN	tokoo	
	FORMAL	tokimashoo	

	Affirmative		*Affirmative*
POTENTIAL	tokeru	HONORIFIC	otoki ni naru
			otoki nasaru
PASSIVE	tokareru	HUMBLE	otoki suru
			otoki itasu
CAUSATIVE	tokaseru		
CAUS. PASSIVE	tokaserareru		
	tokasareru		

Examples:

1. *Hako o akeru tame ni himo o toita.*
   I unfastened the string to open up the box.
2. *Chiisai kodomo wa kutsu no himo o joozu ni tokemasen.*
   A small child can't untie his shoes well.
3. *Watashi wa yatto sono nazo o tokimashita.*
   I have finally solved the puzzle.
4. *Kare no gokai o toku no ni kuroo shimashita.*
   We had difficulty convincing him otherwise. (*lit.*, untie his misunderstanding)
5. *Shachoo wa kanojo no shoku o toita.*
   The president relieved her of her post.

止まる to stop, halt; 泊まる to stay the night, lodge: (both intrans.)

		Affirmative	*Negative*
PLAIN FORM:	PRESENT	tomaru	tomaranai
	PAST	tomatta	tomaranakatta
MASU FORM:	PRESENT	tomarimasu	tomarimasen
	PAST	tomarimashita	tomarimasen deshita
IMPERATIVE		tomare	tomaru na
TE FORM		tomatte	tomaranakute
CONDITIONAL:	PLAIN	tomareba	tomaranakereba
		tomatta ra	tomaranakatta ra
	FORMAL	tomarimashita ra	tomarimasen deshita ra
PRESUMPTIVE:	PLAIN	tomaru daroo	tomaranai daroo
	FORMAL	tomaru deshoo	tomaranai deshoo
VOLITIONAL:	PLAIN	tomaroo	
	FORMAL	tomarimashoo	

	Affirmative		*Affirmative*
POTENTIAL	tomareru	HONORIFIC	otomari ni naru
			otomari nasaru
PASSIVE	tomarareru	HUMBLE	(otomari suru)
			(otomari itasu)
CAUSATIVE	tomaraseru		
CAUS. PASSIVE	tomaraserareru		
	tomarasareru		

Examples:

1. *Watashi no uchi no mae de akai kuruma ga tomatta.*
   A red car stopped in front of my house.
2. *Anata no tokei wa tomatte imasu.*
   Your watch has stopped running.
3. *Taifuu no tame denki ga tomatta.*
   Because of the typhoon, the electricity went off.
4. *Oji wa uchi ni tomatte imasu.*
   My uncle is staying with us.
5. *Kanojo wa kesshite soto de tomaranai.*
   She never stays out overnight.

止める to stop; 泊める to give lodging; 留める to fasten, fix, attach to: (all trans.)

		Affirmative	*Negative*
PLAIN FORM:	PRESENT	tomeru	tomenai
	PAST	tometa	tomenakatta
MASU FORM:	PRESENT	tomemasu	tomemasen
	PAST	tomemashita	tomemasen deshita
IMPERATIVE		tomero	tomeru na
TE FORM		tomete	tomenakute
CONDITIONAL:	PLAIN	tomereba	tomenakereba
		tometa ra	tomenakatta ra
	FORMAL	tomemashita ra	tomemasen deshita ra
PRESUMPTIVE:	PLAIN	tomeru daroo	tomenai daroo
	FORMAL	tomeru deshoo	tomenai deshoo
VOLITIONAL:	PLAIN	tomeyoo	
	FORMAL	tomemashoo	

	Affirmative		*Affirmative*
POTENTIAL	tomerareru	HONORIFIC	otome ni naru
	tomereru		otome nasaru
PASSIVE	tomerareru	HUMBLE	otome suru
			otome itasu
CAUSATIVE	tomesaseru		
CAUS. PASSIVE	tomesaserareru		

Examples:

1. *Sono kikai o tomete kudasai.*
   Please stop that machine.
2. *Kare wa kodomo ga koinu o ijimeru no o tometa.*
   He stopped the child from teasing the puppy.
3. *Ashita kooji no tame denki o juu-ji kara tomemasu.*
   The electricity will be shut off from ten o'clock tomorrow due to construction.
4. *Yuujin o hito-ban tomete ageta.*
   I let my friend stay with me for a night.
5. *Sono chizu o kabe ni shikkari tomete oite kudasai.*
   Please affix that map firmly to the wall.

通る to pass, pass through: (intrans.)*

		Affirmative	*Negative*
PLAIN FORM:	PRESENT	tooru	tooranai
	PAST	tootta	tooranakatta
MASU FORM:	PRESENT	toorimasu	toorimasen
	PAST	toorimashita	toorimasen deshita
IMPERATIVE		toore	tooru na
TE FORM		tootte	tooranakute
CONDITIONAL:	PLAIN	tooreba	tooranakereba
		tootta ra	tooranakatta ra
	FORMAL	toorimashita ra	toorimasen deshita ra
PRESUMPTIVE:	PLAIN	tooru daroo	tooranai daroo
	FORMAL	tooru deshoo	tooranai deshoo
VOLITIONAL:	PLAIN	tooroo	
	FORMAL	toorimashoo	

	Affirmative		*Affirmative*
POTENTIAL	tooreru	HONORIFIC	otoori ni naru
			otoori nasaru
PASSIVE	toorareru	HUMBLE	(otoori suru)
			(otoori itasu)
CAUSATIVE	tooraseru		
CAUS. PASSIVE	tooraserareru		
	toorasareru		

Examples:

1. *Kono michi wa kuruma ga yoku tooru.*
   Many cars use this road.
2. *Kono michi o tootte, gakkoo e kayoimasu.*
   We go to school using this road.
3. *Migi-gawa o tootte kudasai.*
   Keep to the right, please.
4. *Kare wa shiken ni toorimashita.*
   He passed the examination.
5. *Kanojo no koe wa tooku made yoku tooru.*
   Her voice carries far.

* As with other verbs indicating movement, *tooru* may take a direct object, thus giving an idea of "going through a defined area." (*See* examples 2 and 3.)

取れる to come off, be able to catch; 撮れる be taken (a photo): (both intrans.)

		Affirmative	*Negative*
PLAIN FORM:	PRESENT	toreru	torenai
	PAST	toreta	torenakatta
MASU FORM:	PRESENT	toremasu	toremasen
	PAST	toremashita	toremasen deshita
IMPERATIVE		(torero)	(toreru na)
TE FORM		torete	torenakute
CONDITIONAL:	PLAIN	torereba	torenakereba
		toreta ra	torenakatta ra
	FORMAL	toremashita ra	toremasen deshita ra
PRESUMPTIVE:	PLAIN	toreru daroo	torenai daroo
	FORMAL	toreru deshoo	torenai deshoo
VOLITIONAL:	PLAIN	(toreyoo)	
	FORMAL	(toremashoo)	

	Affirmative		*Affirmative*
POTENTIAL	(torerareru)	HONORIFIC	otore ni naru
			otore nasaru
PASSIVE	(torerareru)	HUMBLE	(otore suru)
			(otore itasu)
CAUSATIVE	(toresaseru)		
CAUS. PASSIVE	(toresaserareru)		

Examples:

1. *Uwagi no botan ga toreta.*
   A button has come off my coat.
2. *Inku no shimi wa nakanaka torenai.*
   Ink stains will not come out easily.
3. *Kotoshi wa amari maguro ga torenakatta.*
   This year they weren't able to catch many tuna.
4. *Kono bun wa iku-toori ni mo toreru.*
   This sentence can be interpreted in several ways.
5. *Shashin ga yoku toreta ra, ichi-mai agemasu yo.*
   If the picture comes out well, I'll give you a copy.

取る to get, take, catch: (trans.)

		Affirmative	*Negative*
PLAIN FORM:	PRESENT	toru	toranai
	PAST	totta	toranakatta
MASU FORM:	PRESENT	torimasu	torimasen
	PAST	torimashita	torimasen deshita
IMPERATIVE		tore	toru na
TE FORM		totte	toranakute
CONDITIONAL:	PLAIN	toreba	toranakereba
		totta ra	toranakatta ra
	FORMAL	torimashita ra	torimasen deshita ra
PRESUMPTIVE:	PLAIN	toru daroo	toranai daroo
	FORMAL	toru deshoo	toranai deshoo
VOLITIONAL:	PLAIN	toroo	
	FORMAL	torimashoo	

	Affirmative		*Affirmative*
POTENTIAL	toreru	HONORIFIC	otori ni naru
			otori nasaru
PASSIVE	torareru	HUMBLE	otori suru
			otori itasu
CAUSATIVE	toraseru		
CAUS. PASSIVE	toraserareru		
	torasareru		

Examples:

1. *Sono hon o totte kudasai.*
   Please take (let me have) that book.
2. *Kare wa ittoo-shoo o totta.*
   He took first prize.
3. *Kanojo wa watashi no puropoozu o joodan to torimashita.*
   She took my marriage proposal for a joke.
4. *Zubon no shimi o torimashita.*
   I removed the stains from the trousers.
5. *Watashi-tachi wa kawa de sakana o takusan torimashita.*
   We caught many fish in the river.

捕まえる to catch, take hold of, arrest: (trans.)

		Affirmative	*Negative*
PLAIN FORM:	PRESENT	tsukamaeru	tsukamaenai
	PAST	tsukamaeta	tsukamaenakatta
MASU FORM:	PRESENT	tsukamaemasu	tsukamaemasen
	PAST	tsukamaemashita	tsukamaemasen deshita
IMPERATIVE		tsukamaero	tsukamaeru na
TE FORM		tsukamaete	tsukamaenakute
CONDITIONAL:	PLAIN	tsukamaereba	tsukamaenakereba
		tsukamaeta ra	tsukamaenakatta ra
	FORMAL	tsukamaemashita ra	tsukamaemasen deshita ra
PRESUMPTIVE:	PLAIN	tsukamaeru daroo	tsukamaenai daroo
	FORMAL	tsukamaeru deshoo	tsukamaenai deshoo
VOLITIONAL:	PLAIN	tsukamaeyoo	
	FORMAL	tsukamaemashoo	

	Affirmative		*Affirmative*
POTENTIAL	tsukamaerareru	HONORIFIC	otsukamae ni naru
	tsukamaereru		otsukamae nasaru
PASSIVE	tsukamaerareru	HUMBLE	(otsukamae suru)
			(otsukamae itasu)
CAUSATIVE	tsukamaesaseru		
CAUS. PASSIVE	tsukamaesaserareru		

Examples:

1. *Keisatsu wa doroboo o tsukamaemashita.*
   The police caught the robber.
2. *Kare ga dekakeru mae ni tsukamae-tai.*
   I want to catch him before he goes out.
3. *Roopu o shikkari tsukamaete iro.*
   Keep a tight hold of the rope.
4. *Kanojo wa oo-ganemochi o tsukamaeta.*
   She has managed to hook a very rich man.
5. *Yonaka ni takushii o tsukamaeru no wa muzukashii.*
   It's difficult to catch a taxi late at night.

捕む to catch, grasp, take hold of: (trans.)

		Affirmative	*Negative*
PLAIN FORM:	PRESENT	tsukamu	tsukamanai
	PAST	tsukanda	tsukamanakatta
MASU FORM:	PRESENT	tsukamimasu	tsukamimasen
	PAST	tsukamimashita	tsukamimasen deshita
IMPERATIVE		tsukame	tsukamu na
TE FORM		tsukande	tsukamanakute
CONDITIONAL:	PLAIN	tsukameba	tsukamanakereba
		tsukanda ra	tsukamanakatta ra
	FORMAL	tsukamimashita ra	tsukamimasen deshita ra
PRESUMPTIVE:	PLAIN	tsukamu daroo	tsukamanai daroo
	FORMAL	tsukamu deshoo	tsukamanai deshoo
VOLITIONAL:	PLAIN	tsukamoo	
	FORMAL	tsukamimashoo	

	Affirmative		*Affirmative*
POTENTIAL	tsukameru	HONORIFIC	otsukami ni naru
			otsukami nasaru
PASSIVE	tsukamareru	HUMBLE	(otsukami suru)
			(otsukami itasu)
CAUSATIVE	tsukamaseru		
CAUS. PASSIVE	tsukamaserareru		
	tsukamasareru		

Examples:

1. *Kare wa kanojo no ude o tsukanda.*
   He grabbed her by the arm.
2. *Kono roopu o tsukame.*
   Take hold of this rope.
3. *Kare no itte iru imi ga tsukamenakatta.*
   I could not grasp what he said.
4. *Keisatsu wa nani ka atarashii joohoo o tsukanda rashii.*
   The police seem to have gotten hold of some new information.
5. *Oboreru mono wa wara o mo tsukamu.*
   A drowning man will grasp at even a straw.

疲れる to be tired, be weary; つかれる to be possessed: (both intrans.)

		Affirmative	*Negative*
PLAIN FORM:	PRESENT	tsukareru	tsukarenai
	PAST	tsukareta	tsukarenakatta
MASU FORM:	PRESENT	tsukaremasu	tsukaremasen
	PAST	tsukaremashita	tsukaremasen deshita
IMPERATIVE		(tsukarero)	(tsukareru na)
TE FORM		tsukarete	tsukarenakute
CONDITIONAL:	PLAIN	tsukarereba	tsukarenakereba
		tsukareta ra	tsukarenakatta ra
	FORMAL	tsukaremashita ra	tsukaremasen deshita ra
PRESUMPTIVE:	PLAIN	tsukareru daroo	tsukarenai daroo
	FORMAL	tsukareru deshoo	tsukarenai deshoo
VOLITIONAL:	PLAIN	(tsukareyoo)	
	FORMAL	(tsukaremashoo)	

	Affirmative		*Affirmative*
POTENTIAL	(tsukarerareru)	HONORIFIC	otsukare ni naru
			otsukare nasaru
PASSIVE	(tsukarerareru)	HUMBLE	(otsukare suru)
			(otsukare itasu)
CAUSATIVE	tsukaresaseru		
CAUS. PASSIVE	tsukaresaserareru		

Examples:

1. *Amari tsukarete ita node, nani mo taberaremasen deshita.*
   I was too tired to eat anything.
2. *Kare wa tsukareta kao de, uchi ni kaette kita.*
   He came home looking tired.
3. *Kodomo-tachi wa asobi-tsukareta rashii.*
   The children seem to be tired from playing.
4. *Kare wa tsukareta uwagi o kite imasu.*
   He is wearing a worn-out jacket.
5. *Kare wa nani ka ni tsukareta yoo ni tatakatta.*
   He fought like one who was possessed.

使う to use, handle, employ; 遣う to spend, consume: (both trans.)

		Affirmative	*Negative*
PLAIN FORM:	PRESENT	tsukau	tsukawanai
	PAST	tsukatta	tsukawanakatta
MASU FORM:	PRESENT	tsukaimasu	tsukaimasen
	PAST	tsukaimashita	tsukaimasen deshita
IMPERATIVE		tsukae	tsukau na
TE FORM		tsukatte	tsukawanakute
CONDITIONAL:	PLAIN	tsukaeba	tsukawanakereba
		tsukatta ra	tsukawanakatta ra
	FORMAL	tsukaimashita ra	tsukaimasen deshita ra
PRESUMPTIVE:	PLAIN	tsukau daroo	tsukawanai daroo
	FORMAL	tsukau deshoo	tsukawanai deshoo
VOLITIONAL:	PLAIN	tsukaoo	
	FORMAL	tsukaimashoo	

	Affirmative		*Affirmative*
POTENTIAL	tsukaeru	HONORIFIC	otsukai ni naru
			otsukai nasaru
PASSIVE	tsukawareru	HUMBLE	(otsukai suru)
			(otsukai itasu)
CAUSATIVE	tsukawaseru		
CAUS. PASSIVE	tsukawaserareru		
	tsukawasareru		

Examples:

1. *Denwa o tsukatte mo ii desu ka.*
   May I use your telephone?
2. *Ei-go wa kokusai-go to shite tsukawarete iru.*
   English is used as an international language.
3. *Kono mise de kanojo o tsukatte itadakemasen ka.*
   Could you employ her at this store?
4. *Kare wa kasegu yori tsukau hoo ga ooi.*
   He spends more than he earns.
5. *Sono shigoto ni kore ijoo jikan o tsukau na.*
   Don't spend any more time on that work.

付ける *or* 着ける to put on, fix, to tail (a person); つける to switch on: (all trans.)

		Affirmative	*Negative*
PLAIN FORM:	PRESENT	tsukeru	tsukenai
	PAST	tsuketa	tsukenakatta
MASU FORM:	PRESENT	tsukemasu	tsukemasen
	PAST	tsukemashita	tsukemasen deshita
IMPERATIVE		tsukero	tsukeru na
TE FORM		tsukete	tsukenakute
CONDITIONAL:	PLAIN	tsukereba	tsukenakereba
		tsuketa ra	tsukenakatta ra
	FORMAL	tsukemashita ra	tsukemasen deshita ra
PRESUMPTIVE:	PLAIN	tsukeru daroo	tsukenai daroo
	FORMAL	tsukeru deshoo	tsukenai deshoo
VOLITIONAL:	PLAIN	tsukeyoo	
	FORMAL	tsukemashoo	

	Affirmative		*Affirmative*
POTENTIAL	tsukerareru tsukereru	HONORIFIC	otsuke ni naru otsuke nasaru
PASSIVE	tsukerareru	HUMBLE	otsuke suru otsuke itasu
CAUSATIVE	tsukesaseru		
CAUS. PASSIVE	tsukesaserareru		

Examples:

1. *Kanojo wa fuku ni buroochi o tsukete imasu.*
   She has a brooch on her dress.
2. *Kare wa to ni atarashii beru o tsuketa.*
   He put a new bell on the door.
3. *Kega o shita ashi ni kusuri o tsukemashita.*
   I put some medicine on my injured foot.
4. *Kare wa keiji ni tsukerareta.*
   He was tailed by a police detective.
5. *Terebi o tsuketa mama ni shite oita.*
   I left the television on.

付く to stick to, attend; 着く arrive; つく to be lighted: (all intrans.)*

		Affirmative	*Negative*
PLAIN FORM:	PRESENT	tsuku	tsukanai
	PAST	tsuita	tsukanakatta
MASU FORM:	PRESENT	tsukimasu	tsukimasen
	PAST	tsukimashita	tsukimasen deshita
IMPERATIVE		tsuke	tsuku na
TE FORM		tsuite	tsukanakute
CONDITIONAL:	PLAIN	tsukeba	tsukanakereba
		tsuita ra	tsukanakatta ra
	FORMAL	tsukimashita ra	tsukimasen deshita ra
PRESUMPTIVE:	PLAIN	tsuku daroo	tsukanai daroo
	FORMAL	tsuku deshoo	tsukanai deshoo
VOLITIONAL:	PLAIN	tsukoo	
	FORMAL	tsukimashoo	

	Affirmative		*Affirmative*
POTENTIAL	tsukeru	HONORIFIC	otsuki ni naru
			otsuki nasaru
PASSIVE	tsukareru	HUMBLE	(otsuki suru)
			(otsuki itasu)
CAUSATIVE	tsukaseru		
CAUS. PASSIVE	tsukaserareru		
	tsukasareru		

Examples:

1. *Nekutai ni inku no shimi ga tsuita.*
   There is an inkstain on my tie.
2. *Byoonin ni wa kangofu ga tsuite imasu.*
   The patient is attended by a nurse.
3. *Keisatsu wa genba ni jup-pun-go ni tsuita.*
   The police arrived on the scene ten minutes later.
4. *Kare wa tenjoo ni atama ga tsuku hodo se ga takai.*
   He is so tall that his head reaches the ceiling.
5. *Kare no heya ni akari ga tsuite iru.*
   The light is on in his room.

* The verb *tsuku* つく meaning "to be lighted" generally does not use the imperative, volitional, potential, passive, humble, causative, or causative passive forms.

作る *or* 造る to make, create, produce: (trans.)

		Affirmative	*Negative*
PLAIN FORM:	PRESENT	tsukuru	tsukuranai
	PAST	tsukutta	tsukuranakatta
MASU FORM:	PRESENT	tsukurimasu	tsukurimasen
	PAST	tsukurimashita	tsukurimasen deshita
IMPERATIVE		tsukure	tsukuru na
TE FORM		tsukutte	tsukuranakute
CONDITIONAL:	PLAIN	tsukureba	tsukuranakereba
		tsukutta ra	tsukuranakatta ra
	FORMAL	tsukurimashita ra	tsukurimasen deshita ra
PRESUMPTIVE:	PLAIN	tsukuru daroo	tsukuranai daroo
	FORMAL	tsukuru deshoo	tsukuranai deshoo
VOLITIONAL:	PLAIN	tsukuroo	
	FORMAL	tsukurimashoo	

	Affirmative		*Affirmative*
POTENTIAL	tsukureru	HONORIFIC	otsukuri ni naru
			otsukuri nasaru
PASSIVE	tsukurareru	HUMBLE	otsukuri suru
			otsukuri itasu
CAUSATIVE	tsukuraseru		
CAUS. PASSIVE	tsukuraserareru		
	tsukurasareru		

Examples:

1. *Chichi wa ki de hondana o tsukurimashita.*
   My father made a bookshelf out of wood.
2. *Kanojo ni aeru kikai o tsukutte yaroo.*
   I'll arrange an opportunity for you to be able to meet her.
3. *Kanojo wa tomodachi o tsukuru no ga hayai.*
   She is quick to make friends.
4. *Karera wa enjin o tsukutta.*
   They formed themselves into a circle.
5. *Kami wa ten to chi o tsukutta.*
   God created heaven and earth.

伝える to tell, report, introduce, transmit: (trans.)

		Affirmative	*Negative*
PLAIN FORM:	PRESENT	tsutaeru	tsutaenai
	PAST	tsutaeta	tsutaenakatta
MASU FORM:	PRESENT	tsutaemasu	tsutaemasen
	PAST	tsutaemashita	tsutaemasen deshita
IMPERATIVE		tsutaero	tsutaeru na
TE FORM		tsutaete	tsutaenakute
CONDITIONAL:	PLAIN	tsutaereba	tsutaenakereba
		tsutaeta ra	tsutaenakatta ra
	FORMAL	tsutaemashita ra	tsutaemasen deshita ra
PRESUMPTIVE:	PLAIN	tsutaeru daroo	tsutaenai daroo
	FORMAL	tsutaeru deshoo	tsutaenai deshoo
VOLITIONAL:	PLAIN	tsutaeyoo	
	FORMAL	tsutaemashoo	

	Affirmative		*Affirmative*
POTENTIAL	tsutaerareru	HONORIFIC	otsutae ni naru
	tsutaereru		otsutae nasaru
PASSIVE	tsutaerareru	HUMBLE	otsutae suru
			otsutae itasu
CAUSATIVE	tsutaesaseru		
CAUS. PASSIVE	tsutaesaserareru		

Examples:

1. *Ato de anata ni denwa suru yoo ni kare ni tsutaete okimasu.*
   I will tell him to phone you later.
2. *Kooshoo ga shuuketsu ni chikazuite kita to shinbun wa tsutaete iru.*
   Newspapers report that the negotiations are nearing a settlement.
3. *Harigane wa denki o tsutaeru.*
   Wires transmit electricity.
4. *Bukkyoo wa Chuugoku kara Nihon ni tsutaerareta.*
   Buddhism was introduced into Japan from China.
5. *Sono katana wa chichi kara ko e daidai tsutaerareta.*
   That sword has for generations been handed down from father to child.

伝わる to be handed down, be transmitted, be introduced: (intrans.)

		Affirmative	*Negative*
PLAIN FORM:	PRESENT	tsutawaru	tsutawaranai
	PAST	tsutawatta	tsutawaranakatta
MASU FORM:	PRESENT	tsutawarimasu	tsutawarimasen
	PAST	tsutawarimashita	tsutawarimasen deshita
IMPERATIVE		(tsutaware)	(tsutawaru na)
TE FORM		tsutawatte	tsutawaranakute
CONDITIONAL:	PLAIN	tsutawareba	tsutawaranakereba
		tsutawatta ra	tsutawaranakatta ra
	FORMAL	tsutawarimashita ra	tsutawarimasen deshita ra
PRESUMPTIVE:	PLAIN	tsutawaru daroo	tsutawaranai daroo
	FORMAL	tsutawaru deshoo	tsutawaranai deshoo
VOLITIONAL:	PLAIN	(tsutawaroo)	
	FORMAL	(tsutawarimashoo)	

	Affirmative		*Affirmative*
POTENTIAL	(tsutawareru)	HONORIFIC	otsutawari ni naru
			otsutawari nasaru
PASSIVE	(tsutawarareru)	HUMBLE	(otsutawari suru)
			(otsutawari itasu)
CAUSATIVE	tsutawaraseru		
CAUS. PASSIVE	tsutawaraserareru		

Examples:

1. *Kono katana wa sofu no dai kara tsutawatta.*
   This sword has been handed down from my grandfather's time.
2. *Kono harigane ni wa denki ga tsutawatte iru.*
   This wire is charged with electricity.
3. *Kare no kinchoo ga kanojo ni mo tsutawatta yoo da.*
   His tension seems to have transferred itself to her too.
4. *Sono uwasa wa machi-juu ni tsutawatte shimaimashita.*
   That rumor ended up spreading throughout the town.
5. *Bukkyoo wa Chuugoku kara Nihon ni tsutawarimashita.*
   Buddhism was introduced into Japan from China.

包む to wrap, veil, envelop in: (trans.)

		Affirmative	*Negative*
PLAIN FORM:	PRESENT	tsutsumu	tsutsumanai
	PAST	tsutsunda	tsutsumanakatta
MASU FORM:	PRESENT	tsutsumimasu	tsutsumimasen
	PAST	tsutsumimashita	tsutsumimasen deshita
IMPERATIVE		tsutsume	tsutsumu na
TE FORM		tsutsunde	tsutsumanakute
CONDITIONAL:	PLAIN	tsutsumeba	tsutsumanakereba
		tsutsunda ra	tsutsumanakatta ra
	FORMAL	tsutsumimashita ra	tsutsumimasen deshita ra
PRESUMPTIVE:	PLAIN	tsutsumu daroo	tsutsumanai daroo
	FORMAL	tsutsumu deshoo	tsutsumanai deshoo
VOLITIONAL:	PLAIN	tsutsumoo	
	FORMAL	tsutsumimashoo	

	Affirmative		*Affirmative*
POTENTIAL	tsutsumeru	HONORIFIC	otsutsumi ni naru
			otsutsumi nasaru
PASSIVE	tsutsumareru	HUMBLE	otsutsumi suru
			otsutsumi itasu
CAUSATIVE	tsutsumaseru		
CAUS. PASSIVE	tsutsumaserareru		
	tsutsumasareru		

Examples:

1. *Kore o kami ni tsutsunde kudasai.*
   Please wrap this up in paper.
2. *Kare wa ooki na manto ni mi o tsutsunde ita.*
   He was wrapped up in a big cloak.
3. *Sanchoo wa kiri ni tsutsumarete ita.*
   The mountaintop was veiled in mist.
4. *Kanojo no shussei wa shinpi ni tsutsumarete imasu.*
   Her birth is veiled in mystery.
5. *Ie wa honoo ni tsutsumarete ita.*
   The house was enveloped in flames.

通じる to make oneself understood, to lead to, be well informed, connect with (telephone): (intrans.)

		Affirmative	*Negative*
PLAIN FORM:	PRESENT	tsuujiru	tsuujinai
	PAST	tsuujita	tsuujinakatta
MASU FORM:	PRESENT	tsuujimasu	tsuujimasen
	PAST	tsuujimashita	tsuujimasen deshita
IMPERATIVE		(tsuujiro)	(tsuujiru na)
TE FORM		tsuujite	tsuujinakute
CONDITIONAL:	PLAIN	tsuujireba	tsuujinakereba
		tsuujita ra	tsuujinakatta ra
	FORMAL	tsuujimashita ra	tsuujimasen deshita ra
PRESUMPTIVE:	PLAIN	tsuujiru daroo	tsuujinai daroo
	FORMAL	tsuujiru deshoo	tsuujinai deshoo
VOLITIONAL:	PLAIN	(tsuujiyoo)	
	FORMAL	(tsuujimashoo)	

	Affirmative		*Affirmative*
POTENTIAL	(tsuujirareru)	HONORIFIC	otsuuji ni naru
			otsuuji nasaru
PASSIVE	(tsuujirareru)	HUMBLE	(otsuuji suru)
			(otsuuji itasu)
CAUSATIVE	tsuujisaseru		
CAUS. PASSIVE	tsuujisaserareru		

Examples:

1. *Furansu-go o shabetta ga, aite ni tsuujinakatta.*
   I spoke in French, but couldn't make myself understood.
2. *Kare ni wa joodan ga tsuujimasen.*
   He doesn't understand jokes.
3. *Koko kara Kyooto made tetsudoo ga tsuujite imasu.*
   A railroad runs from here to Kyoto.
4. *Kare wa gendai ongaku ni tsuujite iru.*
   He is well informed about modern music.
5. *Hanashi-chuu de denwa ga tsuujinai.*
   The line is busy and I can't reach him.

続ける to continue, go on, proceed, carry on: (trans.)

		Affirmative	*Negative*
PLAIN FORM:	PRESENT	tsuzukeru	tsuzukenai
	PAST	tsuzuketa	tsuzukenakatta
MASU FORM:	PRESENT	tsuzukemasu	tsuzukemasen
	PAST	tsuzukemashita	tsuzukemasen deshita
IMPERATIVE		tsuzukero	tsuzukeru na
TE FORM		tsuzukete	tsuzukenakute
CONDITIONAL:	PLAIN	tsuzukereba	tsuzukenakereba
		tsuzuketa ra	tsuzukenakatta ra
	FORMAL	tsuzukemashita ra	tsuzukemasen deshita ra
PRESUMPTIVE:	PLAIN	tsuzukeru daroo	tsuzukenai daroo
	FORMAL	tsuzukeru deshoo	tsuzukenai deshoo
VOLITIONAL:	PLAIN	tsuzukeyoo	
	FORMAL	tsuzukemashoo	

	Affirmative		*Affirmative*
POTENTIAL	tsuzukerareru	HONORIFIC	otsuzuke ni naru
	tsuzukereru		otsuzuke nasaru
PASSIVE	tsuzukerareru	HUMBLE	otsuzuke suru
			otsuzuke itasu
CAUSATIVE	tsuzukesaseru		
CAUS. PASSIVE	tsuzukesaserareru		

Examples:

1. *Hanashi o tsuzukete kudasai.*
   Please proceed with your story.
2. *Karera wa yonaka made hanashi-tsuzukemashita.*
   They went on talking until late at night.
3. *Jishin no saichuu mo kare wa enzetsu o tsuzuketa.*
   He continued with his speech even during the earthquake.
4. *Tsukarete imashita ga, kare wa shigoto o tsuzukemashita.*
   Though he was tired, he kept on with his work.
5. *Kinoo wa juu-jikan tsuzukete hataraita.*
   Yesterday I worked for ten hours without a break.

続く to continue, last, lead to, follow: (intrans.)

		Affirmative	*Negative*
PLAIN FORM:	PRESENT	tsuzuku	tsuzukanai
	PAST	tsuzuita	tsuzukanakatta
MASU FORM:	PRESENT	tsuzukimasu	tsuzukimasen
	PAST	tsuzukimashita	tsuzukimasen deshita
IMPERATIVE		tsuzuke	tsuzuku na
TE FORM		tsuzuite	tsuzukanakute
CONDITIONAL:	PLAIN	tsuzukeba	tsuzukanakereba
		tsuzuita ra	tsuzukanakatta ra
	FORMAL	tsuzukimashita ra	tsuzukimasen deshita ra
PRESUMPTIVE:	PLAIN	tsuzuku daroo	tsuzukanai daroo
	FORMAL	tsuzuku deshoo	tsuzukanai deshoo
VOLITIONAL:	PLAIN	tsuzukoo	
	FORMAL	tsuzukimashoo	

	Affirmative		*Affirmative*
POTENTIAL	(tsuzukeru)	HONORIFIC	otsuzuki ni naru
			otsuzuki nasaru
PASSIVE	(tsuzukareru)	HUMBLE	(otsuzuki suru)
			(otsuzuki itasu)
CAUSATIVE	tsuzukaseru		
CAUS. PASSIVE	tsuzukaserareru		
	tsuzukasareru		

Examples:

1. *Ame ga ichi-nichi-juu furi-tsuzuita.*
   The rain continued falling all day.
2. *Tsugi no peeji ni tsuzuku.*
   It continues on the next page.
3. *Ii tenki wa asatte made tsuzuku daroo ka.*
   I wonder if the fine weather will last till the day after tomorrow.
4. *Kono michi wa kooen ni tsuzuite imasu.*
   This road leads to the park.
5. *Haru wa fuyu ni tsuzuku.*
   Spring follows winter.

ugokasu

動かす to move, operate, influence: (trans.)

		Affirmative	*Negative*
PLAIN FORM:	PRESENT	ugokasu	ugokasanai
	PAST	ugokashita	ugokasanakatta
MASU FORM:	PRESENT	ugokashimasu	ugokashimasen
	PAST	ugokashimashita	ugokashimasen deshita
IMPERATIVE		ugokase	ugokasu na
TE FORM		ugokashite	ugokasanakute
CONDITIONAL:	PLAIN	ugokaseba	ugokasanakereba
		ugokashita ra	ugokasanakatta ra
	FORMAL	ugokashimashita ra	ugokashimasen deshita ra
PRESUMPTIVE:	PLAIN	ugokasu daroo	ugokasanai daroo
	FORMAL	ugokasu deshoo	ugokasanai deshoo
VOLITIONAL:	PLAIN	ugokasoo	
	FORMAL	ugokashimashoo	

	Affirmative		*Affirmative*
POTENTIAL	ugokaseru	HONORIFIC	ougokashi ni naru
			ougokashi nasaru
PASSIVE	ugokasareru	HUMBLE	ougokashi suru
			ougokashi itasu
CAUSATIVE	ugokasaseru		
CAUS. PASSIVE	ugokasaserareru		
	ugokasasareru		

Examples:

1. *Kono teeburu o sukoshi migi e ugokashite kudasai.*
   Please move this table a little farther to the right.
2. *Byoonin o ugokashite wa ikenai. Sono mama ni shite oki-nasai.*
   Don't move the patient. Leave him where he is.
3. *Imaya yotei o ugokasenai.*
   We can't change the schedule at this point.
4. *Kono kikai o ugokasu no wa kantan da.*
   This machine is easy to run.
5. *Watashi wa kare no kotoba ni ugokasareta.*
   I was deeply moved by his words.

動く to move, change, run (intrans.)

		Affirmative	*Negative*
PLAIN FORM:	PRESENT	ugoku	ugokanai
	PAST	ugoita	ugokanakatta
MASU FORM:	PRESENT	ugokimasu	ugokimasen
	PAST	ugokimashita	ugokimasen deshita
IMPERATIVE		ugoke	ugoku na
TE FORM		ugoite	ugokanakute
CONDITIONAL:	PLAIN	ugokeba	ugokanakereba
		ugoita ra	ugokanakatta ra
	FORMAL	ugokimashita ra	ugokimasen deshita ra
PRESUMPTIVE:	PLAIN	ugoku daroo	ugokanai daroo
	FORMAL	ugoku deshoo	ugokanai deshoo
VOLITIONAL:	PLAIN	ugokoo	
	FORMAL	ugokimashoo	

	Affirmative		*Affirmative*
POTENTIAL	ugokeru	HONORIFIC	ougoki ni naru
			ougoki nasaru
PASSIVE	ugokareru	HUMBLE	(ougoki suru)
			(ougoki itasu)
CAUSATIVE	ugokaseru		
CAUS. PASSIVE	ugokaserareru		

Examples:

1. *Kono tokei wa ugokanai.*
   This watch doesn't work.
2. *Ano hito wa kantan ni kane de ugoku.*
   He is easily influenced by money.
3. *Kono kuruma wa denki de ugokimasu.*
   This car runs on electricity.
4. *Sekai joosei wa ugoite imasu.*
   The world situation is changing.
5. *Ugoku to, inochi wa nai zo.*
   Move, and you are a dead man.

浮かべる to float, rise to the surface, appear: (trans.)

		Affirmative	*Negative*
PLAIN FORM:	PRESENT	ukaberu	ukabenai
	PAST	ukabeta	ukabenakatta
MASU FORM:	PRESENT	ukabemasu	ukabemasen
	PAST	ukabemashita	ukabemasen deshita
IMPERATIVE		ukabero	ukaberu na
TE FORM		ukabete	ukabenakute
CONDITIONAL:	PLAIN	ukabereba	ukabenakereba
		ukabeta ra	ukabenakatta ra
	FORMAL	ukabemashita ra	ukabemasen deshita ra
PRESUMPTIVE:	PLAIN	ukaberu daroo	ukabenai daroo
	FORMAL	ukaberu deshoo	ukabenai deshoo
VOLITIONAL:	PLAIN	ukabeyoo	
	FORMAL	ukabemashoo	

	Affirmative		*Affirmative*
POTENTIAL	ukaberareru	HONORIFIC	oukabe ni naru
			oukabe nasaru
PASSIVE	ukaberareru	HUMBLE	(oukabe suru)
			(oukabe itasu)
CAUSATIVE	ukabesaseru		
CAUS. PASSIVE	ukabesaserareru		

Examples:

1. *Shoonen wa mizu ni kami no fune o ukabemashita.*
   The boy floated his paper boat on the water.
2. *Sono shirase o kiite kare wa shitsuboo no iro o kao ni ukabeta.*
   A look of disappointment appeared on his face after hearing that news.
3. *Kanojo wa kotoba de arawasenai kansha no kimochi o kao ni ukabeta.*
   Her face showed a gratitude that she couldn't express in words.
4. *Shoojo wa me ni namida o ukabete imashita.*
   The girl had tears in her eyes.
5. *Kanojo wa emi o ukabete, ojigi o shita.*
   She bowed with a smile about her lips.

浮かぶ to float, rise to the surface: (intrans.)

		Affirmative	*Negative*
PLAIN FORM:	PRESENT	ukabu	ukabanai
	PAST	ukanda	ukabanakatta
MASU FORM:	PRESENT	ukabimasu	ukabimasen
	PAST	ukabimashita	ukabimasen deshita
IMPERATIVE		ukabe	ukabu na
TE FORM		ukande	ukabanakute
CONDITIONAL:	PLAIN	ukabeba	ukabanakereba
		ukanda ra	ukabanakatta ra
	FORMAL	ukabimashita ra	ukabimasen deshita ra
PRESUMPTIVE:	PLAIN	ukabu daroo	ukabanai daroo
	FORMAL	ukabu deshoo	ukabanai deshoo
VOLITIONAL:	PLAIN	ukaboo	
	FORMAL	ukabimashoo	

	Affirmative		*Affirmative*
POTENTIAL	(ukaberu)	HONORIFIC	oukabi ni naru
			oukabi nasaru
PASSIVE	(ukabareru)	HUMBLE	(oukabi suru)
			(oukabi itasu)
CAUSATIVE	ukabaseru		
CAUS. PASSIVE	ukabaserareru		
	ukabasareru		

Examples:

1. *Ki wa mizu ni ukabu.*
   Wood floats on water.
2. *Shiroi kumo ga sora ni ukande imasu.*
   White clouds are floating in the sky.
3. *Kare no kao ni wa fuan no iro ga ukanda.*
   A look of uneasiness appeared on his face.
4. *Kanojo no me ni namida ga ukabimashita.*
   Tears came to her eyes.
5. *Meian ga ukanda.*
   A good idea occurred to me.

生まれる *or* 産まれる to be born, arise: (intrans.)

		Affirmative	*Negative*
PLAIN FORM:	PRESENT	umareru	umarenai
	PAST	umareta	umarenakatta
MASU FORM:	PRESENT	umaremasu	umaremasen
	PAST	umaremashita	umaremasen deshita
IMPERATIVE		(umarero)	(umareru na)
TE FORM		umarete	umarenakute
CONDITIONAL:	PLAIN	umarereba	umarenakereba
		umareta ra	umarenakatta ra
	FORMAL	umaremashita ra	umaremasen deshita ra
PRESUMPTIVE:	PLAIN	umareru daroo	umarenai daroo
	FORMAL	umareru deshoo	umarenai deshoo
VOLITIONAL:	PLAIN	(umareyoo)	
	FORMAL	(umaremashoo)	

	Affirmative		*Affirmative*
POTENTIAL	(umarerareru)	HONORIFIC	oumare ni naru
			oumare nasaru
PASSIVE	(umarerareru)	HUMBLE	(oumare suru)
			(oumare itasu)
CAUSATIVE	umaresaseru		
CAUS. PASSIVE	umaresaserareru		

Examples:

1. *Watashi wa sen kyuuhyaku yonjuu-kyuu nen, ku-gatsu muika ni Tookyoo de umaremashita.*
   I was born in Tokyo on September 6, 1949.
2. *Yamada-san no tokoro ni onna no ko ga umaremashita.*
   A baby girl was born to Mr. Yamada.
3. *Raigetsu ane ni kodomo ga umareru yotei da.*
   My sister is going to have a baby next month.
4. *Kono koto kara juudai na kekka ga umareru kamo-shirenai.*
   Serious results may arise from this.
5. *Atarashii kokka ga umareta.*
   A new nation has been founded.

生む *or* 産む to give birth, produce, yield: (trans.)

		Affirmative	*Negative*
PLAIN FORM:	PRESENT	umu	umanai
	PAST	unda	umanakatta
MASU FORM:	PRESENT	umimasu	umimasen
	PAST	umimashita	umimasen deshita
IMPERATIVE		ume	umu na
TE FORM		unde	umanakute
CONDITIONAL:	PLAIN	umeba	umanakereba
		unda ra	umanakatta ra
	FORMAL	umimashita ra	umimasen deshita ra
PRESUMPTIVE:	PLAIN	umu daroo	umanai daroo
	FORMAL	umu deshoo	umanai deshoo
VOLITIONAL:	PLAIN	umoo	
	FORMAL	umimashoo	

	Affirmative		*Affirmative*
POTENTIAL	umeru	HONORIFIC	oumi ni naru
			oumi nasaru
PASSIVE	umareru	HUMBLE	(oumi suru)
			(oumi itasu)
CAUSATIVE	umaseru		
CAUS. PASSIVE	umaserareru		
	umasareru		

Examples:

1. *Ane wa kinoo kodomo o umimashita.*
   My older sister had a baby yesterday.
2. *Kono niwatori wa mainichi tamago o umu.*
   This hen lays eggs everyday.
3. *Kare wa Nihon ga unda saidai no geijutsuka da.*
   He is the greatest artist that Japan has ever produced.
4. *Kare no okonatta tooshi wa genzai kyuu-paasento no rieki o unde iru.*
   The investment which he made now yields a nine-percent interest.
5. *Kane ga kane o umu.*
   Money begets money.

売る to sell: (trans.)

		Affirmative	*Negative*
PLAIN FORM:	PRESENT	uru	uranai
	PAST	utta	uranakatta
MASU FORM:	PRESENT	urimasu	urimasen
	PAST	urimashita	urimasen deshita
IMPERATIVE		ure	uru na
TE FORM		utte	uranakute
CONDITIONAL:	PLAIN	ureba	uranakereba
		utta ra	uranakatta ra
	FORMAL	urimashita ra	urimasen deshita ra
PRESUMPTIVE:	PLAIN	uru daroo	uranai daroo
	FORMAL	uru deshoo	uranai deshoo
VOLITIONAL:	PLAIN	uroo	
	FORMAL	urimashoo	

	Affirmative		*Affirmative*
POTENTIAL	ureru	HONORIFIC	ouri ni naru
			ouri nasaru
PASSIVE	urareru	HUMBLE	ouri suru
			ouri itasu
CAUSATIVE	uraseru		
CAUS. PASSIVE	uraserareru		
	urasareru		

Examples:

1. *Hitotsu gojuu en de urimasu.*
   I will sell them at fifty yen apiece.
2. *Shio wa ichi pondo tan'i de urarete iru.*
   Salt is sold by the pound. (*lit.*, one-pound basis)
3. *Kore wa ikura de urimasu ka.*
   How much are you asking for this?
4. *Wareware wa zaiko o sugu ni uri-kitta.*
   We sold out the whole stock in no time.
5. *Kare wa jibun no kuni o utta.*
   He betrayed his own country.

疑う to doubt, suspect: (trans.)

		Affirmative	*Negative*
PLAIN FORM:	PRESENT	utagau	utagawanai
	PAST	utagatta	utagawanakatta
MASU FORM:	PRESENT	utagaimasu	utagaimasen
	PAST	utagaimashita	utagaimasen deshita
IMPERATIVE		utagae	utagau na
TE FORM		utagatte	utagawanakute
CONDITIONAL:	PLAIN	utagaeba	utagawanakereba
		utagatta ra	utagawanakatta ra
	FORMAL	utagaimashita ra	utagaimasen deshita ra
PRESUMPTIVE:	PLAIN	utagau daroo	utagawanai daroo
	FORMAL	utagau deshoo	utagawanai deshoo
VOLITIONAL:	PLAIN	utagaoo	
	FORMAL	utagaimashoo	

	Affirmative		*Affirmative*
POTENTIAL	utagaeru	HONORIFIC	outagai ni naru
			outagai nasaru
PASSIVE	utagawareru	HUMBLE	outagai suru
			outagai itasu
CAUSATIVE	utagawaseru		
CAUS. PASSIVE	utagawaserareru		
	utagawasareru		

Examples:

1. *Anata wa mada watashi o utagau no desu ka.*
   Do you still doubt me?
2. *Boku wa kimi no nooryoku o utagawanai.*
   I do not doubt your ability.
3. *Kare no seikoo o utagawazaru o enai.*
   I can't help being doubtful of his success.
4. *Watashi wa jibun no mimi o utagatta.*
   I could hardly believe my ears.
5. *Kare wa hannin da to utagawareta.*
   He was suspected to be the criminal.

歌う to sing; うたう to express: (both trans.)

		Affirmative	*Negative*
PLAIN FORM:	PRESENT	utau	utawanai
	PAST	utatta	utawanakatta
MASU FORM:	PRESENT	utaimasu	utaimasen
	PAST	utaimashita	utaimasen deshita
IMPERATIVE		utae	utau na
TE FORM		utatte	utawanakute
CONDITIONAL:	PLAIN	utaeba	utawanakereba
		utatta ra	utawanakatta ra
	FORMAL	utaimashita ra	utaimasen deshita ra
PRESUMPTIVE:	PLAIN	utau daroo	utawanai daroo
	FORMAL	utau deshoo	utawanai deshoo
VOLITIONAL:	PLAIN	utaoo	
	FORMAL	utaimashoo	

	Affirmative		*Affirmative*
POTENTIAL	utaeru	HONORIFIC	outai ni naru
			outai nasaru
PASSIVE	utawareru	HUMBLE	outai suru
			outai itasu
CAUSATIVE	utawaseru		
CAUS. PASSIVE	utawaserareru		
	utawasareru		

Examples:

1. *Doozo watashi-tachi ni uta o utatte kudasai.*
   Please sing us a song.
2. *Kanojo wa piano o hiki-nagara utatta.*
   She sang, accompanying herself on the piano.
3. *Kare wa hataraki-nagara utaimashita.*
   He sang while he worked.
4. *Kare wa jinsei no yorokobi to kanashimi o shi ni utatta.*
   He sang a song of the joys and sorrows of life.
5. *Wareware no hooshin wa gen'an ni hakkiri utawarete iru.*
   Our policies are clearly expressed in the original draft.

打つ to beat, strike, hit; 撃つ to shoot: (both trans.)

		Affirmative	*Negative*
PLAIN FORM:	PRESENT	utsu	utanai
	PAST	utta	utanakatta
MASU FORM:	PRESENT	uchimasu	uchimasen
	PAST	uchimashita	uchimasen deshita
IMPERATIVE		ute	utsu na
TE FORM		utte	utanakute
CONDITIONAL:	PLAIN	uteba	utanakereba
		utta ra	utanakatta ra
	FORMAL	uchimashita ra	uchimasen deshita ra
PRESUMPTIVE:	PLAIN	utsu daroo	utanai daroo
	FORMAL	utsu deshoo	utanai deshoo
VOLITIONAL:	PLAIN	utoo	
	FORMAL	uchimashoo	

	Affirmative		*Affirmative*
POTENTIAL	uteru	HONORIFIC	ouchi ni naru
			ouchi nasaru
PASSIVE	utareru	HUMBLE	(ouchi suru)
			(ouchi itasu)
CAUSATIVE	utaseru		
CAUS. PASSIVE	utaserareru		
	utasareru		

Examples:

1. *Roojin wa shoonen o tsue de utta.*
   The old man beat the boy with a stick.
2. *Nami ga kaigan o utte ita.*
   The waves were beating against the shore.
3. *Kare wa kaminari ni utarete shinda.*
   He was struck dead by lightning.
4. *Keikan wa ashi o utaremashita.*
   The policeman was shot in the leg.
5. *Ugoku na, samonai to utsu zo.*
   Don't move, or I'll shoot.

移る to move, transfer; 映る to be reflected: (both intrans.)*

		Affirmative	*Negative*
PLAIN FORM:	PRESENT	utsuru	utsuranai
	PAST	utsutta	utsuranakatta
MASU FORM:	PRESENT	utsurimasu	utsurimasen
	PAST	utsurimashita	utsurimasen deshita
IMPERATIVE		utsure	utsuru na
TE FORM		utsutte	utsuranakute
CONDITIONAL:	PLAIN	utsureba	utsuranakereba
		utsutta ra	utsuranakatta ra
	FORMAL	utsurimashita ra	utsurimasen deshita ra
PRESUMPTIVE:	PLAIN	utsuru daroo	utsuranai daroo
	FORMAL	utsuru deshoo	utsuranai deshoo
VOLITIONAL:	PLAIN	utsuroo	
	FORMAL	utsurimashoo	

	Affirmative		*Affirmative*
POTENTIAL	utsureru	HONORIFIC	outsuri ni naru
			outsuri nasaru
PASSIVE	utsurareru	HUMBLE	(outsuri suru)
			(outsuri itasu)
CAUSATIVE	utsuraseru		
CAUS. PASSIVE	utsuraserareru		
	utsurasareru		

Examples:

1. *Watashi wa Kyooto ni utsutta bakari desu.*
   I have just moved to Kyoto.
2. *Tomodachi no kaze ga utsutta.*
   I caught a cold from my friend.
3. *Tanaka-san wa jinji-bu ni utsurimashita.*
   Mr. Tanaka moved to the personnel section.
4. *Sakura no ki ga mizu ni utsutte imasu.*
   The cherry trees are reflected in the water.
5. *Ayashii kage ga kaaten ni utsutta.*
   A strange shadow fell on the curtain.

* In general, the verb *utsuru* 映る meaning "to be reflected" does not use the imperative, volitional, potential, or passive forms.

移す to move to, transfer; 写す to copy; 映す to reflect: (all trans.)

		Affirmative	*Negative*
PLAIN FORM:	PRESENT	utsusu	utsusanai
	PAST	utsushita	utsusanakatta
MASU FORM:	PRESENT	utsushimasu	utsushimasen
	PAST	utsushimashita	utsushimasen deshita
IMPERATIVE		utsuse	utsusu na
TE FORM		utsushite	utsusanakute
CONDITIONAL:	PLAIN	utsuseba	utsusanakereba
		utsushita ra	utsusanakatta ra
	FORMAL	utsushimashita ra	utsushimasen deshita ra
PRESUMPTIVE:	PLAIN	utsusu daroo	utsusanai daroo
	FORMAL	utsusu deshoo	utsusanai deshoo
VOLITIONAL:	PLAIN	utsusoo	
	FORMAL	utsushimashoo	

	Affirmative		*Affirmative*
POTENTIAL	utsuseru	HONORIFIC	outsushi ni naru
			outsushi nasaru
PASSIVE	utsusareru	HUMBLE	outsushi suru
			outsushi itasu
CAUSATIVE	utsusaseru		
CAUS. PASSIVE	utsusaserareru		

Examples:

1. *Kazoku o kaigan ni utsushita bakari desu.*
   I have just moved my family to the seashore.
2. *Kare wa watashi ni kaze o utsushimashita.*
   He has given me his cold.
3. *Yoshida-san wa soomu-bu ni utsusaremashita.*
   Mr. Yoshida was transferred to the general affairs section.
4. *San-peeji kara yon-peeji made nooto ni utsushite kudasai.*
   Please copy from page three to page four in your notebook.
5. *Kodomo wa oya o utsusu kagami desu.*
   Children are mirrors reflecting their parents.

分れる *or* 別れる to part, separate from, be divided: (intrans.)

		Affirmative	*Negative*
PLAIN FORM:	PRESENT	wakareru	wakarenai
	PAST	wakareta	wakarenakatta
MASU FORM:	PRESENT	wakaremasu	wakaremasen
	PAST	wakaremashita	wakaremasen deshita
IMPERATIVE		wakarero	wakareru na
TE FORM		wakarete	wakarenakute
CONDITIONAL:	PLAIN	wakarereba	wakarenakereba
		wakareta ra	wakarenakatta ra
	FORMAL	wakaremashita ra	wakaremasen deshita ra
PRESUMPTIVE:	PLAIN	wakareru daroo	wakarenai daroo
	FORMAL	wakareru deshoo	wakarenai deshoo
VOLITIONAL:	PLAIN	wakareyoo	
	FORMAL	wakaremashoo	

	Affirmative		*Affirmative*
POTENTIAL	wakarerareru	HONORIFIC	owakare ni naru
			owakare nasaru
PASSIVE	wakarerareru	HUMBLE	owakare suru
			owakare itasu
CAUSATIVE	wakaresaseru		
CAUS. PASSIVE	wakaresaserareru		

Examples:

1. *Watashi wa kanojo to eki mae de wakaremashita.*
   I parted from her in front of the station.
2. *Karera wa muttsu no chiisana guruupu ni wakareta.*
   They separated into six small groups.
3. *Gakkoo wa hachi kurasu ni wakarete imasu.*
   Our school is divided into eight classes.
4. *Too wa ni-ha ni wakareta.*
   The political party split into two factions.
5. *Kare wa tsuma to wakaremashita.*
   He separated from his wife.

分かる to understand, know, find out: (intrans.)

		Affirmative	*Negative*
PLAIN FORM:	PRESENT	wakaru	wakaranai
	PAST	wakatta	wakaranakatta
MASU FORM:	PRESENT	wakarimasu	wakarimasen
	PAST	wakarimashita	wakarimasen deshita
IMPERATIVE		wakare	wakaru na
TE FORM		wakatte	wakaranakute
CONDITIONAL:	PLAIN	wakareba	wakaranakereba
		wakatta ra	wakaranakatta ra
	FORMAL	wakarimashita ra	wakarimasen deshita ra
PRESUMPTIVE:	PLAIN	wakaru daroo	wakaranai daroo
	FORMAL	wakaru deshoo	wakaranai deshoo
VOLITIONAL:	PLAIN	wakaroo	
	FORMAL	wakarimashoo	

	Affirmative		*Affirmative*
POTENTIAL	(wakareru)	HONORIFIC	owakari ni naru
			owakari nasaru
PASSIVE	(wakarareru)	HUMBLE	(owakari suru)
			(owakari itasu)
CAUSATIVE	wakaraseru		
CAUS. PASSIVE	wakaraserareru		
	wakarasareru		

Examples:

1. *Watashi ni wa anata no iu koto ga wakarimasen.*
   I don't understand what you are saying.
2. *Dooshite yoi no ka wakarimasen.*
   I don't know what to do.
3. *Karera ga Amerika-jin da to dooshite kare ni wakatta no kashira.*
   I wonder how he knew they were Americans.
4. *Watashi no machigatte iru koto ga wakatta.*
   I found out that I was mistaken.
5. *Kare ni wa shi ga wakaranai.*
   He has no understanding of poetry.

分ける to divide, separate, classify: (trans.)

		Affirmative	Negative
PLAIN FORM:	PRESENT	wakeru	wakenai
	PAST	waketa	wakenakatta
MASU FORM:	PRESENT	wakemasu	wakemasen
	PAST	wakemashita	wakemasen deshita
IMPERATIVE		wakero	wakeru na
TE FORM		wakete	wakenakute
CONDITIONAL:	PLAIN	wakereba	wakenakereba
		waketa ra	wakenakatta ra
	FORMAL	wakemashita ra	wakemasen deshita ra
PRESUMPTIVE:	PLAIN	wakeru daroo	wakenai daroo
	FORMAL	wakeru deshoo	wakenai deshoo
VOLITIONAL:	PLAIN	wakeyoo	
	FORMAL	wakemashoo	

	Affirmative		Affirmative
POTENTIAL	wakerareru wakereru	HONORIFIC	owake ni naru owake nasaru
PASSIVE	wakerareru	HUMBLE	owake suru owake itasu
CAUSATIVE	wakesaseru		
CAUS. PASSIVE	wakesaserareru		

Examples:

1. *Kanojo wa keeki o itsutsu ni waketa.*
   She divided the cake into five pieces.
2. *Sensei wa danshi o joshi kara wakemashita.*
   The teacher separated the boys from the girls.
3. *Kare wa kenka o waketa.*
   He broke up the fight.
4. *Kaado wa arufabetto-jun ni wakerarete iru.*
   The cards are classified in alphabetical order.
5. *Daidokoro o heya to shite wakereba, go heya arimasu.*
   We have five rooms, if you classify a kitchen as a room.

笑う to laugh, smile (intrans. and trans.)

		Affirmative	*Negative*
PLAIN FORM:	PRESENT	warau	warawanai
	PAST	waratta	warawanakatta
MASU FORM:	PRESENT	waraimasu	waraimasen
	PAST	waraimashita	waraimasen deshita
IMPERATIVE		warae	warau na
TE FORM		waratte	warawanakute
CONDITIONAL:	PLAIN	waraeba	warawanakereba
		waratta ra	warawanakatta ra
	FORMAL	waraimashita ra	waraimasen deshita ra
PRESUMPTIVE:	PLAIN	warau daroo	warawanai daroo
	FORMAL	warau deshoo	warawanai deshoo
VOLITIONAL:	PLAIN	waraoo	
	FORMAL	waraimashoo	

	Affirmative			*Affirmative*
POTENTIAL	waraeru	HONORIFIC		owarai ni naru
				owarai nasaru
PASSIVE	warawareru	HUMBLE		(owarai suru)
				(owarai itasu)
CAUSATIVE	warawaseru			
CAUS. PASSIVE	warawaserareru			
	warawasareru			

Examples:

1. *Saigo ni warau mono ga ichiban oogoe de warau.*
   He who laughs last laughs the loudest.
2. *Sonna koto o shita ra, warawareru yo.*
   You'll be laughed at if you do such a thing.
3. *Sono kookei o mite, warawanaide wa irarenakatta.*
   I could not help laughing at the sight.
4. *Kanojo wa kodomo-tachi ga asobu no o mite waratta.*
   She smiled as she watched the children playing.
5. *Kanojo ga eiga sutaa ni nari-tai-tte? Warawaseru ne.*
   You say she wishes to become a movie star? That's a laugh.

割れる to break, be divided, split: (intrans.)

		Affirmative	*Negative*
PLAIN FORM:	PRESENT	wareru	warenai
	PAST	wareta	warenakatta
MASU FORM:	PRESENT	waremasu	waremasen
	PAST	waremashita	waremasen deshita
IMPERATIVE		(warero)	(wareru na)
TE FORM		warete	warenakute
CONDITIONAL:	PLAIN	warereba	warenakereba
		wareta ra	warenakatta ra
	FORMAL	waremashita ra	waremasen deshita ra
PRESUMPTIVE:	PLAIN	wareru daroo	warenai daroo
	FORMAL	wareru deshoo	warenai deshoo
VOLITIONAL:	PLAIN	(wareyoo)	
	FORMAL	(waremashoo)	

	Affirmative		*Affirmative*
POTENTIAL	(warerareru)	HONORIFIC	oware ni naru
			oware nasaru
PASSIVE	(warerareru)	HUMBLE	(oware suru)
			(oware itasu)
CAUSATIVE	waresaseru		
CAUS. PASSIVE	waresaserareru		

Examples:

1. *Tamago wa ware-yasui.*
   Eggs break easily.
2. *Koppu wa futatsu ni wareta.*
   The cup broke in two.
3. *Hyaku wa go de waremasu.*
   A hundred can be divided by five.
4. *Kaiin no iken ga sono ten de wareta.*
   The members' opinions were divided on that point.
5. *Too wa futatsu no ha ni wareta.*
   The party split into two factions.

割る to break, divide: (trans.)

		Affirmative	*Negative*
PLAIN FORM:	PRESENT	waru	waranai
	PAST	watta	waranakatta
MASU FORM:	PRESENT	warimasu	warimasen
	PAST	warimashita	warimasen deshita
IMPERATIVE		ware	waru na
TE FORM		watte	waranakute
CONDITIONAL:	PLAIN	wareba	waranakereba
		watta ra	waranakatta ra
	FORMAL	warimashita ra	warimasen deshita ra
PRESUMPTIVE:	PLAIN	waru daroo	waranai daroo
	FORMAL	waru deshoo	waranai deshoo
VOLITIONAL:	PLAIN	waroo	
	FORMAL	warimashoo	

	Affirmative		*Affirmative*
POTENTIAL	wareru	HONORIFIC	owari ni naru
			owari nasaru
PASSIVE	warareru	HUMBLE	(owari suru)
			(owari itasu)
CAUSATIVE	waraseru		
CAUS. PASSIVE	waraserareru		
	warasareru		

Examples:

1. *Booru de mado o watta.*
   I broke the window with a ball.
2. *Juu o ni de waru to, go ni naru.*
   Ten divided by two equals five.
3. *Kare wa booru de megane o wararemashita.*
   His glasses were broken by the ball.
4. *Karera wa too o futatsu no ha ni waroo to takurande iru.*
   They are plotting to split the political party into two factions.
5. *Watashi wa mizu-wari o nomi-tai.*
   I'd like to drink a whiskey-and-water.

忘れる to forget, leave a thing behind: (trans.)

		Affirmative	*Negative*
PLAIN FORM:	PRESENT	wasureru	wasurenai
	PAST	wasureta	wasurenakatta
MASU FORM:	PRESENT	wasuremasu	wasuremasen
	PAST	wasuremashita	wasuremasen deshita
IMPERATIVE		wasurero	wasureru na
TE FORM		wasurete	wasurenakute
CONDITIONAL:	PLAIN	wasurereba	wasurenakereba
		wasureta ra	wasurenakatta ra
	FORMAL	wasuremashita ra	wasuremasen deshita ra
PRESUMPTIVE:	PLAIN	wasureru daroo	wasurenai daroo
	FORMAL	wasureru deshoo	wasurenai deshoo
VOLITIONAL:	PLAIN	wasureyoo	
	FORMAL	wasuremashoo	

	Affirmative		*Affirmative*
POTENTIAL	wasurerareru	HONORIFIC	owasure ni naru
	wasurereru		owasure nasaru
PASSIVE	wasurerareru	HUMBLE	(owasure suru)
			(owasure itasu)
CAUSATIVE	wasuresaseru		
CAUS. PASSIVE	wasuresaserareru		

Examples:

1. *Kare no namae o wasuremashita.*
   I forget his name.
2. *Anata no shinsetsu wa kesshite wasuremasen.*
   I shall never forget your kindness.
3. *Kyoo yakusoku ga aru no o wasureru tokoro deshita.*
   I almost forgot that I had an appointment today.
4. *Sensei, hon o uchi ni wasurete kimashita.*
   Teacher, I left my book at home.
5. *Kare wa sono koto o kesshite wasurenakatta.*
   He has never forgotten that.

渡る to cross, be brought over; わたる to range (from ~), cover (both intrans.)

		Affirmative	*Negative*
PLAIN FORM:	PRESENT	wataru	wataranai
	PAST	watatta	wataranakatta
MASU FORM:	PRESENT	watarimasu	watarimasen
	PAST	watarimashita	watarimasen deshita
IMPERATIVE		watare	wataru na
TE FORM		watatte	wataranakute
CONDITIONAL:	PLAIN	watareba	wataranakereba
		watatta ra	wataranakatta ra
	FORMAL	watarimashita ra	watarimasen deshita ra
PRESUMPTIVE:	PLAIN	wataru daroo	wataranai daroo
	FORMAL	wataru deshoo	wataranai deshoo
VOLITIONAL:	PLAIN	wataroo	
	FORMAL	watarimashoo	

	Affirmative		*Affirmative*
POTENTIAL	watareru	HONORIFIC	owatari ni naru
			owatari nasaru
PASSIVE	watarareru	HUMBLE	(owatari suru)
			(owatari itasu)
CAUSATIVE	wataraseru		
CAUS. PASSIVE	wataraserareru		
	watarasareru		

Examples:

1. *Kono kawa o oyoide wataremasu ka.*
   Can you swim across this river?
2. *Watashi-tachi ga watatta toki, kaikyoo wa arete imashita.*
   The channel was rough when we crossed over.
3. *Bukkyoo wa Chuugoku kara watatte kita.*
   Buddhism was brought over from China.
4. *Karera no nenrei wa juu-go sai kara ni-juu-yon sai ni watatte iru.*
   Their ages range from fifteen to twenty-four.
5. *Kare no kenkyuu wa hiroi han'i ni watatte imasu.*
   His studies cover a wide field.

* As with other verbs indicating movement, *wataru* 渡る meaning "to cross" may take a direct object, thus giving an idea of "going through a defined area."

渡す to hand, give, transfer: (trans.)

		Affirmative	*Negative*
PLAIN FORM:	PRESENT	watasu	watasanai
	PAST	watashita	watasanakatta
MASU FORM:	PRESENT	watashimasu	watashimasen
	PAST	watashimashita	watashimasen deshita
IMPERATIVE		watase	watasu na
TE FORM		watashite	watasanakute
CONDITIONAL:	PLAIN	wataseba	watasanakereba
		watashita ra	watasanakatta ra
	FORMAL	watashimashita ra	watashimasen deshita ra
PRESUMPTIVE:	PLAIN	watasu daroo	watasanai daroo
	FORMAL	watasu deshoo	watasanai deshoo
VOLITIONAL:	PLAIN	watasoo	
	FORMAL	watashimashoo	

	Affirmative		*Affirmative*
POTENTIAL	wataseru	HONORIFIC	owatashi ni naru
			owatashi nasaru
PASSIVE	watasareru	HUMBLE	owatashi suru
			owatashi itasu
CAUSATIVE	watasaseru		
CAUS. PASSIVE	watasaserareru		

Examples:

1. *Kono tegami o kare ni watashite kudasai.*
   Please hand him this letter.
2. *Doroboo wa keisatsu ni watasareta.*
   The burglar was handed over to the police.
3. *Atarashii hashi ga kawa ni watasaremashita.*
   A new bridge was built across the river.
4. *Kare wa ie o musuko ni watashita.*
   He transferred his house to his son.
5. *Suutsu wa reshiito to hikikae ni owatashi shimasu.*
   We will give you your suit in exchange for the receipt.

破れる to tear, break;* 敗れる to lose a game, be defeated: (both intrans.)

		Affirmative	*Negative*
PLAIN FORM:	PRESENT	yabureru	yaburenai
	PAST	yabureta	yaburenakatta
MASU FORM:	PRESENT	yaburemasu	yaburemasen
	PAST	yaburemashita	yaburemasen deshita
IMPERATIVE		yaburero	yabureru na
TE FORM		yaburete	yaburenakute
CONDITIONAL:	PLAIN	yaburereba	yaburenakereba
		yabureta ra	yaburenakatta ra
	FORMAL	yaburemashita ra	yaburemasen deshita ra
PRESUMPTIVE:	PLAIN	yabureru daroo	yaburenai daroo
	FORMAL	yabureru deshoo	yaburenai deshoo
VOLITIONAL:	PLAIN	yabureyoo	
	FORMAL	yaburemashoo	

	Affirmative		*Affirmative*
POTENTIAL	(yaburerareru)	HONORIFIC	oyabure ni naru
			oyabure nasaru
PASSIVE	(yaburerareru)	HUMBLE	(oyabure suru)
			(oyabure itasu)
CAUSATIVE	yaburesaseru		
CAUS. PASSIVE	yaburesaserareru		

Examples:

1. *Kono kami wa kantan ni yaburenai.*
   This paper does not tear easily.
2. *Uwagi ga kugi ni hikkakatte yabureta.*
   My jacket caught on a nail and tore.
3. *Ryookoku-kan no wahei kooshoo wa yaburemashita.*
   The peace talks between the two countries were broken off.
4. *Naze shiai ni yabureta no desu ka.*
   Why did we lose the game?
5. *Kanojo no yume wa kotogotoku yabureta.*
   All her dreams were shattered.

* The verb *yabureru* 破れる meaning "to tear, break" does not generally use the imperative, volitional, potential, or passive forms.

yaburu

破る to tear, break; 敗る to beat, defeat: (both trans.)

		Affirmative	*Negative*
PLAIN FORM:	PRESENT	yaburu	yaburanai
	PAST	yabutta	yaburanakatta
MASU FORM:	PRESENT	yaburimasu	yaburimasen
	PAST	yaburimashita	yaburimasen deshita
IMPERATIVE		yabure	yaburu na
TE FORM		yabutte	yaburanakute
CONDITIONAL:	PLAIN	yabureba	yaburanakereba
		yabutta ra	yaburanakatta ra
	FORMAL	yaburimashita ra	yaburimasen deshita ra
PRESUMPTIVE:	PLAIN	yaburu daroo	yaburanai daroo
	FORMAL	yaburu deshoo	yaburanai deshoo
VOLITIONAL:	PLAIN	yaburoo	
	FORMAL	yaburimashoo	

	Affirmative		*Affirmative*
POTENTIAL	yabureru	HONORIFIC	oyaburi ni naru
			oyaburi nasaru
PASSIVE	yaburareru	HUMBLE	(oyaburi suru)
			(oyaburi itasu)
CAUSATIVE	yaburaseru		
CAUS. PASSIVE	yaburaserareru		
	yaburasareru		

Examples:

1. *Kanojo wa kugi ni hikkakatte, sukaato o yabutte shimatta.*
   She caught her skirt on a nail and tore it.
2. *Kare wa shibashiba yakusoku o yaburu.*
   He often breaks his promise.
3. *Gootoo wa doa o yabutte haitta.*
   The burglar broke in through the door.
4. *Kanojo no yume wa yaburareta.*
   Her dreams were shattered.
5. *Kare wa tenisu no shiai de kyooteki o yaburimashita.*
   He beat a powerful opponent in the tennis match.

焼ける to be burned, grilled; やける to be jealous: (both intrans.)

		Affirmative	*Negative*
PLAIN FORM:	PRESENT	yakeru	yakenai
	PAST	yaketa	yakenakatta
MASU FORM:	PRESENT	yakemasu	yakemasen
	PAST	yakemashita	yakemasen deshita
IMPERATIVE		(yakero)	(yakeru na)
TE FORM		yakete	yakenakute
CONDITIONAL:	PLAIN	yakereba	yakenakereba
		yaketa ra	yakenakatta ra
	FORMAL	yakemashita ra	yakemasen deshita ra
PRESUMPTIVE:	PLAIN	yakeru daroo	yakenai daroo
	FORMAL	yakeru deshoo	yakenai deshoo
VOLITIONAL:	PLAIN	(yakeyoo)	
	FORMAL	(yakemashoo)	

	Affirmative		*Affirmative*
POTENTIAL	(yakerareru)	HONORIFIC	oyake ni naru
			oyake nasaru
PASSIVE	(yakerareru)	HUMBLE	(oyake suru)
			(oyake itasu)
CAUSATIVE	yakesaseru		
CAUS. PASSIVE	yakesaserareru		

Examples:

1. *Kare no ie wa kaji de yaketa.*
   His house was burned down by fire.
2. *Kono niku wa yoku yakete inai.*
   This meat is underdone.
3. *Watashi wa hada ga yaketa.*
   I got sunburnt.
4. *Kare wa okusan ga totemo miryokuteki na node yakete imasu.*
   He is jealous because his wife is so attractive.
5. *Kare no kooun ni wa mattaku yakeru.*
   I am really envious of his good luck.

焼く to burn, grill; やく to be jealous of, envy: (both trans.)

		Affirmative	*Negative*
PLAIN FORM:	PRESENT	yaku	yakanai
	PAST	yaita	yakanakatta
MASU FORM:	PRESENT	yakimasu	yakimasen
	PAST	yakimashita	yakimasen deshita
IMPERATIVE		yake	yaku na
TE FORM		yaite	yakanakute
CONDITIONAL:	PLAIN	yakeba	yakanakereba
		yaita ra	yakanakatta ra
	FORMAL	yakimashita ra	yakimasen deshita ra
PRESUMPTIVE:	PLAIN	yaku daroo	yakanai daroo
	FORMAL	yaku deshoo	yakanai deshoo
VOLITIONAL:	PLAIN	yakoo	
	FORMAL	yakimashoo	

	Affirmative		*Affirmative*
POTENTIAL	yakeru	HONORIFIC	oyaki ni naru
			oyaki nasaru
PASSIVE	yakareru	HUMBLE	oyaki suru
			oyaki itasu
CAUSATIVE	yakaseru		
CAUS. PASSIVE	yakaserareru		
	yakasareru		

Examples:

1. *Sakuya no kaji de kare wa ie o yakarete shimatta.*
   His house burnt down in last night's fire.
2. *Watashi wa pan o yaku no ga suki desu.*
   I like to bake bread.
3. *Pan o ichi-mai yaita.*
   I toasted a slice of bread.
4. *Kaigan de hada o yakimashita.*
   I got a suntan at the beach.
5. *Kare wa tsuma ga miryokuteki na no o yaite imasu.*
   He is jealous of his wife since she is so attractive.

止める to stop doing, abandon; 辞める to resign, retire: (both trans.)

		Affirmative	*Negative*
PLAIN FORM:	PRESENT	yameru	yamenai
	PAST	yameta	yamenakatta
MASU FORM:	PRESENT	yamemasu	yamemasen
	PAST	yamemashita	yamemasen deshita
IMPERATIVE		yamero	yameru na
TE FORM		yamete	yamenakute
CONDITIONAL:	PLAIN	yamereba	yamenakereba
		yameta ra	yamenakatta ra
	FORMAL	yamemashita ra	yamemasen deshita ra
PRESUMPTIVE:	PLAIN	yameru daroo	yamenai daroo
	FORMAL	yameru deshoo	yamenai deshoo
VOLITIONAL:	PLAIN	yameyoo	
	FORMAL	yamemashoo	

	Affirmative		*Affirmative*
POTENTIAL	yamerareru	HONORIFIC	oyame ni naru
	yamereru		oyame nasaru
PASSIVE	yamerareru	HUMBLE	(oyame suru)
			(oyame itasu)
CAUSATIVE	yamesaseru		
CAUS. PASSIVE	yamesaserareru		

Examples:

1. *Kanojo ga haitte kita ra, karera wa hanashi o yameta.*
   They stopped talking when she came in.
2. *Tabako o yameta hoo ga ii yo.*
   You'd better quit smoking.
3. *Wareware wa kono keiyaku o yameru koto ni shita.*
   We have decided to abandon this contract.
4. *Kare wa ni-nen no toki, daigaku o yamemashita.*
   He left college in his second year.
5. *Kare wa shachoo o yameta.*
   He resigned as president.

やる　to do, to give, send:* (trans.)

		Affirmative	*Negative*
PLAIN FORM:	PRESENT	yaru	yaranai
	PAST	yatta	yaranakatta
MASU FORM:	PRESENT	yarimasu	yarimasen
	PAST	yarimashita	yarimasen deshita
IMPERATIVE		yare	yaru na
TE FORM		yatte	yaranakute
CONDITIONAL:	PLAIN	yareba	yaranakereba
		yatta ra	yaranakatta ra
	FORMAL	yarimashita ra	yarimasen deshita ra
PRESUMPTIVE:	PLAIN	yaru daroo	yaranai daroo
	FORMAL	yaru deshoo	yaranai deshoo
VOLITIONAL:	PLAIN	yaroo	
	FORMAL	yarimashoo	

	Affirmative		*Affirmative*
POTENTIAL	yareru	HONORIFIC	nasaru
			oyari ni naru
			oyari nasaru
PASSIVE	yarareru	HUMBLE	itasu
CAUSATIVE	yaraseru		
CAUS. PASSIVE	yaraserareru		
	yarasareru		

Examples:

1. *Kare wa ima shukudai o yatte iru.*
   He is doing his homework now.
2. *Otoosan wa nani o nasatte irasshaimasu ka. Hon'ya o yatte imasu.*
   What does your father do? He runs a bookstore.
3. *Watashi wa kare ni hyaku en yatta.*
   I gave him one hundred yen.
4. *Kanojo ga musuko o daigaku ni yaru no wa taihen datta.*
   It was not easy for her to send her son to college.
5. *Watashi wa osake mo tabako mo yarimasen.*
   I neither drink nor smoke.

* The verb *yaru* meaning "to give, send" generally does not use the honorific or humble forms.

やせる to lose weight, become thin, become infertile: (intrans.)

		Affirmative	*Negative*
PLAIN FORM:	PRESENT	yaseru	yasenai
	PAST	yaseta	yasenakatta
MASU FORM:	PRESENT	yasemasu	yasemasen
	PAST	yasemashita	yasemasen deshita
IMPERATIVE		yasero	yaseru na
TE FORM		yasete	yasenakute
CONDITIONAL:	PLAIN	yasereba	yasenakereba
		yaseta ra	yasenakatta ra
	FORMAL	yasemashita ra	yasemasen deshita ra
PRESUMPTIVE:	PLAIN	yaseru daroo	yasenai daroo
	FORMAL	yaseru deshoo	yasenai deshoo
VOLITIONAL:	PLAIN	yaseyoo	
	FORMAL	yasemashoo	

	Affirmative		*Affirmative*
POTENTIAL	yaserareru	HONORIFIC	oyase ni naru
	yasereru		oyase nasaru
PASSIVE	yaserareru	HUMBLE	(oyase suru)
			(oyase itasu)
CAUSATIVE	yasesaseru		
CAUS. PASSIVE	yasesaserareru		

Examples:

1. *Kanojo wa zuibun yasete shimatta.*
   She has become much thinner.
2. *Kanojo wa yaseru hoohoo o sagashite imasu.*
   She is looking for a way to lose weight.
3. *Koko sanka-getsu de, go kiro yaseta.*
   I have lost five kilograms in the past three months.
4. *Kanojo wa yaseyoo to kurushinde imasu.*
   She is having a hard time losing weight.
5. *Kono tochi wa hidoku yasete iru.*
   This soil is terribly infertile.

休む to take a rest, sleep, be absent from, take a vacation: (intrans.)

		Affirmative	Negative
PLAIN FORM:	PRESENT	yasumu	yasumanai
	PAST	yasunda	yasumanakatta
MASU FORM:	PRESENT	yasumimasu	yasumimasen
	PAST	yasumimashita	yasumimasen deshita
IMPERATIVE		yasume	yasumu na
TE FORM		yasunde	yasumanakute
CONDITIONAL:	PLAIN	yasumeba	yasumanakereba
		yasunda ra	yasumanakatta ra
	FORMAL	yasumimashita ra	yasumimasen deshita ra
PRESUMPTIVE:	PLAIN	yasumu daroo	yasumanai daroo
	FORMAL	yasumu deshoo	yasumanai deshoo
VOLITIONAL:	PLAIN	yasumoo	
	FORMAL	yasumimashoo	

	Affirmative		Affirmative
POTENTIAL	yasumeru	HONORIFIC	oyasumi ni naru
			oyasumi nasaru
PASSIVE	yasumareru	HUMBLE	(oyasumi suru)
			(oyasumi itasu)
CAUSATIVE	yasumaseru		
CAUS. PASSIVE	yasumaserareru		
	yasumasareru		

Examples:

1. *Hito-yasumi shite, koohii o nomoo.*
   Let's take a break for coffee.
2. *Sakuya wa yoku oyasumi ni naremashita ka.*
   Were you able to sleep well last night?
3. *Chichi wa moo yasumimashita.*
   My father has already gone to bed.
4. *Kare wa kinoo gakkoo o yasunda.*
   He was absent from school yesterday.
5. *Hon'ya wa kyoo yasunde iru.*
   The bookstore is closed today.

雇う to employ, hire: (trans.)

		Affirmative	*Negative*
PLAIN FORM:	PRESENT	yatou	yatowanai
	PAST	yatotta	yatowanakatta
MASU FORM:	PRESENT	yatoimasu	yatoimasen
	PAST	yatoimashita	yatoimasen deshita
IMPERATIVE		yatoe	yatou na
TE FORM		yatotte	yatowanakute
CONDITIONAL:	PLAIN	yatoeba	yatowanakereba
		yatotta ra	yatowanakatta ra
	FORMAL	yatoimashita ra	yatoimasen deshita ra
PRESUMPTIVE:	PLAIN	yatou daroo	yatowanai daroo
	FORMAL	yatou deshoo	yatowanai deshoo
VOLITIONAL:	PLAIN	yatooo	
	FORMAL	yatoimashoo	

	Affirmative		*Affirmative*
POTENTIAL	yatoeru	HONORIFIC	oyatoi ni naru
			oyatoi nasaru
PASSIVE	yatowareru	HUMBLE	(oyatoi suru)
			(oyatoi itasu)
CAUSATIVE	yatowaseru		
CAUS. PASSIVE	yatowaserareru		
	yatowasareru		

Examples:

1. *Sono kaisha wa sen nin roodoosha o yatotte iru.*
   That company employs a thousand workers.
2. *Kare wa kaisha ni untenshu to shite yatowarete imasu.*
   He is employed as a driver in the firm.
3. *Uekiya o ichi-nichi yatoimashita.*
   We hired a gardener for a day.
4. *Ensoku no tame ni basu o yatotta.*
   We chartered a bus for the excursion.
5. *Kaisha ni yatowarete iru kagiri, kisoku o mamoranakereba naranai.*
   For as long as you are employed by the company, you must follow
   the regulations.

呼ぶ to call, invite, attract (customers): (trans.)

		Affirmative	*Negative*
PLAIN FORM:	PRESENT	yobu	yobanai
	PAST	yonda	yobanakatta
MASU FORM:	PRESENT	yobimasu	yobimasen
	PAST	yobimashita	yobimasen deshita
IMPERATIVE		yobe	yobu na
TE FORM		yonde	yobanakute
CONDITIONAL:	PLAIN	yobeba	yobanakereba
		yonda ra	yobanakatta ra
	FORMAL	yobimashita ra	yobimasen deshita ra
PRESUMPTIVE:	PLAIN	yobu daroo	yobanai daroo
	FORMAL	yobu deshoo	yobanai deshoo
VOLITIONAL:	PLAIN	yoboo	
	FORMAL	yobimashoo	

	Affirmative			*Affirmative*
POTENTIAL	yoberu	HONORIFIC		oyobi ni naru
				oyobi nasaru
PASSIVE	yobareru	HUMBLE		oyobi suru
				oyobi itasu
CAUSATIVE	yobaseru			
CAUS. PASSIVE	yobaserareru			
	yobasareru			

Examples:

1. *Okaasan ga anata o yonde imasu yo.*
   Your mother is calling you.
2. *Kare o uchi ni yoboo.*
   Let's invite him over.
3. *Denwa de takushii o yonde kudasai.*
   Please call for a taxi.
4. *Daitooryoo no hatsugen ga giron o yonda.*
   The President's speech aroused much public discussion.
5. *Ano depaato wa kyaku o yobu no ni arayuru shudan o kokoromite iru.*
   That department store is trying every means to attract customers.

読む to read: (trans.)

		Affirmative	*Negative*
PLAIN FORM:	PRESENT	yomu	yomanai
	PAST	yonda	yomanakatta
MASU FORM:	PRESENT	yomimasu	yomimasen
	PAST	yomimashita	yomimasen deshita
IMPERATIVE		yome	yomu na
TE FORM		yonde	yomanakute
CONDITIONAL:	PLAIN	yomeba	yomanakereba
		yonda ra	yomanakatta ra
	FORMAL	yomimashita ra	yomimasen deshita ra
PRESUMPTIVE:	PLAIN	yomu daroo	yomanai daroo
	FORMAL	yomu deshoo	yomanai deshoo
VOLITIONAL:	PLAIN	yomoo	
	FORMAL	yomimashoo	

	Affirmative		*Affirmative*
POTENTIAL	yomeru	HONORIFIC	oyomi ni naru
			oyomi nasaru
PASSIVE	yomareru	HUMBLE	oyomi suru
			oyomi itasu
CAUSATIVE	yomaseru		
CAUS. PASSIVE	yomaserareru		
	yomasareru		

Examples:

1. *Watashi wa sore o shinbun de yomimashita.*
   I read about it in a newspaper.
2. *Kono hon wa Nihon no gakusei-tachi ni hiroku yomarete iru.*
   This book is widely read by Japanese students.
3. *Kanojo no kangae ga yomenakatta.*
   I couldn't read her thoughts.
4. *Kanojo wa kodomo ni doowa o yonde yatta.*
   She read a nursery story to the children.
5. *Omoshiroi kara kono bubun o yonde hoshii.*
   Because it's interesting, I'd like you to read this section.

喜ぶ to be glad, be delighted: (intrans. and trans.)

		Affirmative	*Negative*
PLAIN FORM:	PRESENT	yorokobu	yorokobanai
	PAST	yorokonda	yorokobanakatta
MASU FORM:	PRESENT	yorokobimasu	yorokobimasen
	PAST	yorokobimashita	yorokobimasen deshita
IMPERATIVE		yorokobe	yorokobu na
TE FORM		yorokonde	yorokobanakute
CONDITIONAL:	PLAIN	yorokobeba	yorokobanakereba
		yorokonda ra	yorokobanakatta ra
	FORMAL	yorokobimashita ra	yorokobimasen deshita ra
PRESUMPTIVE:	PLAIN	yorokobu daroo	yorokobanai daroo
	FORMAL	yorokobu deshoo	yorokobanai deshoo
VOLITIONAL:	PLAIN	yorokoboo	
	FORMAL	yorokobimashoo	

	Affirmative		*Affirmative*
POTENTIAL	yorokoberu	HONORIFIC	oyorokobi ni naru
			oyorokobi nasaru
PASSIVE	yorokobareru	HUMBLE	oyorokobi suru
			oyorokobi itasu
CAUSATIVE	yorokobaseru		
CAUS. PASSIVE	yorokobaserareru		
	yorokobasareru		

Examples:

1. *Haha wa watashi no seikoo o yorokobimashita.*
   Mother was delighted with my success.
2. *Anata ga buji da to kiite, wareware wa ooini yorokonda.*
   We were very glad to hear that you were safe.
3. *Kanojo o yorokobaseru tame ni wa watashi wa nan-demo suru.*
   I'll do anything to please her.
4. *Anata no tame ni sore o watashi wa yorokonde shimashoo.*
   I shall be glad to do it for you.
5. *Issho ni osake o nomimasen ka. Mochiron yorokonde.*
   Will you have a drink with me? Sure, with pleasure.

寄る to draw near, drop in; 因る to depend on, be due to: (both intrans.)

		Affirmative	*Negative*
PLAIN FORM:	PRESENT	yoru	yoranai
	PAST	yotta	yoranakatta
MASU FORM:	PRESENT	yorimasu	yorimasen
	PAST	yorimashita	yorimasen deshita
IMPERATIVE		yore	yoru na
TE FORM		yotte	yoranakute
CONDITIONAL:	PLAIN	yoreba	yoranakereba
		yotta ra	yoranakatta ra
	FORMAL	yorimashita ra	yorimasen deshita ra
PRESUMPTIVE:	PLAIN	yoru daroo	yoranai daroo
	FORMAL	yoru deshoo	yoranai deshoo
VOLITIONAL:	PLAIN	yoroo	
	FORMAL	yorimashoo	

	Affirmative		*Affirmative*
POTENTIAL	yoreru	HONORIFIC	oyori ni naru
			oyori nasaru
PASSIVE	yorareru	HUMBLE	oyori suru
			oyori itasu
CAUSATIVE	yoraseru		
CAUS. PASSIVE	yoraserareru		
	yorasareru		

Examples:

1. *Kanojo wa watashi ni yotte kita.*
   She came up to me.
2. *Gakkoo no kaeri ni anata no ie ni yorimasu.*
   I'll drop in at your house on my way back from school.
3. *Karera wa teeburu no mawari ni yotta.*
   They circled round the table.
4. *Nedan wa omosa ni yotte chigaimasu.*
   The price depends on the weight.
5. *Sono jiko wa kare no fuchuui unten ni yoru mono deshita.*
   That accident was due to his careless driving.

酔う to get drunk, become intoxicated: (intrans.)

		Affirmative	*Negative*
PLAIN FORM:	PRESENT	you	yowanai
	PAST	yotta	yowanakatta
MASU FORM:	PRESENT	yoimasu	yoimasen
	PAST	yoimashita	yoimasen deshita
IMPERATIVE		yoe	you na
TE FORM		yotte	yowanakute
CONDITIONAL:	PLAIN	yoeba	yowanakereba
		yotta ra	yowanakatta ra
	FORMAL	yoimashita ra	yoimasen deshita ra
PRESUMPTIVE:	PLAIN	you daroo	yowanai daroo
	FORMAL	you deshoo	yowanai deshoo
VOLITIONAL:	PLAIN	yooo	
	FORMAL	yoimashoo	

	Affirmative		*Affirmative*
POTENTIAL	yoeru	HONORIFIC	oyoi ni naru
			oyoi nasaru
PASSIVE	yowareru	HUMBLE	(oyoi suru)
			(oyoi itasu)
CAUSATIVE	yowaseru		
CAUS. PASSIVE	yowaserareru		
	yowasareru		

Examples:

1. *Yuube osake o nomi-sugite, yotte shimaimashita.*
   Last night I drank too much and got drunk.
2. *Doomo chotto yotta rashii.*
   I think I'm a bit drunk.
3. *Yotte, kuruma o unten suru no wa kiken desu.*
   It is dangerous to drive a car while intoxicated.
4. *Karera wa shoori ni yotta.*
   They were elated at having won.
5. *Kanojo no utsukushii koe ga chooshuu o yowasemashita.*
   Her beautiful voice enchanted the audience.

許す to forgive, permit, allow, admit into: (trans.)

		Affirmative	*Negative*
PLAIN FORM:	PRESENT	yurusu	yurusanai
	PAST	yurushita	yurusanakatta
MASU FORM:	PRESENT	yurushimasu	yurushimasen
	PAST	yurushimashita	yurushimasen deshita
IMPERATIVE		yuruse	yurusu na
TE FORM		yurushite	yurusanakute
CONDITIONAL:	PLAIN	yuruseba	yurusanakereba
		yurushita ra	yurusanakatta ra
	FORMAL	yurushimashita ra	yurushimasen deshita ra
PRESUMPTIVE:	PLAIN	yurusu daroo	yurusanai daroo
	FORMAL	yurusu deshoo	yurusanai deshoo
VOLITIONAL:	PLAIN	yurusoo	
	FORMAL	yurushimashoo	

	Affirmative		*Affirmative*
POTENTIAL	yuruseru	HONORIFIC	oyurushi ni naru
			oyurushi nasaru
PASSIVE	yurusareru	HUMBLE	(oyurushi suru)
			(oyurushi itasu)
CAUSATIVE	yurusaseru		
CAUS. PASSIVE	yurusaserareru		

Examples:

1. *Watashi no ayamachi o oyurushi kudasai.*
   Please forgive my mistake.
2. *Kyooshitu de no kitsuen wa yurusarete imasen.*
   Smoking is not allowed in classrooms.
3. *Haha wa watashi ga ryokoo suru no o yurushite kurenakatta.*
   My mother wouldn't permit me to take a trip.
4. *Moshi jikan ga yuruseba, watashi wa soko e ikimasu.*
   I will go there if time permits.
5. *Hyaku-mei no gakusei ga daigaku ni nyuugaku o yurusaremashita.*
   A hundred students were admitted to the university.

A LIST OF COMPOUND VERBS

Compound verbs are formed by adding a verb to the pre-*masu* form of another verb. Thus, the original meaning of the verb (in pre-*masu* form) is modified by the attached verb. Following are twenty common examples of such verbs:

ayumi-yoru 歩み寄る to walk up to: (intrans.)
　Kanojo wa sono kuruma ni ayumi-yotta.
　She walked up to the car.

fumi-taosu 踏み倒す to avoid paying: (trans.)
　Shakuya-nin wa yachin o fumi-taoshite nigeta.
　The tenant vanished without paying his rent.

furi-wakeru 振り分ける to divide: (trans.)
　Kare wa zaisan o san-nin no kodomo ni furi-waketa.
　He divided his property among his three children.

hiki-tsukeru 引き付ける to fascinate, attract: (trans.)
　Kare wa kanojo no miryoku ni hiki-tsukerareta.
　He was attracted by her charm.

ii-tateru 言い立てる to state, maintain: (trans.)
　Shachoo ni iken o ii-tateta.
　We stated our opinions to the president.

iki-wataru 行き渡る to spread, go around: (intrans.)
　Wain ga minna ni iki-watarimashita ka.
　Has everyone been served with wine?

ire-komu いれ込む to be crazy about: (intrans.)
Kare wa keiba ni ire-konde iru.
He is crazy about horse racing.

kangae-tsuku 考え付く to think of: (intrans.)
Ii keikaku o kangae-tsuita.
I hit upon a good plan.

kiki-toru 聞き取る to hear, be audible: (trans.)
Kanojo ga itte iru koto ga kiki-torenai.
I can't catch what she is saying.

mi-suteru 見捨てる to abandon: (trans.)
Watashi o mi-sutenaide kudasai.
Please don't abandon me.

mi-wakeru 見分ける to distinguish: (trans.)
Ano futago o mi-wakeraremasu ka.
Can you tell those twins apart?

mi-yaburu 見破る to see through: (trans.)
Watashi wa kanojo no furi ni damasarenaide, honshin o mi-yabure-mashita.
Not being fooled by her act, I was able to see what her real intentions were.

ochi-tsuku 落ち着く to calm down, become quiet: (intrans.)
Kimochi ga ochi-tsukanai.
I can't calm down.
Yatto kaze ga ochi-tsuita.
The wind finally died down.

shire-wataru 知れ渡る to become widely known: (intrans.)
Sono jiken wa sugu shire-watatta.
News of that incident quickly spread.

sumi-tsuku 住み着く to settle down: (intrans.)
Nihon ni sumi-tsuita.
I settled down in Japan.

tachi-yoru 立ち寄る to drop in: (intrans.)
Hon'ya ni tachi-yotta.
I dropped into a bookstore.

yomi-toru 読み取る to understand the meaning, read between the lines: (trans.)

Kono bunmyaku wa yomi-tori-nikui.

It is difficult to grasp the meaning of this passage.

tori-tateru 取り立てる to collect, levy taxes: (trans.)

Kare wa zeikin o tori-taterareta.

He was made to pay his taxes.

tori-tsuku 取り付く to possess, be taken ill: (intrans.)

Kare wa byooki ni tori-tsukarete iru.

He has fallen ill.

yomi-ageru 読み上げる to read aloud: (trans.)

Koe o dashite, hon o yomi-agete kudasai.

Please read the book aloud.

A LIST OF SURU VERBS

Many verbs simply consist of a noun followed by *suru*. The different forms of these verbs are made by conjugating *suru* (see page 255); for instance, the present *masu* form of *annai suru* is *annai shimasu,* the causative form is *annai sasemasu,* and so forth. Following are 277 commonly used noun + *suru* verbs.

aiyoo suru 愛用する (trans.) to use regularly, patronize
anji suru 暗示する (trans.) to hint, suggest
annai suru 案内する (trans.) to guide, lead
anshin suru 安心する (intrans.) be relieved, feel secure
antei suru 安定する (intrans.) be steady, stable

bakuhatsu suru 爆発する (intrans.) to explode, burst, blow up
bengo suru 弁護する (trans.) to defend, testify for
benkyoo suru 勉強する (trans.) to study, to give a discount
benshoo suru 弁償する (trans.) to compensate, repay for loss
boogai suru 妨害する (trans.) to barricade, disturb
booshi suru 防止する (trans.) to prevent, keep in check
boshuu suru 募集する (trans.) to recruit, collect
bunkatsu suru 分割する (trans.) to divide, split
bunseki suru 分析する (trans.) to analyze, break down

chikoku suru 遅刻する (intrans.) to be late, tardy
chokin suru 貯金する (intrans.) to save money
choosa suru 調査する (trans.) to investigate, inquire into, examine

choosei suru 調整する (trans.) to regulate, adjust
choosen suru 挑戦する (intrans.) to challenge
chuucho suru ちゅうちょする (trans.) to hesitate, waver, vacillate
chuui suru 注意する (intrans.) to be careful of, pay attention to
chuukei suru 中継する (trans.) to relay (a broadcast)
chuukoku suru 忠告する (intrans.) to warn
chuumoku suru 注目する (trans. or intrans.) to observe, take notice of
chuumon suru 注文する (trans.) to order (food, goods)
chuushi suru 中止する (trans.) to stop, discontinue, call off

daihyoo suru 代表する (trans.) to represent, act for
dakyoo suru 妥協する (intrans.) to compromise
denwa suru 電話する (intrans.) to make a telephone call
dokuritsu suru 独立する (intrans.) to become independent
dooi suru 同意する (intrans.) to agree, approve
doonyuu suru 導入する (trans.) to bring in, introduce
doryoku suru 努力する (intrans.) to make an effort, work hard

eigyoo suru 営業する (intrans.) to do business, be open
eikyoo suru 影響する (intrans.) to influence, affect
enchoo suru 延長する (intrans.) to extend, lengthen
engi suru 演技する (intrans.) to act, perform
enjo suru 援助する (trans.) to assist, help, support, aid
enki suru 延期する (trans.) to postpone, put off
enryo suru 遠慮する (trans.) to refrain, hold back
enzetsu suru 演説する (intrans.) to make a speech

fukkatsu suru 復活する (trans. or intrans.) to revive, restore
fukushuu suru 復習する (trans.) to review, go over
fukushuu suru 復讐する (intrans.) to revenge
fukyuu suru 普及する (intrans.) to spread, diffuse
funin suru 赴任する (intrans.) to leave for one's new post
fusoku suru 不足する (intrans.) to be short of, be lacking
futan suru 負担する (trans.) to bear the weight of

gaman suru 我慢する (trans.) to be patient, endure

genkyuu suru 言及する (intrans.) to refer to, touch upon, mention
genshoo suru 減少する (intrans. or trans.) to decrease
gentei suru 限定する (trans.) to limit, restrict
giron suru 議論する (intrans.) to argue, discuss, debate
gokai suru 誤解する (trans.) to misunderstand
gookaku suru 合格する (intrans.) to pass an examination
gookei suru 合計する (trans.) to add up, total

haishi suru 廃止する (trans.) to abolish, do away with, repeal
haitatsu suru 配達する (trans.) to deliver
hakai suru 破壊する (trans. or intrans.) to destroy, break, ruin
hakkoo suru 発行する (trans.) to publish, issue, bring out
han'ei suru 反映する (trans. or intrans.) to reflect
han'ei suru 繁栄する (intrans.) to prosper, flourish
handan suru 判断する (trans.) to judge, conclude
hansei suru 反省する (trans.) to reflect on oneself, reconsider
hantai suru 反対する (intrans.) to be against, be opposed
hatsubai suru 発売する (trans.) to begin selling, put on the market
hatsumei suru 発明する (trans.) to invent
hatten suru 発展する (intrans.) to develop, expand
heikin suru 平均する (trans.) to average, balance
henka suru 変化する (intrans.) to change, alter, be transformed
henshuu suru 編集する (trans.) to edit, compile
hihan suru 批判する (trans.) to criticize
hitei suru 否定する (trans.) to deny, negate
hon'yaku suru 翻訳する (trans.) to translate
hookoku suru 報告する (trans.) to report, inform
hoomon suru 訪問する (trans.) to visit, call on, pay a visit
hoshoo suru 保障する (trans.) to make secure
hoshoo suru 保証する (trans.) to guarantee, warrant
hoshoo suru 補償する (trans.) to compensate, make up for
hyooka suru 評価する (trans.) to appraise, value

ihan suru 違反する (intrans.) to violate
iji suru 維持する (trans.) to maintain, support, keep
intai suru 引退する (intrans.) to retire, give up one's position

irai suru 依頼する (trans.) to request, ask
itchi suru 一致する (intrans.) to agree with, be in unison
ito suru 意図する (trans.) to intend to do, make a goal

jikken suru 実験する (trans.) to experiment
jikkoo suru 実行する (trans.) to carry out, execute
jiman suru 自慢する (trans.) to be proud, boast of, take pride in
jiritsu suru 自立する (intrans.) to become independent
jisatsu suru 自殺する (intrans.) to commit suicide
jishoku suru 辞職する (trans. or intrans.) to resign
jitsugen suru 実現する (intrans. or trans.) to be realized, come true
jooei suru 上映する (trans.) to show a film
jooho suru 譲歩する (trans.) to concede, give way to
jooshoo suru 上昇する (intrans.) to go up, rise, ascend
junbi suru 準備する (trans.) to prepare

kaifuku suru 回復する (intrans. or trans.) to restore, recuperate
kaihatsu suru 開発する (trans.) to develop, exploit
kaihoo suru 開放する (trans.) to open a place to the public
kaihoo suru 解放する (trans.) to release, set a prisoner free
kaikaku suru 改革する (trans.) to reform, improve
kaiketsu suru 解決する (trans.) to settle, resolve
kaisai suru 開催する (trans.) to hold (an event)
kaisei suru 改正する (trans.) to revise, amend, improve
kaishaku suru 解釈する (trans.) to interpret, explain
kaitaku suru 開拓する (trans.) to reclaim, exploit, develop
kakudai suru 拡大する (trans.) to magnify, enlarge, expand
kakunin suru 確認する (trans.) to confirm, ascertain
kakoo suru 下降する (intrans.) to come down, descend, drop
kakoo suru 加工する (trans.) to process, manufacture
kankei suru 関係する (intrans.) to be related, have a relationship
kanri suru 管理する (trans.) to manage, control, administer
kansatsu suru 観察する (trans.) to observe, watch closely
kansei suru 完成する (intrans. or trans.) to finish, complete
kanshin suru 感心する (intrans. or trans.) to admire, be impressed
kanshoo suru 干渉する (intrans.) to intervene, interfere, meddle with

kanshoo suru 鑑賞する (trans.) to appreciate

katei suru 仮定する (intrans. or trans.) to assume, suppose

katsudoo suru 活動する (intrans.) to be active,

katsuyaku suru 活躍する (intrans.) be active in, take an active part

keiei suru 経営する (trans.) to manage, conduct, run (a business)

keika suru 経過する (intrans.) to pass, elapse, expire

keikaku suru 計画する (trans.) to plan

keiken suru 経験する (trans.) to experience, undergo

keisan suru 計算する (trans.) to count, calculate, sum up

keiyaku suru 契約する (intrans.) to contract, make a contract with

kekkon suru 結婚する (intrans.) to marry

kenbutsu suru 見物する (trans.) to go sightseeing

kenka suru けんかする (intrans.) to quarrel, fight

kenkyuu suru 研究する (trans.) to study, research

kenshuu suru 研修する (trans.) to study, train, intern

kentoo suru 検討する (intrans.) to examine, investigate, think over

kesseki suru 欠席する (intrans.) to be absent

kesshin suru 決心する (intrans.) to make up one's mind, decide

kettei suru 決定する (trans.) to decide, determine

kinchoo suru 緊張する (intrans.) to be tense, nervous

kinen suru 記念する (trans.) to commemorate

kiroku suru 記録する (trans.) to record, write down

kitai suru 期待する (trans.) to expect, hope

konran suru 混乱する (intrans.) to be confused, be in disorder

koogeki suru 攻撃する (trans.) to attack, charge, criticize

kooji suru 工事する (intrans.) to construct

kooji suru 公示する (trans.) to announce publicly

kookai suru 後悔する (trans.) to regret, repent, be sorry

kookan suru 交換する (trans.) to exchange

kooryo suru 考慮する (trans.) to consider, think over

kooryuu suru 交流する (intrans.) to exchange (ideas, culture)

kooshoo suru 交渉する (intrans.) to negotiate

kootai suru 交代する (intrans.) to take turns, take a person's place

kootai suru 後退する (intrans.) to retreat, go back, recede

kootei suru 肯定する (trans.) to affirm, acknowledge

koshoo suru 故障する (intrans.) to break down

kyohi suru 拒否する (trans.) to refuse, reject, deny
kyoka suru 許可する (trans.) to permit
kyooiku suru 教育する (trans.) to educate
kyookyuu suru 供給する (intrans.) to supply, furnish, provide
kyoosei suru 強制する (trans.) to compel, force a person to do
kyoosei suru 矯正する (trans.) to reform, correct, rectify, straighten
kyoosoo suru 競争する (intrans.) to compete
kyuujo suru 救助する (trans.) to rescue, help
kyuukei suru 休憩する (intrans.) to rest, take a break
kyuushuu suru 吸収する (trans.) to absorb

meiwaku suru 迷惑する (intrans.) to be troubled, annoyed
mensetsu suru 面接する (intrans.) to interview
mokunin suru 黙認する (trans.) to permit or approve tacitly
mujun suru 矛盾する (intrans.) to be contradictory, to conflict
mushi suru 無視する (trans.) to ignore, disregard

nattoku suru 納得する (trans.) to be convinced
ninmei suru 任命する (trans.) to appoint, nominate
ninshiki suru 認識する (trans.) to recognize, realize, understand
nyuugaku suru 入学する (intrans.) to enter a school
nyuuin suru 入院する (intrans.) to be hospitalized

ooen suru 応援する (trans.) to aid, support, encourage, cheer
oofuku suru 往復する (intrans.) to go and return
ooyoo suru 応用する (intrans.) to apply, put into practice

rakudai suru 落第する (intrans.) to fail an exam, be rejected
rakusen suru 落選する (intrans.) to be defeated in an election
renraku suru 連絡する (intrans. or trans.) to contact, get in touch
renshuu suru 練習する (trans.) to practice, exercise
rikai suru 理解する (trans.) to understand, comprehend
rikon suru 離婚する (intrans.) to divorce
riyoo suru 利用する (trans.) to make use of
rokuon suru 録音する (trans.) to record (sound)
roohi suru 浪費する (trans.) to waste (money or time), throw away

ryokoo suru 旅行する (intrans.) to travel
ryoori suru 料理する (trans.) to cook
ryuugaku suru 留学する (intrans.) to study abroad
ryuukoo suru 流行する (intrans.) to be in fashion, be widespread

saiban suru 裁判する (intrans.) to hold a trial
saiyoo suru 採用する (trans.) to employ, adopt (measures)
sanka suru 参加する (intrans.) to join, take part in
sanpo suru 散歩する (intrans.) to take a walk
sansei suru 賛成する (intrans.) to agree, approve
seikatsu suru 生活する (intrans.) to make a living, support oneself
seikoo suru 成功する (intrans.) to succeed
seisan suru 生産する (trans.) to produce, manufacture
senkoo suru 選考する (trans.) to select, choose
senkoo suru 専攻する (trans.) to specialize, major in
senkyo suru 選挙する (trans.) to elect
senkyo suru 占拠する (trans.) to occupy
sensoo suru 戦争する (intrans.) to make war
sentaku suru 選択する (trans.) to choose, select
sentaku suru 洗濯する (trans.) to wash (clothes)
setsumei suru 説明する (trans.) to explain
setsuyaku suru 節約する (trans.) to economize, skimp, save
settoku suru 説得する (trans.) to persuade
sewa suru 世話する (trans.) to take care of, look after (someone)
shidoo suru 指導する (trans.) to lead, guide
shigeki suru 刺激する (trans.) to stimulate, irritate, excite
shihai suru 支配する (trans.) to control, dominate
shiji suru 指示する (trans.) to instruct
shimei suru 指名する (trans.) to nominate, designate
shinpai suru 心配する (trans. or intrans.) to be anxious, feel uneasy
shinpo suru 進歩する (intrans.) to make progress, advance
shinryaku suru 侵略する (trans.) to invade
shinsei suru 申請する (trans.) to make out an application
shinyoo suru 信用する (trans.) to trust, believe, place confidence in
shippai suru 失敗する (intrans.) to fail
shishutsu suru 支出する (trans.) to spend (expenditures)

shiteki suru 指摘する (trans.) to point out
shitsumon suru 質問する (intrans.) to ask a question
shiyoo suru 使用する (trans.) to use, employ
shokuji suru 食事する (intrans.) to take a meal
shoohi suru 消費する (trans.) to consume, expend
shookai suru 紹介する (trans.) to introduce, present
shoomei suru 証明する (trans.) to prove, testify, certify
shooshin suru 昇進する (intrans.) to be promoted
shootai suru 招待する (trans.) to invite
shoyuu suru 所有する (trans.) to own, possess
shozoku suru 所属する (intrans.) to belong to
shuchoo suru 主張する (trans.) to insist on, assert, emphasize
shukushoo suru 縮小する (trans. or intrans.) to reduce, cut, curtail
shuppan suru 出版する (trans.) to publish, issue
shuppatsu suru 出発する (intrans.) to leave for, depart
shusseki suru 出席する (intrans.) to attend
shutchoo suru 出張する (intrans.) to go on a business trip
shuuchuu suru 集中する (intrans.) to concentrate, centralize
shuuri suru 修理する (trans.) to repair, mend, fix
shuushoku suru 就職する (intrans.) to find employment
shuuyoo suru 収容する (trans.) to accommodate, seat, intern
sokushin suru 促進する (intrans.) to accelerate, promote, quicken
sonzai suru 存在する (intrans.) to exist
soodan suru 相談する (trans.) to consult, discuss
sooji suru 掃除する (trans.) to clean
soosa suru 捜査する (trans.) to investigate, search
soosa suru 操作する (trans.) to operate, handle
soozoo suru 想像する (trans.) to imagine, guess
soshiki suru 組織する (trans.) to organize, form
sotsugyoo suru 卒業する (trans.) to graduate from
suisen suru 推薦する (trans.) to recommend

taiho suru 逮捕する (trans.) to arrest, apprehend
taiin suru 退院する (intrans.) to be released from a hospital
tairitsu suru 対立する (intrans.) to be opposed
tanken suru 探検する (intrans.) to explore

tantoo suru 担当する (trans.) to take charge of
tassei suru 達成する (trans.) to achieve, attain, accomplish
teian suru 提案する (trans.) to propose, suggest
teishutsu suru 提出する (trans.) to submit, present
tetsuya suru 徹夜する (intrans.) to work all night
toochaku suru 到着する (intrans.) to arrive
toohyoo suru 投票する (intrans.) to vote, cast a ballot
tooitsu suru 統一する (trans.) to unify, unite
toosen suru 当選する (intrans.) to be elected
tooshi suru 投資する (intrans.)* to invest
tooshi suru 透視する (trans.) to see through
torihiki suru 取り引きする (intrans.) to have dealings with
tsuihoo suru 追放する (trans.) to banish, expel, deport
tsuika suru 追加する (trans.) to supplement, add
tsuikyuu suru 追求する (trans.) to pursue, seek
tsuikyuu suru 追究する (trans.) to investigate thoroughly
tsuuchi suru 通知する (trans.) to inform, give notice
tsuuka suru 通過する (intrans.) to pass, go through without stopping

un'ei suru 運営する (trans.) to manage, run, administer
unsoo suru 運送する (trans.) to transport, convey, carry
unten suru 運転する (trans.) to drive, to manage (money)

wakai suru 和解する (intrans.) to be reconciled with

yakusoku suru 約束する (trans.) to promise
yoboo suru 予防する (trans.) to prevent, protect
yookyuu suru 要求する (trans.) to demand, claim
yoosei suru 要請する (trans.) to request, claim
yoosei suru 養成する (trans.) to train, develop (a person)
yoshuu suru 予習する (trans.) to study beforehand
yosoo suru 予想する (intrans.) to predict, anticipate
yoyaku suru 予約する (trans.) to reserve, book
yunyuu suru 輸入する (trans.) to import

* Classified as an intransitive, but often used like a transitive verb.

yushutsu suru 輸出する (trans.) to export

yuukai suru 誘拐する (trans.) to kidnap

yuushi suru 融資する (intrans.) to finance, furnish with funds

yuushoo suru 優勝する (intrans.) to win a contest or championship

yuusoo suru 郵送する (trans.) to send by mail

yuuwaku suru 誘惑する (trans.) to tempt, lure, entice

zetsuboo suru 絶望する (intrans.) to have no hope, be in despair

zooka suru 増加する (intrans.) to increase, grow, augment